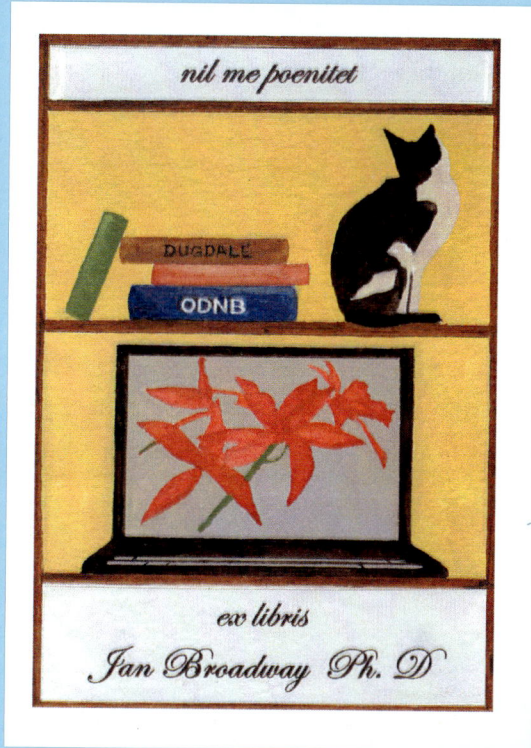

nil me poenitet

DUGDALE

ODNB

ex libris

Jan Broadway Ph. D

The Bristol and Gloucestershire Archaeological Society
Gloucestershire Record Series

Hon. General Editor

J. D. Hodsdon, B.A., Ph.D.

Volume 26

The Forest of Dean Eyre of 1634

THE
FOREST OF DEAN EYRE
OF
1634

Edited by Nicholas Herbert

The Bristol and Gloucestershire Archaeological Society

2012

The Bristol and Gloucestershire Archaeological Society
Gloucestershire Record Series

© The Bristol and Gloucestershire Archaeological Society

ISBN 978 0 900197 80 2

British Library Cataloguing in Publication Data
A catalogue entry for this book is available from the British Library

The illustration on the title page is taken from a sketch in H.G. Nicholls, The Forest of Dean (1858) and shows an incised figure from a tomb slab formerly in Newland churchyard (now in the south aisle of the church). It probably commemorates a holder of the office of bow-bearer under the Throckmortons of Clearwell, chief foresters-of-fee of Dean in the 17th century.

Printed in Great Britain by 4word Ltd, Bristol

CONTENTS

PREFACE AND ACKNOWLEDGEMENTS

This volume had its origin back in 1997 in a suggestion made to me by Cyril Hart that the record of the Forest of Dean swanimote of June 1634, held in connexion with Charles I's revival of the system of forest eyres, would be worth editing for publication. The late Dr Hart, who became well known to all those interested in the history of the Forest through his series of books on its administration and industry, earned their further gratitude by making much of the original source material available in copious extracts in his books and in a large collection of photocopies and other material he deposited with the Gloucestershire Archives; but the Harleian manuscript which includes the record of the swanimote was one of the few sources which had hitherto escaped his notice. Less surprisingly, it was a source that I had overlooked when writing an account of the Forest's administration for the recently-published Volume Five of the Victoria County History of Gloucestershire, so I was interested in discovering what further light it cast on the Forest at a troubled period of its history. On taking up the project again after retirement some years later, it seemed that the most appropriate plan was to present the record of the swanimote in its context by editing with it other documentation produced by the Dean eyre of 1634.

The subject matter of this volume was accepted for the Gloucestershire Record Series by the former editor, the late Christopher Elrington, who (continuing a role that benefited much of my career as a professional local historian) gave valuable advice on the content and format. His task as editor has been continued to the same high standard by James Hodsdon, for whose careful setting of the text and general attention to detail I am most grateful. My former colleague John Juřica kindly read and commented on the Introduction. My thanks are due to the British Library, the National Archives, the Bodleian Library, and Gloucestershire Archives for making available in photographic, digital, or actual form the various parts of the documentation published. Re-acquaintance with Forest of Dean history has been a reminder of how much of the source material still remains little known and difficult of access, and I hope the present volume will not be the last in this series to deal with what is historically one of the most unusual and intriguing parts of any English county.

Nicholas Herbert
June 2012

SELECT BIBLIOGRAPHY

J. Atkinson, *Plan of Her Majesty's Forest of Dean with High Meadow and Great Doward Woods* (1847)

Calendar of State Papers, Domestic Series, Charles I (23 vols. HMSO, 1858–97)

George Hammersley, 'The Revival of the Forest Laws under Charles I', *History*, (new series) xlv. 85–102

Cyril (C.E.) Hart, *The Free Miners of the Royal Forest of Dean and Hundred of St. Briavels*, 2nd. edn. (Lydney, 2002)

Cyril Hart, *The Industrial History of the Forest of Dean* (Newton Abbot, 1971)

Cyril Hart, *Royal Forest: A History of Dean's Woods as Producers of Timber* (Oxford, 1966)

Cyril Hart, 'Metes and Bounds of the Forest of Dean', *BGAS Transactions*, lxvi. 166–207

Manwood's Treatise of the Forest Laws, 4th edn. corrected and enlarged by William Nelson (London, 1717)

H.G. Nicholls, *The Forest of Dean; an Historical and Descriptive Account* (1858)

Les Reports de Sir William Jones, Chevalier, jades Un des Justices Del Banck le Roy et devant Un des Justices del' Court de Common Banck, de Divers Special Cases ... (London, 1675) (BL shelf mark: 506.g.5.)

Victoria History of the Counties of England: Gloucestershire, Volume Five: the Forest of Dean, edited by N.M. Herbert (Oxford University Press for the Institute of Historical Research, 1996): articles on 'Bounds' and 'Forest Administration' (N.M.H.); and on 'Settlement' and 'Industry' (A.R.J. Juřica)

ABBREVIATIONS

BL   The British Library, London
BGAS Bristol and Gloucestershire Archaeological Society
GA   Gloucestershire Archives, Gloucester
ODNB Oxford Dictionary of National Biography
OED   Oxford English Dictionary
TNA   The National Archives, Kew
VCH   Victoria History of the Counties of England

A representative folio (f. 51) of Harleian MS. 4850; see pp. 100–1.

INTRODUCTION

'This forlorn, disowned piece of ground, so much talked of, and so little cared for in reality' was how John Wade, one of the many public servants to grapple with its problems over the centuries, described the Forest of Dean.[1] An administrator's nightmare and a lawyer's delight, the Forest was a tangle of conflicting interests. Miners, ironmasters, quarrymen, wood-workers, landowners, farmers, and humble cottagers all laid claim to its assets, while, presiding over all, the Crown and its advisers pursued a policy that veered between short-term exploitation and far-sighted preservation for national needs. Adding to the confusion were historic uncertainties over what constituted the Forest as a geographical and juridical entity. The distinction between the 'royal demesne', a central tract of woodland and waste owned and managed directly for the Crown, and the adjoining areas, which were parochial and manorial but subject nevertheless to the system of forest law, was not always understood by contemporaries, and the bounds between the demesne and the parochial lands were never so clearly established as to be immune from challenge by this or that interested community or landowner. As was implied by Wade's remark – made in 1660 as dispiritedly he prepared to quit his post as the Forest's administrator under the Commonwealth – there had been no lack of attention from officialdom to this problematical region. The previous fifty years had seen frequent commissions of enquiry, surveys, and other documentation; and the flood of paperwork would continue unabated in later years – through an energetic reorganization in the late 17th century, a relapse to administrative lethargy in the 18th, a busy era of parliamentary legislation in the early 19th, and on through the successive regimes of the Commissioners of Crown Woods and the Forestry Commission.

In the long and complex history of Dean and the wealth of documentation relating to it one of the landmarks is the forest eyre of 1634. The eyre provides a picture of the state of the Forest in the early Stuart period and of the personnel then attempting to administer or profit from it. By playing a part in fuelling opposition to Charles I in the years preceding the Civil War, it also has significance in national political history.

[1] *Cal. S.P. Dom.* 1659–60, p. 413.

THE FOREST OF DEAN IN THE EARLY 17TH CENTURY

The eyre of 1634 comes near the middle of an unusually troubled period in the Forest's history. It was a time when the centuries-old pressures – the claims of the local inhabitants to dig minerals, take fuel and building material, and pasture animals in the royal demesne land, and the historic temptation to supplement their income and diet by the theft of the king's timber and deer – were augmented by a new element, the partial privatisation of the Forest's resources. Influential courtiers and local landowners were permitted to inclose parts of the demesne for their own use, and ironmasters were empowered to establish furnaces and forges and manage large areas of the woodland to produce the charcoal to fuel them.

Ironworking in Dean, carried on for centuries in numerous small and inefficient 'bloomery' forges often peripatetic in the woodlands, entered a new era at the close of the 16th century with the introduction of blast furnaces and forges using water power to drive their bellows and hammers. Several landowners in adjoining parishes, both within and outside the bounds of the Forest jurisdiction as then accepted, began to employ that new technology. Among them were the Winter family at Lydney, the earls of Essex at Lydbrook and Bishopswood, the Hall family of Highmeadow at Redbrook, and the governors of the Company of the Mineral and Battery Works who built wireworks at Tintern and Whitebrook across the river Wye in Monmouthshire. The new works, which used up the produce of the privately-owned woodlands at a startling rate, soon began to impinge on the Crown land of the central Forest: the ironmasters lobbied for the right to coppice parts of the woodland, while the ready market for wood added further incentives to the established local culture of timber-stealing. The response of James I and his ministers was to allow the building of furnaces and forges within the demesne itself and, to fuel them, grant quotas of cordwood (standard-sized bundles of coppice wood) taken at a set rate of payment from the Crown woodlands. This inaugurated the 60-year era in Dean of what became known as 'the king's ironworks'.[1]

The first large cordwood concession of James's reign appears to have been that granted in 1610 to Sir Edward Winter, owner of the Lydney estate and its ironworks. He secured the right to take the wood in 520 a. on Bradley hill on the eastern edge of the demesne woodlands, an area that had been managed as coppice by the Forest officials for sales to local ironmakers since the 1560s or earlier. Winter renegotiated his concession the following year, paying £800 for a five-year lease.[2] More significantly, under a 21-year lease in February 1612 William Herbert, earl of Pembroke and warden of the Forest, was empowered to build works in the demesne, dig iron ore and 'cinders' (the waste material left by earlier, less efficient ironworking), and take 12,000 cords of wood each year.[3]

---

[1] For the general history of the ironworks at this period, Hart, *Ind. Hist. of Dean*, pp. 8–13.
[2] BL, Lansdowne MS. 166, ff. 348–56; and for earlier use of the coppices, *VCH Glos.* v. pp. 362.
[3] TNA, C 99/4.

Under Pembroke's grant four blast furnaces with three forges (to fashion into bar iron the pig iron produced by the furnaces) were built in the valleys of the Cannop, Soudley, and Greathough (or Lyd) brooks and carried on by a succession of sub-lessees under the earl. At the time of the eyre the works were operated under a further lease granted to Pembroke in 1627 and assigned by him the following year to a partnership comprising a prominent industrialist Sir Basil Brooke, owner and developer of mines and iron works at Coalbrookdale on his manor of Madeley in Shropshire, George Mynne, the deputy governor of the Company of Mineral and Battery Works, and Thomas Hackett, manager of that company's Tintern wireworks. The partners, who were entitled under Pembroke's grant to an annual quota of 10,000 cords of wood from the demesne, spent a large sum (over £14,000, Brooke claimed later) on refurbishing the king's ironworks and expanding them with three additional forges. Hackett left the partnership after a few years, and in 1634, a month or two before the eyre convened, Mynne sold out to a new partnership formed by Brooke and Sir John Winter, the son and successor of Sir Edward Winter at Lydney. Winter was already in possession of a separate concession of 2,500 cords a year that had been granted to Pembroke in 1629.[1]

Under James I another scheme for profiting from the Forest was a levy of fines on ancient assarts that had been taken out of the royal demesne and absorbed into the adjoining manorial lands. That was a somewhat cynical exercise, seeing that much of the land in question was held legitimately under licences granted by the king's predecessors as long ago as the early 14th century. Over 10,000 acres, mainly in the Newland and St. Briavels area to the west of the demesne, were affected, the owners finding themselves in effect obliged to buy their land back from intermediaries to whom the Crown sold its rights in 1618 and 1619.[2] James also leased out parts of the demesne: the wood called Chestnuts on its north-eastern edge, another part of the woodland traditionally managed as coppice, was granted to Richard Brayne of Littledean for 21 years in 1624.[3]

Charles I went further, permitting the creation of large freeholds in the demesne. Soon after coming to throne in 1625, he granted to Sir Edward Villiers, a half-brother of the royal favourite Buckingham,[4] a tract of the demesne woodland called Mailscot covering over 800 a. in the Wye valley adjoining English Bicknor. Villiers died the following year, Mailscot passing to his widow Barbara and, by the time of the eyre, to her son William, Viscount Grandison.[5] In 1627 the king granted to John Gibbons, secretary to his Lord Treasurer, a long lease of over 500 a. in the Cannop area, land which had already been inclosed

---

[1] TNA, C 99/21–2, 36; SP 16/293, no. 69; and for Brooke, see also *VCH Shropshire*, xi. pp. 35, 46, 48.
[2] *VCH Glos*. v. 364.
[3] Ibid. 362; GA, D 421/E 5.
[4] *ODNB*, lvi. p. 482.
[5] TNA, C 99/28; *VCH Glos*. v. pp. 101, 109. The grant and later references give the wood's area as *c*. 430 a., presumably using the larger 'forest acre'.

and coppiced under James I presumably with a view to profit by supplying the ironworks. In 1629 the same land was included in a grant in fee of a total of *c*.1,100 a. to Sir Allen Apsley, who shortly afterwards sold his rights to Gibbons. According to evidence presented at the eyre, the land in the first grant lay in two separate parcels and in the course of forming them into a single enclosure Gibbons contrived to take possession of the whole of the wider area covered by the later grant. The details of the transactions given in various accounts are contradictory, but, by whatever means, Gibbons secured for himself a substantial private estate, usually known as Cannop Vallets, lying in the heart of the demesne. He walled it off from the surrounding woodland, felled and sold much of the timber, and built himself a residence.[1] In a reminder to the king that innovations in the management of the Forest tended to provoke a violent response, his grants led to a serious outbreak of rioting in 1631 when the grantees and their agents attempted to exclude the commoners from pasturing animals on their lands. The disturbances, which were part of a pattern of anti-inclosure riots in the royal forests known as the 'Skimmington' riots from the alias adopted by one of the ringleaders, were directed mainly against the Mailscot enclave but also involved incursions into Cannop Vallets.[2] Leases of several other parts of the demesne woodland were secured by courtiers in the early years of Charles's reign,[3] and grants to other individuals of the right to take wood, bark, and the roots of felled trees further complicated the situation.[4]

The results of the grants of land and cordwood are made clear in the records of various government commissions of enquiry and in the litany of destruction that forms the bulk of the evidence presented at the eyre. The ironmasters, their agents, and workmen were generally lax in their interpretation of the cordwood concessions and they, as well as the new owners and lessees of parts of the demesne, often failed to observe the restrictions imposed in their grants on the felling of large timber trees, earmarked for the Crown's shipyards. During the period of their operations, the demesne woodlands saw an influx of settlers, many more than the limited numbers that the Crown and its advisers had envisaged might be needed for operating the works and managing the coppices. The incomers formed hamlets of primitive cabins and were soon busy stealing wood, not only to construct their dwellings and for firewood but also to supplement their income by woodworking crafts such as the fashioning of

---

[1] Below, pp. 12, 23–4; GA, D 9125/1/2937, f. 38 and v. The estate comprised the lands that later formed the bulk of Sallowvallets and New Beechenhurst Inclosures, lying on either side of the Cannop brook and between the two main roads passing through the demesne (to Monmouth and to Coleford): below, pp. 43 (no. 4), 130 (no. 14), 149 (nos. 28–9); TNA, F 17/7 (a plan of *c.* 1680, which appears to show the estate as still walled off).

[2] *VCH Glos.* v. 364; GA, D 9125/1/2937, ff. 12–13.

[3] e.g. TNA, C 99/26 (1626, the Snead and Kidnalls, near Lydney); GA, D 421/E 5 (1630, a new lease of the Bradley hill coppices).

[4] *Cal. S.P. Dom.* 1627–8, p. 314; 1628–9, p. 269; 1629–31, pp. 277, 509.

trenchers, saddle-trees, shovels, and the hoops and staves used in barrel-making.[1] The last, usually termed 'coopers' wares', became a major Dean trade, finding a ready market in the adjoining cider-producing regions of Severnside and Herefordshire as well as being shipped out in large quantities to Bristol. Also, for inhabitants of the villages bordering the demesne woodlands, particularly tradesmen such as tanners, carpenters, and smiths, the extensive felling, cording, and charcoaling operations under way in the demesne gave additional opportunities to carry off bark, useful small timber, and firewood.

THE FOREST ADMINISTRATION IN 1634

The new elements introduced under the early Stuart kings and the associated abuses taxed the administrative machinery of the Forest, an antiquated and unwieldy hierarchy of officials with overlapping, and sometimes ill-defined, responsibilities.[2] At its head was the constable of St. Briavels, who under the Crown held St. Briavels castle, the historic headquarters of the administration, together with the royal manors of St. Briavels and Newland, and *ex officio* was warden of the Forest with overall responsibility for its management. He, or more usually a deputy constable acting for him, presided over the mine-law court, which regulated Dean's 'free miners' and their closely-guarded customs and restrictive practices, and over a court for exercising petty jurisdiction (mainly in cases of debt) over St. Briavels hundred, the 11 parishes which with the royal demesne constituted the historic core of the Forest. He also appointed seven under-foresters or keepers, headed by an officer known as the bow-bearer. For most of the 90 years preceding the eyre the joint offices of constable and warden had been held by members of the Herbert family, earls of Pembroke, Philip Herbert succeeding to the post after the death of his brother William in 1630.[3]

Under the constable was a tier of senior woodwards who held office by right of their tenure of manors within St. Briavels hundred and exercised responsibilities in ten Forest bailiwicks, sections of the royal demesne to which those manors adjoined.[4] At the time of the eyre there were only six woodwards in all, for three bailiwicks (Ruardean, Abenhall, and Littledean also called Badcocks Bailey), were held with their parent manors by a widow Joan Vaughan, heir to the prominent late-medieval family of Baynham, two others (Mitcheldean and Lea) were held by Nicholas Roberts, and two others (Staunton and English Bicknor) by Benedict Hall, who in 1633 marked his increasing status in the Forest region by building a large mansion adjoining his family's old farmhouse at Highmeadow, on the boundary of Newland and Staunton parishes. Of the other

---

[1] TNA, E 178/3837, account of cordwood 1612–13, depositions 1614, inquisition 1616.
[2] For the Forest officers and courts, *VCH Glos.* v. 357–60; and for a comprehensive general account of forest law and administration as developed in England: *Select Pleas of the Forest*, ed. G.J. Turner (Selden Society xiii), introduction.
[3] *VCH Glos.* v. p. 415.
[4] For those officers, see below, pp. 30–1; and relevant manorial descents in *VCH Glos.* v (and for Blaize bailiwick, ibid. x. p. 40).

bailiwicks, Blakeney bailiwick was attached to a small manor centred on Over Hall (later the Hayes) in Blakeney and belonged to Edmund Berrow, while Bearse bailiwick, a residual area left by medieval assarting on the western fringes of the demesne, was attached to Sir Baynham Throckmorton's Clearwell manor, and Blaize Bailey, another small bailiwick, was held with an estate called Blythes Court in Newnham parish by Richard Hill. Another group of nine forest officers, termed by the eyre foresters-in-fee, was based originally on small estates in St. Briavels manor. By the early 17th century, however, most of the foresterships-in-fee had become hereditary and most of the holders had little or no involvement in the Forest and its administration; only two, Sir Baynham Throckmorton who still held by right of an estate in St. Briavels and enjoyed the added status of appointing his own bow-bearer, and Sir John Winter of Lydney, bothered to enter claims at the eyre.[1] A more central role in the administration was played by three verderers who, as in other royal forests, were elected in the sheriff's county court under royal writ. Their main responsibility was to preside over the forest courts, which in Dean were an attachment or 'speech' court, held every few weeks to record offences involving damage to the 'vert' (the woodland) and supervise the grant or sale of wood to miners and to those with customary right to 'estovers' (wood for fuel and house repairs), and a swanimote, held two or three times a year to deal with a wider range of offences including poaching, encroachments, and illegal building on the demesne. Two or three other posts in the administration, held by officers called 'rangers', had become sinecures awarded by the Crown to minor court officials, while the offices of 12 'regarders' had lapsed with the system of forest eyres, in which they had specific duties.

The forest eyre, which in the 17th century was more commonly referred to as the 'justice seat', was in theory the final authority for regulating this profusion of offices, courts, and conflicting interests. It was supposed to be convened for each royal forest every few years by a chief justice-in-eyre responsible for all the forests in the parts of England south of the river Trent. Its roles were to punish – almost always by fine but with the sanction of imprisonment for non-compliance – offenders against the forest laws in royal demesne land and in manorial and parochial land within a forest, to determine claims to privileges and exemption from the forest jurisdiction, and to supervise and regulate the local officers. In preparation for the visitation the regarders and the other officers were required to carry out a wide-ranging survey (a 'regard') of the state of the forest and to have ready and enrolled all outstanding offences presented to the courts of attachment and swanimote. Inevitably most of the offences brought to the eyre's attention involved damage to the vert, poaching the king's deer, and encroachment on the demesne (termed 'purprestures' and 'assarts'), but various other matters deemed relevant came within its purview, including the possession of hunting dogs, bows, and other equipment that might

---

[1] Below, pp. 124, 126.

be used for poaching, mining and quarrying, and the keeping of boats that might be used to carry away stolen timber. All of that, together with the requirement to discipline the forest officers, was covered by a comprehensive catalogue of articles or heads of enquiry termed the 'charge', which the judges conducting the eyre put to the grand jury of county freeholders who delivered the final verdicts on offenders.[1] During the 12th and 13th centuries an eyre had visited the Forest of Dean at regular intervals, and on three occasions, in 1258, 1270, and 1282, the records of its sessions survive, with for 1282 also the roll of the regard that preceded it.[2] Since 1282, though royal justices had made sporadic visits to deal with individual matters and gaol-delivery of those imprisoned by the minor forest courts,[3] it seems that the full process had not been activated – that at least was the assumption of the justices in 1634. By the mid 16th century the attachment court had taken on the role of fining for minor vert offences,[4] though technically all punishments were the responsibility of the eyre. In the royal forests generally the system of eyres had fallen into disuse by the end of the 16th century.[5]

By the early 1630s recent efforts to regulate the Forest of Dean by *ad hoc* enquiries by special commissioners and surveys by government officials had produced little more than hand-wringing denunciations, both of the local culture of depredation and of the conduct of the officers, mainly the deputies who carried out most of the executive functions on behalf of the officers by tenure. The revival of an ancient system of maintaining central control on behalf of the Crown might, therefore, have seemed an appropriate move, had not its function been obscured by the short-term need for cash and complicated by growing opposition to the use of the royal prerogative.

PREPARATIONS FOR THE EYRE

The Forest of Dean eyre of July 1634 forms a significant chapter in the exploitation of the forest law by Charles I and his ministers, one of the fiscal expedients resorted to in the years from 1629 to 1640 when the king attempted to rule without Parliament. The political background to the revival of forest eyres has been ably analysed by George Hammersley in an article of 1960.[6] In it he shows that the manner in which the Forest of Dean eyre was conducted set the pattern for subsequent visitations of other royal forests and inflated that aspect of royal policy into one of the major grievances of the king's subjects in the run-up to the Civil War. As a result, the most controversial result of Charles's eyres, the

---

[1] See *Manwood's Forest Laws*, ed. Nelson, pp. 65–77, which recites a charge comprising 84 separate articles, and BL, Harl. MS. 4850, which includes (bound into the front of the volume) a differently worded version covering much the same topics in 91 articles.
[2] TNA, E 32/28–31.
[3] Hart, Royal Forest, 55*n*, p. 70.
[4] *VCH Glos.* v. pp. 359–60.
[5] J. Manwood, *Treatise and Discourse of the Lawes of the Forest* (1598), ff. 51–2.
[6] Hammersley, ' Revival of Forest Laws'; to that article this introduction owes a major debt, both in comprehending the national context and in identifying some of the relevant sources.

extension of forests to ancient and long-disused boundaries, was among the first matters to be addressed by the Long Parliament in 1641, along with ship money, the prerogative courts, and the revival of 'feudal incidents'.

The Dean eyre was the second in the series held for the royal forests. It followed one convened for Windsor and Bagshot forests in September 1632 but it was conducted with less restraint than its predecessor and opened a more controversial phase in royal policy towards the forests.[1] The intention to hold it was possibly under consideration by the close of 1632 when the earl of Pembroke, constable of St. Briavels, appointed as one of his deputies a prominent member of the judiciary, Sir John Bridgeman, chief justice of Chester;[2] Bridgeman was already acquainted with the Forest and its problems, having served on the commission that tried the 'Skimmington' rioters in the previous year,[3] and he would sit as one of the judges at the eyre. In April 1633 a new officer for Dean, a deputy surveyor directly responsible to the surveyor-general of the royal forests, was appointed and ordered to make a detailed survey of the standing timber, probably with a view to collecting some of the necessary evidence.[4] Plans were not, however, made public until early in 1634. In March that year the king dispatched a writ to the sheriff of Gloucestershire ordering him to summon to Mitcheldean on 10 July all the Forest officers together with 'four men and the reeve' from each of its townships. That was followed by a writ addressed to Pembroke by Henry Rich, earl of Holland, the chief justice of the royal forests south of Trent, ordering the attendance of all the Forest officers with their records of offenders and all who as officers or landholders claimed liberties and franchises in the Forest.[5] To join the officers in assembling the necessary evidence, the sheriff was to appoint 12 new regarders for Dean; Justice Bridgeman was to advise him on choosing 'people well affected to the King's service' and instruct them on their duties.[6]

To support Chief Justice Holland, who was essentially a courtier who had acquired his office by influence rather than by any legal ability, a panel of professional judges was constituted, comprising Bridgeman, Sir Thomas Trevor, one of the Barons of the Court of Exchequer, and Sir William Jones, a judge of King's Bench.[7] The key role of counsel for the Crown was intended for Sir William Noy, the attorney-general and the man popularly credited as the architect of the policy of reviving ancient royal prerogatives to raise funds;[8] at the Windsor eyre of 1632 he had virtually directed the proceedings, exhibiting a

---

[1] Hammersley, 'Revival of Forest Laws', pp. 89, 93–4.
[2] TNA, C 99/25.
[3] GA, D 9125/1/2937, f. 13; *Cal. S.P. Dom. 1631–3*, pp. 178, 336.
[4] *Cal. S.P. Dom.* 1633–4, pp. 20, 191.
[5] Below, pp. 1–2.
[6] *Cal. S.P. Dom.* 1633–4, p. 576.
[7] TNA, C 99/31.
[8] *ODNB*, xli. Pp. 241–4.

comprehensive grasp of the finer points of the forest law.[1] Noy's illness and retirement from office, however, caused a significant change of personnel. He was replaced by Sir John Finch, who in a succession of legal and political offices became notorious as an enforcer of the king's policy: as Speaker of the Commons he had figured in the celebrated incident of 1629 when he was prevented from adjourning the session, and later, as chief justice of Common Pleas, he played a major part in securing the verdict against Hampden over ship money.[2]

In Gloucestershire preparations were soon under way that would produce the principal documents published in this volume. The county sheriff drew up lists and issued summons to those required to attend; the Forest's officers compiled a formidable record of over 800 offences against the forest laws for presentation at a preparatory swanimote convened at Mitcheldean on 10 June; and local landowners summoned lawyers to draft, in the required long-winded terminology, their claims to common pasture, to estovers, and to other privileges. Finch meanwhile busied himself searching out past records that could be used to the king's advantage, as well as gathering evidence against the principal holders of rights in the Forest, Sir Basil Brooke, George Mynne, Sir John Winter, and John Gibbons. Having hints that more could be laid to their charge than the offences presented at the swanimote, Finch came down to Gloucestershire several days before the opening of the eyre. There he found useful informants, among them Sir Baynham Throckmorton, who had his own designs on the ironworks and cordwood concession[3] and was happy to disparage the current holders. 'When I came to Gloucester', Finch noted later, 'I heard the bell ring out against them, and with all had information given me that all art and diligence was used to obscure things and to prevent things coming clearly to the notice of the regard and by them to the swanimote court and so to the justice seat'.[4]

THE PROCEEDINGS

The fullest account of the proceedings and the deliberations of the panel of judges at the eyre appears to be that published in this volume, surviving in a copy among the archives of the Highmeadow estate.[5] A shorter account (also included below) concentrating mainly on the matter of the Forest's bounds was prepared by Sir John Finch as a report to the king.[6] Finch's account survives today in an unusual number of copies dispersed among different repositories, a fact which, as Hammersley suggests,[7] reflects the importance attached by contemporaries to the proceedings – by the government as a precedent for future action and by its

---

[1] *Reports de Sir William Jones*, pp. 266–98.
[2] For Finch's career, see *ODNB*, xix. pp. 572–7 (which, however, has only a brief and inaccurate mention of his role in the Dean eyre).
[3] Hart, *Royal Forest*, p. 105.
[4] GA, D 9125/1/2937, ff. 33, 36.
[5] Below, pp. 3–20.
[6] Below, pp. 21–7.
[7] Hammersley, 'Revival of Forest Laws', p. 93*n*.

opponents as a controversial manifestation of the royal prerogative. Also surviving are other (in parts cryptic) notes by Finch covering much the same ground.[1]

The eyre lasted for eight days, from 10 to 18 July 1634. After a token summons and adjournment at Mitcheldean, it met in Gloucester on the mound known as the Barbican, part of the defences of the city's ancient castle.[2] The castle, then used as the county gaol and headquarters of the county sheriff, provided the necessary administrative back-up for the proceedings and a means of temporary imprisonment of recalcitrant offenders, also presumably somewhere for the visiting notables to take shelter if rain disrupted the proceedings. The business opened with considerable ceremonial and strict observance of historical precedent. The full hierarchy of forest officers was summoned, each to make his oath and produce, on pain of a fine, hunting horns, hatchets, and other symbols of office, and the judges and king's counsel showed off their research into the archaic process by bringing up minor procedural matters.[3] Even more scope for abstruse legal argument and dredging up ancient precedent was afforded by a discussion initiated by Finch about the correct boundaries of the Forest. That matter (treated below in this introduction) took up the best part of one day and resulted in the imposition of much wider bounds than those currently accepted.

Much of the eight days was occupied with the principal offenders as presented at the swanimote, Sir Basil Brooke and George Mynne, who for most of previous six years had held the king's ironworks with the main concession to take cordwood, Sir John Winter, the other main ironmaster in Dean and holder of a lesser cordwood concession, and the owners in fee of parts of the royal demesne, Lady Villiers and her son at Mailscot and John Gibbons at Cannop. Lady Villiers was cleared of any offence, the felling of thousands of timber trees on her estate being judged to be within the terms of her grant. The treatment meted out to others by Finch and the judges shows that they could easily have found sufficient quibble with the wording of the grant to support a conviction if they had wished;[4] so no doubt the relationship to the late duke of Buckingham

---

[1] GA, D 9125/1/2937 (formerly Glos. Colln. LF 1.1), ff. 33–38v. What follows in the next few paragraphs is based on those three sources. Another, very brief account of the proceedings was left by Sir William Jones: *Reports de Sir William Jones*, pp.347–8.

[2] *VCH Glos.* iv. pp. 245, 247.

[3] e.g. questioning the apparent absence in Dean of the office of agistor, and warning a woodward about the ancient penalty for failure to produce his accounts: below, pp. 5–7.

[4] See the convoluted discussions concerning the clause *licet sit infra metas foreste*, held to be necessary in a grant of land or rights in a forest in order to waive the usual restrictions. The Mailscot grant did not include that clause but the judges exonerated Lady Villiers on the grounds that other wording 'made clear' that the land was within the Forest; the grants of the Cannop estate also omitted the clause but Gibbons, though he claimed the grant in fee to Sir Allen Apsley had another clause, giving the right to take timber trees, was convicted; while the grant of the site of Rodmore furnace (part of King James's sale of ancient assarts in 1618) did include the clause, but Winter was convicted nevertheless, on the grounds that it contained another and contradictory clause: below, pp. 10–12, 23–4; GA, D 9125/1/2937, f. 38v.; *Reports de Sir William Jones*, p. 347.

still counted in the family's favour.[1] Against the other main offenders Finch proceeded by 'special indictment' rather than on the evidence presented at the swanimote. That, he was at pains to make clear, was to give them the opportunity to make their defence and call witnesses during the eyre itself, but it also wrong-footed them by allowing him to produce additional evidence of abuses not specified in the presentments. The procedure was, he said, the best for the king's 'profit and for justice',[2] an order of words that seems to reveal the priorities of the eyre.

In the case of John Gibbons and his Cannop Vallets estate the eyre upheld the swanimote's presentment against him and Stephen Veynor (presumably his agent) for felling timber trees and enclosing a larger area than his grants had permitted, and added a further indictment concerning timber trees designated for the use of the navy. His total fine was set at *c*. £9,000. Probably expecting that the estate would be forfeit to the Crown, he had sold it shortly before the eyre to Sir Robert Banister,[3] who was left unmolested in his purchase and continued to develop the estate, felling more timber and attempting to stop up traditional highways running through it.[4] The case against Sir Basil Brooke and George Mynne took up the longest time. Mynne, who had recently sold his share in the works and cordwood concession to Brooke and his new partner Sir John Winter, did not attend the proceedings and left Brooke to defend their joint activities. He was probably anxious to keep a low profile, as he was already in trouble for suspect activities in an office he held under the Crown.[5] With Brooke and Mynne the swanimote had not been sparing, recording their felling and charcoaling operations in a total of 2,570 a. of woods all over the demesne, but providing little evidence as to what they were taking in amounts of coppice wood or protected timber trees. Finch after making his further enquiries collated their offences in an indictment for taking 178,200 cords, almost three times their entitlement over the six years they had held the concession, and drew up a list of more specific charges: manipulating the size of the bundles of cordwood, intimidating the officials appointed to supervise the delivery of the wood, taking timber trees under various pretences, and bringing into the demesne numerous and destructive cabiners. After seven hours of debate, including a wrangle over the production of the partnership's books, Brooke gave up the defence and he and Mynne received a massive fine of £57,940.

---

[1] Mailscot was retained by the Villiers family until sold in 1676 to the Halls, owners of the Highmeadow estate, but it returned the Crown woodland of the Forest in 1817 by the sale of that estate to the Commissioners of Woods: *VCH Glos*. v. pp. 109–10, 277–8.

[2] GA, D 9125/1/2937, f. 36v.

[3] Below, p. 24.

[4] Below, pp. 130 (no. 14), 144 (no.16), 149 (nos. 28–9). His heir Banister Maynard was later forced to sell it, under priced, to the Commonwealth government, but he regained it at the Restoration and sold it back to the Crown in 1670: *VCH Glos*. v. p. 366 and *n*.

[5] *ODNB*, xl. p. 85.

Winter, against whom the swanimote had also recorded a catalogue of felling of timber, was indicted for 60,700 cords, four or five times the amount justified by the concession Pembroke had assigned to him in 1629. After witnessing the treatment of Brooke and Mynne, he too confessed and was fined £20,230. He and Brooke evidently saw that as only the prelude to a long process of contesting both the legality of the proceedings and the scale of the fines. Winter was probably confident also that, though he and Brooke might forfeit the king's ironworks and cordwood concession, he would be left unmolested in his other profitable ironworks in the area. His works at Gunn's mill near Abenhall and at Rodmore in St. Briavels incurred (in comparison to the fines imposed for the cordwood offences) a modest total of £700, together with what proved to be a token order to pull them down;[1] he was still working them in 1636.[2] His main works, those at Lydney, were brought back within the Forest by the eyre's revival of the ancient bounds, but he soon freed them from possible sanction by buying his whole estate out of the jurisdiction.[3]

The eyre spent little time on consideration of the many other offenders presented at the swanimote. The bulk of the minor offences went through without challenge or further discussion and with the award of a standard fine, probably assigned by a clerk following general guidelines laid down by the judges. The handful of cases (30 or so) highlighted in the account of the proceedings printed below were possibly the only ones brought to the particular notice of the court, cases where the offender felt he had grounds for seeking a discharge or more lenient treatment and possessed the social status and legal nous to feel confident in doing so. Unsurprisingly, many of the humbler offenders ('many hundreds')[4] did not appear before the judges at Gloucester and in some cases may have been unaware of the charges brought against them.

The role of an eyre in disciplining and regulating forest officialdom, the subject matter of over a quarter of the articles of the 'charge', figures little in the accounts of the proceedings for Dean. The swanimote presentments provided few leads on corruption or other abuses on the part of the officers, which was perhaps not surprising as they were based largely on information gathered by the officers themselves. Finch, preoccupied with his campaign against the ironmasters, seems not to have enquired or encouraged the jury at Gloucester to enquire too deeply into such matters. His claim in his report that the ironmasters had made the officers 'combiners and confederates' in their practices[5] was not followed up. According to the surviving account of the proceedings, the only officials disciplined by the eyre were William Rowles, one of those appointed by the Crown to oversee the cordwood concessions, for selling timber without the

[1] Below, pp. 10, 95 (nos. 699–700).
[2] Below, pp. 149–50 (no. 1).
[3] See below, p. xxiii.
[4] Below, p. 5.
[5] Below, p. 26.

necessary paperwork, and Anthony Callow, deputy woodward of Mitcheldean bailiwick, for accepting a bribe to turn a blind eye to the removal of timber; Callow's substantial fine of £100 was substantially reduced later (to only £10),[1] as was probably Rowles's fine. Otherwise, one or two officers were fined for non-attendance at Gloucester and the three verderers for an inadequate presentment of those keeping unexpeditated dogs.[2]

THE REVIVAL OF THE ANCIENT BOUNDS OF THE FOREST

The bounds of the Forest of Dean, those limits within which inhabitants might expect to find themselves subject to the forest law and administration,[3] had in some minor respects been subject to dispute in fairly recent times. Finch, however, re-opened a major question thought to have been laid to rest centuries before. Under perambulations of 1228 and 1282 the bounds had been confirmed as including all the lands and manors in an area bounded by the rivers Severn and Wye and extending on the north-east to Over bridge outside Gloucester, on the north to Newent town, and on the north-west into Herefordshire as far as Ross-on-Wye. Parts of that area, including the manors of Tidenham and Woolaston in which the lords of Striguil (Chepstow) enjoyed private hunting rights, and a small part of Monmouthshire on the east bank of the Wye belonging to another private hunting chase called Hadnock, secured *de facto* exemption by the late 13th century. Following quarrels between Edward I and his barons over the extent of the royal forests a major reduction was agreed in 1300 and confirmed by Act of Parliament of 1327: by that six parishes in Herefordshire and 15 in Gloucestershire (most of the Severnside parishes and those in the north-west adjoining Herefordshire) were excluded in whole or part from the bounds.[4] A dispute over commoning rights in the royal demesne resulted in Minsterworth parish being declared to be outside the Forest in 1597, and probably at a similar date the large part of Westbury-on-Severn parish belonging to the Duchy of Lancaster manor of Rodley was excluded. That left the juridical Forest as generally accepted at the time of the eyre as the royal demesne, all but one (Hewelsfield) of the 11 parishes of St. Briavels hundred, and the bulk of two large Severnside parishes and a small portion of another (see Table 1, over).

---

[1] Below, pp. 7–9, 12.
[2] Below, pp. 9, 97 (no. 713).
[3] Hart, 'Metes and Bounds of Forest of Dean', traces the history of the bounds in detail and includes transcripts of the various perambulations; *VCH Glos.* v. pp. 295–300 has a more concise re-examination of the evidence.
[4] The original perambulations and other documents relating to them tended to describe the places concerned in terms of tithings or townships based on manorial units; to be more readily understood, this brief summary deals in terms of parishes.

Table 1: CONSTITUENTS OF THE FOREST OF DEAN IN 1634

The extraparochial royal demesne (*c.* 23,000 a.)[1]
Abenhall
Awre (with its tithings of Blakeney, Bledisloe, Etloe, and Hagloe, but
    omitting a small tithing called Box)
English Bicknor
Flaxley
Lea (the part of the parish in Gloucestershire, omitting another part that
    was in Herefordshire)
Littledean
Mitcheldean
Newland (with its tithings of Bream, Clearwell, Coleford, Lea Bailey,
    and various small detached parts)
Newnham (omitting its tithing called Ruddle)
Northwood (a small tithing in Westbury-on-Severn)
Ruardean
St. Briavels
Staunton

Although his original instructions from Noy, the attorney-general, were
to respect the reduced bounds as confirmed in 1327, and though, it seems, well
aware of the damage to the king's credibility in doing otherwise,[2] Finch was
unwilling to pass over an opportunity to bring many more potential offenders into
the net of fines. Unearthing the ancient perambulations from the records in the
Tower of London and wielding the dictum that 'no time runs against the king', he
proposed to the judges to revive the wider bounds and include the many places
where no forest law had operated for three centuries. The arguments for doing so
were flimsy, as even his own report to the king shows, and the selective treatment
of evidence by Finch and Ralph Whitfield, his assistant counsel at the eyre, is
revealed even more clearly in the longer account of the proceedings.
Understandably reluctant to commit themselves, the grand jury of county
freeholders and the assembled forest officers offered a fence-sitting verdict which
confirmed the legality of the wider bounds but added a suggestion that the
decisions of 1300 and 1327 together with the usage of over 300 years made the
restricted bounds also valid. That was not satisfactory to Finch and the judges,
who pressured the jury into omitting the second part of verdict.

---

[1] The acreage as given at the period varied between 21,000 and 25,000, depending whether the
particular estimate included the alienated Mailscot and Cannop estates and other areas of
anomalous status – Abbots wood, which by a grant of 1258 the lords of Flaxley held free of the
forest law but still subject to other rights of the Crown, and Hudnalls, a detached area overlooking
the Wye, in which the men of St. Briavels claimed rights and where the forest law had effectively
lapsed.
[2] GA, D 9125/1/2937, f. 33 and v.

It appears that the sheriff of Gloucestershire, Sir Giles Fettiplace, perhaps prompted by Finch, was also minded to interpret the constituents of the Forest more widely than currently accepted when he drew up lists of those to be summoned to the eyre. His choice of parishes, however, matched none of the disputed perambulations, and to compound the uncertainty his two lists[1] – those parishes or tithings who were to send their manorial reeve and four men, and those whose freeholders were required to attend – differed considerably. The first is fairly close to what had been left in the Forest in 1327 but includes two parishes then excluded (Bulley and Taynton). The second is closer to the wider bounds as perambulated in 1228 and 1282, including even the Tidenham Chase parishes, but it omits some places (Alvington, part of Newent, and surprisingly Taynton) that those perambulations had included.[2] The established usage in the early 17th century is made clear (or as clear as ever could be at the time) by the presentments of the forest officers at the June swanimote and by the claims entered by forest officers and freeholders at the eyre. The catchment area of both (revealed by the parishes where unlicensed felling of timber, building of houses, keeping of guns and dogs, and other infringements of the forest law had occurred and by the manors and freehold estates for which claims were entered) accords well with the list given in Table 1, above.[3]

Although he had swayed the justices and the jury to a decision in his favour, Finch did not go as far as to insist on a retrospective application of the wider bounds. He reported that those living within the added area 'were fearful they should have been questioned for many things done contrary to the forest law. But the king's counsel in regard of long usage thought it not fit to proceed with any of them at that justice seat'.[4] Following the eyre, however, the senior forest officers were required to enforce the wider bounds; under pressure from the justices-in-eyre they probably had no option, however much as local landowners they found it repugnant. Therefore, at swanimotes held between September 1634 and December 1636 (included in this volume) major landowners of Huntley, Longhope, Walford (Herefs.), Hope Mansell (Herefs.), and Dixton (Mon.) found themselves presented for felling their woodlands or building ironworks. Whether any fines were levied as a result of those presentments is not clear. Probably the intention was always to raise further income by encouraging owners to buy out of the forest jurisdiction. During 1637 and 1638 Sir John Winter paid £1,000 to free his Lydney estate while several lesser landowners in Tidenham and Woolaston followed suit with smaller payments,[5] and an order

---

[1] Below, pp. 31–42.

[2] He was not (as sheriff of Gloucestershire) concerned with any of the Herefordshire parishes.

[3] In the claims the main differences are that none is entered for Flaxley, while one is entered for Rodley but with a statement confirming that it was outside the Forest.

[4] Below, p. 23.

[5] TNA, E 401/1924, entries for 29 July, 5 Dec. 1637, 24 Jan., 22 Feb. 1637/8; E 401/1925, entries for 1 May, 12 June 1638.

from the king himself in 1638 seems to imply that all the lands returned to the Forest at the eyre were expected to be bought out.[1] The revived bounds for Dean and for the other royal forests, where later eyres made similar extensions, did not, however, long obtain: by an Act of 1641 the Long Parliament returned all forests to the bounds as they had existed in 1623.[2] For Dean the reduced bounds were confirmed after the Restoration by the Dean Forest Act of 1668. Officially those bounds remained in place until the 19th century, though in practice the forest law was no longer applied in the parochial lands, only in the royal demesne.

OFFENDERS AND OFFENCES

The long list of offences against the forest laws presented to the preparatory swanimote in June 1634 was compiled partly from records that the permanent local officers kept on a routine basis and partly from enquiries conducted following the announcement of the eyre in concert with the newly-appointed regarders. The Forest courts, or at least the attachment court for indicting misdemeanours against the vert, seem to have remained fairly active during the early 17th century.[3] The dating of the offences against vert and venison presented in 1634 indicates that regular checks and reporting to the local courts had been carried out by the officers responsible for the bailiwicks of the demesne during the previous four or five years, and the presentments of cottages and cabins built on the demesne evidently derive from special surveys carried out during 1629 and 1630 with some later updating to the time of the swanimote. Other matters, however, such as fisheries (where the few offences are all dated in early 1634), hawks' eyries, mines, and ironworks, did not come within the standard purview of the attachment and swanimote courts and the presentments for them show signs of having been hastily put together for the purpose of the eyre. As regards the parochial areas of the Forest, the local courts had almost certainly given up collecting and presenting the activities of landowners and their tenants. For fellings in private woodlands vague datings, such as 'within the last 20 years' were offered, and the presentments of 'new cottages' built apparently made use of old records, probably provided by the stewards of the relevant manor courts. For Ruardean a survey made back in 1614 was used and for Flaxley one of 1612, and little effort was made in any of the parishes to update the record to the present. For some parts of the parochial lands that item of the 'charge' was probably not enquired into at all.[4]

---

[1] GA, D 421/E 5, order of 26 Mar. 1638 arranging for grant to Sir John Winter: to be excepted from the grant were 'all such lands as were lately declared forest …which are not *as yet* by letters patent exempted from forest jurisdiction'.
[2] Forest Metes and Bounds Act, 16 Chas. II, c. 16.
[3] *VCH Glos*. v. pp. 359–60.
[4] It might be concluded from the presentments that there had been little or no new building during the early 17th century in Newland parish, containing the populous villages of Coleford and Clearwell (Three or four new cottages are described as 'in Coleford' but appear to have been at that tithing's boundary with the demesne: below, p. 64 (nos. 234–7)). By contrast, at the preparatory

Table 2: Tradesmen from Surrounding Parishes presented for Offences in the Demesne at Swanimotes held 1634–6[1]

	taking wood, bark, etc.	other offences	total
miners	15	6	21
charcoal burners	4	1	5
corders	2	-	2
sawyers	1	-	1
woodcutters	1	4	5
cardboard makers[2]	6	-	6
carpenters	12	3	15
coopers	7	-	7
joiners	-	2	2
saddletree makers	2	-	2
scalemakers[3]	2	-	2
shipwrights[4]	2	1	3
shovel makers	5	-	5
timbermen[5]	9	2	11
treenail makers	1	-	1
trencher makers	1	-	1
turners	2	-	2
masons	3	-	3
nailmakers	1	5	6
pinmakers	2	-	2
potters	-	1	1
smiths	4	4	8
tanners	7	5	12
tilers	-	1	1
butchers	4	2	6
clothiers	1	-	1
feltmakers	-	1	1
glovers	1	1	2
innkeepers	2	1	3
maltmen	1	-	1
mercers	1	1	2
millers	1	1	2
shoemakers	2	-	2
tailors	2	2	4
weavers	-	2	2

swanimote for the Dean eyre of 1656 Newland parish accounted for the majority of the new dwellings presented: GA, D 2026/X 14.

[1] The enumeration is of individuals, not offences; some men were presented several times during the period.

[2] 'Cardboard' at this period was used for thin cuts of timber.

[3] Producers of thin pieces of board (*OED*), probably in effect the same trade as 'cardboard maker'.

[4] Some dealers in ship timber are also mentioned.

[5] A vague term encompassing several of the other categories: some of the individuals given this style occur elsewhere as 'shovel maker', 'turner', etc.

The vert offences which provided the bulk of the presentments at the swanimote of June 1634 and at the sessions held in the years following the eyre underline the findings of other reports and surveys of the Forest at the period – that the illegal taking of timber from the Crown woodlands had become part of the local economy and way of life. The timber and small wood taken by the majority of offenders, usually given the vague description 'labourer', was presumably destined for house repairs and firewood. Many of those would have had a claim to a limited amount by virtue of their occupation of particular dwellings in the Forest parishes but were found to have infringed the restrictions on the type of material to be taken or failed to obtain the required sanction from the attachment court. Other offenders were tradesmen gathering the raw materials of their trades. Such men had probably come to treat the taking of the king's wood and timber as an essential part of their trade and saw the fine, which if detected you paid to the attachment court (at a more modest rate than those the eyre attempted to levy in 1634), as a business overhead. Among them were the miners taking timber to shore up their workings (the men recorded were mostly from Coleford, Clearwell, and other places on the west of the demesne), tanners stripping oak bark for use in their tanneries at Mitcheldean, Blakeney, and elsewhere, and carpenters, coopers, and other woodworkers. Others needed wood to fuel small domestic forges used in nailmaking (a trade centred locally on Littledean), pinmaking, and general smithing.

The fines noted in the margins of the surviving record of the 1634 swanimote appear to have been entered before the proceedings of the eyre opened, probably by a clerk following consultation with the justices-in-eyre, for they represent a first and (from the Crown's point of view) optimistic idea of what might be levied. The fines on the major offenders, as mentioned above, were subsumed in new assessments following Finch's special indictments, a few lesser fines were modified after appeals made by the offenders or their attorneys during the proceedings, and others (mainly on members of the local gentry) were reduced later on petition to the chief justice-in-eyre.[1] For the lesser offences a fairly standard rate was adopted,[2] though there are some odd inconsistencies in the sums. The offences against the vert will be seen to reflect the historic composition of the Forest woodlands, timber trees of oak and beech in roughly equal proportions, with underwood of holly, hawthorn, crab apple, and other species.[3] The venison offences feature only fallow deer (i.e. bucks and does); the red and roe which in medieval times had grazed with them were by the early 17th

---

[1] See the modifications made at a later stage to some of the entries and marginal notes of fines, often recording also payment to a royal receiver, Thomas Leake.

[2] e.g. for taking a whole tree £3 or £5 and for a single branch £1, with a rough scale relating to the tonnage of timber; building a cottage on the demesne £5 or (if wood was stolen for it) £6 13s. 4d.; taking venison £100; keeping a gun £10 or £20.

[3] cf. Hart, *Royal Forest*, pp. 276, 280–2; TNA, E 178/3837, depositions 1611.

century very scarce or no longer present. It was a long time since a reigning monarch had come to hunt in his Forest of Dean, but the deer remained useful as royal largesse in the form of gifts of venison and special licences to hunt, and no doubt they were preserved particularly assiduously by those Forest officers whose traditional perquisites included venison.

EARLY SETTLEMENT IN THE FOREST DEMESNE

An aspect of the presentments at the June 1634 swanimote worth particular mention is the geographical detail provided for an early and temporary phase of settlement on the demesne. That was mainly a result of the arrival of the king's ironworks and mostly affected areas adjoining the works. The grants to the ironmasters permitted them to build what dwellings were necessary for their workmen, but many poor families moved in and put up dwellings and, in some cases, encroached small patches of land around them.

By 1616, within four years of the original grant to the earl of Pembroke, there were, according to one report, already 79 cottages on the demesne occupied by 346 people.[1] The swanimote of 1634 recorded over 150 cottages.[2] The greatest concentration was in the south-western part of the demesne, in and adjoining the valley of the Cannop brook. On the stream stood two of the furnaces of the king's works, one near Cannop bridge and the other at the place downstream known as Parkend from the adjoining enclosure called Whitemead park, and two forges, one at Parkend and another further downstream at Whitecroft. Over 60 dwellings had been built in that area by 1634: their sites are described as at Cannop, at Wet wood (lying south of Cannop bridge and east of the brook), at Parkend, at Whitemead park (which though king's land was held by the constable of St Briavels under his lease of Newland manor and parish), at '*Quiceslade*', a name then used for the valley leading north-westwards from Parkend (now traversed by the Parkend–Coleford road),[3] and at Whitecroft. There were also clusters of dwellings at Bream's Eaves, close to the boundary of the demesne, adjoining the hamlet of Bream, and in the nearby valley of the Oakwood brook. Some of those at Bream's Eaves and Oakwood were possibly built in connexion with Sir John Winter's ironworks in and near Lydney and with his cordwood concession, rather than with the king's works: the swanimote recorded much felling by Winter's agents in woodlands in that part of the demesne.[4] Some cottagers in the same area may have been miners employed in the iron mines on the adjoining parochial lands in Noxon park and elsewhere in Clearwell and Bream tithings.

In the more easterly parts of the demesne over 40 cottages were recorded, including a substantial group at Staple Edge adjoining the valley of the

---

[1] TNA, E 178/3837, inquisition 6 Feb. 1616.
[2] See below, Table 3.
[3] Below, p. 63*n*.
[4] Below, pp. 50–1 (nos. 70–2).

Soudley brook, which powered a furnace and forge of the king's works. A settlement had also formed in Chestnuts wood, part of it on the eastern and lower slopes of the wood adjoining the boundary with Westbury-on-Severn parish, in an area then called Blackmore's Hale but later usually known as Pope's Hill;[1] a Giles Pope was among the cottagers living there in 1634.[2] Some of the cottages in Chestnuts may have been occupied by men servicing the forges on the nearby Flaxley estate, where the Forest officers also noted a number of houses built on parochial lands in recent years. Winter's Gunn's mill furnace, higher up the Flaxley stream below Shapridge, may also have helped to encourage settlement in those eastern parts of the demesne. The northern fringes of the demesne were relatively free of settlement, with just a few cottages at Howbrook, Hangerberry, and other places on the hillsides above English Bicknor and Ruardean parishes. The ironworks on that side of the Forest, principally the king's furnace above Lydbrook, a forge of Benedict Hall's at Lydbrook within his Bicknor manor, and works at Bishopswood, partly within Ruardean and partly on lands of the earls of Essex in Walford (Herefs.), presumably drew sufficient labour from the nearby parochial lands. Ruardean significantly is the parish within the Forest bounds where the largest number of 'new' cottages were recorded by the swanimote: 18 were noted as having been built by 1614, by which time both the Lydbrook and Bishopswood works had begun production. A straggle of cottages marked on a plan of *c.* 1680 just within Ruardean's boundary with the demesne was possibly the result of that early 17th-century development.[3] The Bishopswood works stimulated similar building within Walford parish: a swanimote held in December 1634, after that area had been returned to the Forest jurisdiction, recorded 14 dwellings built at Bishopswood in the previous few years.[4]

Table 3: LOCATION OF COTTAGES RECORDED ON THE DEMESNE IN 1634[5]

Parkend and Park Forge	21	Blakeney's Eaves	2
Staple Edge	20	'in Blakeney bailiwick'	2
Chestnuts and Blackmore's Hale	16	Viney	1
Bream's Eaves	13	Ellwood	1
Cannop	10	Gorsty Knoll	1
Wet wood	10	Milkwall	1
Quiceslade	9	'next to Broadwell'	1

[1] *VCH Glos.* v. p. 315; x. p. 84.
[2] Below, p. 58 (no. 137).
[3] TNA, F 17/7.
[4] Below, pp. 132–4.
[5] The enumeration excludes some larger dwellings apparently built by the ironmasters and grantees of estates for their own use and a few cottages where the location, whether in demesne or parochial land, is left unclear by the description. There were probably others on the demesne that escaped the notice of the officers.

Whitemead Park	7	'near Cinderford bridge'	1
Whitecroft	6	Mirystock	1
Oakwood	6	Hangerberry	1
'near Abenhall'	4	*Little Hocke*	1
'near Lea and Lea Bailey'	3	*Telhockhead*	1
Thorneyhills	3	*Denalmore*	1
Soudley	2	*Brookehill*	1
Howbrook	2	*Syndry hill*	1
'near Ruardean'	2	*Le Hayend*	1
Waynewaye	2	(no location given)	2

total 156

Most of the cottagers settled on the demesne were described by the blanket term 'labourer'; only in the case of some places in Blakeney bailiwick – Staple Edge, Soudley, *Thorneyhills* (near Blackpool bridge), and Blakeney's Eaves (the later Blakeney Hill) – did the relevant officers, who had apparently carried out a check in late 1633 when it was known the eyre was imminent, provide more specific occupational descriptions: ten woodcutters, nine charcoal burners, two 'coal (probably charcoal) carriers', and a corder were recorded.[1] Many of the settlers in other parts no doubt followed such trades: for example, Philip James of Parkend and Thomas Phillips of *Quiceslade*, 'labourers', are presumably the same men styled respectively woodcutter and corder in other presentments.[2]

The proportion of settlers who had no direct connexion with the king's ironworks but were attempting to gain a living by other means is not evident. When in 1637 the deputy surveyor John Broughton claimed that, whereas the lessees had allowed 160 cabins to be built, they actually needed no more than 20 to house their employees, he almost certainly set the last figure unrealistically low, for his aim was to secure the concession for himself.[3] According to Sir Basil Brooke, he and George Mynne employed 129 people from the cabins at one time,[4] and the scale of the ironmasters' operations and the labour required is indicated again in 1649 when Thomas Pury, a former parliamentary army officer who secured a share of the works following the Civil War, was said to have 40 packhorses carrying charcoal, each making two or three trips a day.[5] It is clear that to keep the furnaces and forges at work required a large workforce and one based reasonably near at hand. Though some lived in the immediately adjoining parochial lands, it cannot have been practical, particularly when the furnaces

---

[1] Below, pp. 67–9.
[2] Below, pp. 63 (nos. 207–8), 66 (no. 257), 90 (no. 627), 92 (no. 652).
[3] *Cal. S.P. Dom.* 1637, p. 205; Hart, *Royal Forest*, p. 119.
[4] TNA, SP 16/293, no. 69.
[5] Ibid. LRRO 5/7A, inquisition Sept. 1649.

were in blast for weeks on end, to rely on workers tramping from many miles away. Another complaint sometimes made against the ironmasters was that they brought their workers from distant parts of the country.[1] A few skilled men appear to have come from other ironmaking areas to act as forgemen and overseers, but it is likely the great majority moved into the demesne from adjoining parishes, as was the case during the later and permanent settlement during the 18th and early 19th centuries. The considerable number of Welsh patronymics (and some Welsh forenames) recorded among the cottagers in 1634 does not necessarily indicate a sudden recent migration from across the Wye, for such names had long been common in the parishes of the Forest area.[2]

The dwellings of the settlers on the demesne are described both as cottages and cabins. One reference suggests that the two terms are used indiscriminately,[3] so there is probably no need to assume the former term was reserved for something less primitive than the latter. In the 1640s dwellings in the demesne might sell for as little as 30s.,[4] no more than the price of a pair of oxen or horses, and some were valued by the officers in 1634 at a nominal 5s. or 12s. a year.[5] Presentments giving the tonnage of timber used to build cottages and recording materials being carted away (perhaps to be re-erected on another site) show that basically they were of timber.[6] The dwellings put up by squatters on the demesne in the 18th century, though still primitive in character – often windowless and with roofs of turf supported on rough timbers – are described as having drystone walls.[7] Perhaps the difference related to the greater availability of timber for the taking in the former period, perhaps to the wider development of quarrying in the latter. The new dwellings at Bishopswood were described in 1634 in terms of 'bays', which suggests a more conventional and less primitive type of framed timber structure than those on the demesne; put up on manorial land and presumably by permission of the landowner, there would have been more leisure to build and more expectation of permanence.

Following the eyre ineffectual efforts made to tighten up the Forest administration[8] included a move to limit the number of settlers. In 1635 the county sheriff was instructed to send an inventory of all the cottages and other encroachments[9] to Chief Justice Holland, who ordered him to take them all into

[1] e.g. Hart, *Royal Forest*, p. 93.
[2] *Bristol and Glos. Lay Subsidy 1523–7*, ed. M.A. Faraday (BGAS, Glos. Record Series, xxiii, 2009), li–lii, pp. 89–112.
[3] Below, p. 128 (no. 7).
[4] TNA, LRRO 5/7A, certificate by preservators Aug.–Oct. 1648.
[5] Below, p. 69 (nos. 303–6).
[6] e.g. pp. 128 (nos. 7–8, 10), 134 (nos. 61, 63).
[7] Nicholls, *Forest of Dean*, pp. 151–2.
[8] Hart (*Royal Forest*, pp. 114–15) quotes in this connexion a document (in TNA, C 99/31) giving detailed instructions to the deputies of the constable of St. Briavels to take action to redress the abuses, dating it as 1635; but the original document is undated and from internal evidence precedes the eyre, probably c. 1632.
[9] In it he merely repeated the findings of the June 1635 swanimote.

the king's hands.[1] It is doubtful that any action in the form of expulsions followed, and during the chaotic years of the Civil War and its aftermath even more settlers moved in. It was not until the administration of John Wade during the Commonwealth that the bulk of the cottages on the demesne (a later account said as many as 400) were pulled down and the occupants ejected.[2] Some remained to be removed by the reformed Forest administration of Charles II in the 1670s and early 1680s, following which there may have been a period when the demesne was entirely free of illegal settlers. By the 1730s, however, squatter dwellings had begun to appear again,[3] in some cases re-colonising areas of the former invasion, such as Pope's Hill and Bream's Eaves, but forming eventually a much more extensive ring of settlements on the outer hillsides of the demesne.

THE CLAIMS MADE AT THE EYRE

Most of the 120 claims registered at the eyre were by holders of freehold lands in parishes surrounding the demesne for their right to common pasture, estovers, housebote and heybote, and pannage (i.e. to graze animals, take wood for fuel and for building repairs, and to feed pigs on the beech-mast). With the sole exception of the men of Rodley manor,[4] all of the claimants occupied lands within the bounds of the Forest as then accepted.[5] That limitation is puzzling, for it was well established that freeholders in various other parishes and tithings, near adjoining and with reasonably easy access to the demesne, exercised commoning rights on the grounds that their lands were former parts of the Forest ('purlieus'). In 1612, when the first grant of the king's ironworks and cordwood caused concern among the commoners, Alvington, Blaisdon, Hewelsfield, Longhope, the various tithings of Lydney parish, Ruddle (in Newnham), and Rodley, and, in Herefordshire, Hope Mansell, Weston under Penyard with its tithing of Pontshill, and Huntsham (in Goodrich) were among the places claiming rights, along with the parishes and tithings within the Forest.[6] Even more conclusively, in 1628 Sir John Winter, Benedict Hall, and other leading gentry acting on behalf of the commoners secured a decree from the Court of Exchequer which confirmed the eligibility of those same Gloucestershire places (plus Huntsham).[7] The decree followed a careful enquiry and a re-definition of the rights, made by the attorney-general.[8] It seems most unlikely that the judges at

---

[1] TNA, C 99/27.

[2] Hart, *Royal Forest*, p. 289.

[3] *VCH Glos*. v. pp. 300–1.

[4] Below, p. 112 (no.12).

[5] For which, cf. above, Table 1.

[6] TNA, E 112/82, no. 300.

[7] Ibid. E 125/4, ff. 269–74.

[8] The grounds on which a local inhabitant might claim common rights in a royal forest were many and complex: see *Manwood's Forest Laws*, ed. Nelson, pp. 85–93. In Dean, the attorney-general's report declared that rights should be enjoyed only in respect of the occupation of an ancient

the eyre intended to flout a recent finding by one of the highest courts in the land, so the exclusion of the purlieu parishes from the claims as they survive among the records perhaps reflects little more than misguided tidy-mindedness on the part of officialdom. Certainly it did not have the effect of limiting the exercise of commoning rights: five or six purlieu parishes and tithings continued to pasture animals in the demesne during the 18th century and pay herbage money in respect of it. By the late years of that century, however, the general laxity of the administration had made the question of who was entitled largely irrelevant; the Forest keepers were admitting any animals turned in, regardless of origin.[1] By ancient custom the rights extended also to tenants and sub-tenants under the holders of the ancient manors and freeholds, so that at any period the total of individuals who might exercise them probably ran into the thousands. From the mid 18th century the animals pastured were swelled in number by those kept by the new wave of squatters on the demesne. The squatters could have no claim on any legal grounds but as the years passed, with no determined action to expel them, they came to form a majority among the commoners.

Another matter the claims left unresolved and open to discussion was the type of animals the commoners might pasture. Under the forest law as anciently established sheep were not commonable in a royal forest.[2] By the period of the eyre, however, they were pastured in considerable numbers, as several recently-built sheepcots on the fringes of the demesne testified,[3] and the Exchequer decree of 1628 confirmed a claim by the commoners to pasture them in unwooded parts of the demesne.[4] In the late 19th century, when the regulation of the large flocks then being pastured became a major concern of the administration, the Commissioners of Woods sought legal advice to support its contention that the sheep were allowed only on sufferance rather than by ancient custom. The claims made at the eyre were thought to have particular relevance, for an Act of Parliament passed to regulate the Forest in 1668 had provided that commoning should be enjoyed in the same manner as in 1634. Recourse to the claims, however, revealed that the lawyers responsible had described the commonable livestock by the word *averia*, an unhelpfully imprecise term but one usually understood to comprise only cattle and horses.[5]

The claims figured as a precedent to better effect in other legal disputes. In the mid 18th century Thomas Gage, Lord Gage, a notably litigious individual

---

dwelling ('common appurtenant' in the legal terminology) in the eligible parishes. His report also ruled regarding estovers; they were to be taken only in the form of dead and dry wood.
[1] Berkeley Castle Muniments, general series no. 16, survey of the Forest of Dean 1746; *Third Report of Commissioners to Enquire into the Crown Woods, Forests, and Land Revenues* (1788), 38, 85, 109–10.
[2] *Manwood's Forest Laws*, ed. Nelson, p. 93.
[3] Below, pp. 55 (no. 113), 58 (no. 142), 73 (nos. 358–9).
[4] TNA, E 125/4, ff. 269, 272, 273v.–4.
[5] *Report of the Forest of Dean Committee, 1958* (Cmnd. 686), H.C. (1958–9), xiii, pp. 21–4 (reviewing earlier enquiries into the legal position).

who troubled the Forest administration of his day with a series of lawsuits, unearthed the claim of his predecessor Benedict Hall when his right to take windfall trees and the bark of timber felled for the Crown in his bailiwicks of Staunton and Bicknor was challenged.[1] The holder of Abenhall bailiwick similarly employed his predecessor's claim at the same period.[2]

A noticeable omission, in view of its responsibility for testing and determining all rights and privileges, was the eyre's failure to define those affecting mining and quarrying in the Forest. Dean's miners attempted to put in a claim, but the judges, either on orders from the Crown or anticipating its wishes, dismissed it on the grounds that the miners were not incorporated and therefore ineligible to make a joint claim;[3] no miner at the time was apparently found able or wealthy enough to employ lawyers to enter an claim individually or to challenge the judges' decision. It was common knowledge and easily shown by past records that mining rights had been allowed for centuries to the 'free miners' of St. Briavels hundred – their complex customs even secured the Crown's interest, laying down rules by which the king would profit from each pit that was dug. In 1634, however, Charles and his advisers were probably anxious to leave the exact position undefined, since some of the recent grants to the ironmasters and courtiers effectively contravened the miners' rights. The king's policies had led to litigation and violent action on the part of the miners at the time of the lease to Pembroke in 1612, and they would do so again a few years after the eyre when the king granted all coal and grindstone mines in the Forest to one of his privy councillors.[4] So the issue was sidestepped at the eyre and, as with much else concerning the Forest, the basis on which the free miners operated was left unclear until 19th-century legislation.

THE AFTERMATH OF THE EYRE

The Dean eyre caused much comment among contemporaries, focusing in particular on the role played by Sir John Finch, who shortly afterwards was appointed chief justice of Common Pleas and moved on to apply the methods he had used at Gloucester at eyres held for other royal forests. The scale of the fines imposed also attracted comment,[5] but those on the principal offenders were merely, as seems to have been usual at the period, the opening moves in negotiations over what was to be paid. The process against Sir Basil Brooke and George Mynne was transferred to Chancery and eventually to King's Bench, where their attorney attempted a challenge on the technical point that the proceedings had been invalid because held outside the Forest's bounds. As might

[1] GA, D 1677/GG 1230, 1235, 1259–65.
[2] Ibid. D 23/L 2.
[3] Below, p. 18.
[4] Hart, *Free Miners*, pp. 152–9, 169–77.
[5] Hammersley, 'Revival of Forest Laws', pp. 99–101; *Cal. S.P. Dom.* 1634–5, p. 182; Historical Manuscripts Commission, *3rd Report* (1872), p. 282; *Calendar of State Papers and Manuscripts relating to English Affairs …in Venice* (HMSO), xxiii. pp. 263–4, 293, 346.

have been expected from past form, the Crown's lawyer Ralph Whitfield, who had assisted Finch at the eyre, had no trouble in coming up with numerous historical precedents to dispose of that argument.[1] The quest for a reduction in the fines on the former partnership was left mainly to Brooke, who during the next two years bombarded the king and his ministers with petitions. Apart from offering much detail to challenge Finch's calculations about the amount of cordwood used, he advanced further proposals in the hope of preserving the ironworks and cordwood concession for his new partnership with Sir John Winter. In one long and obsequious entreaty to the king he claimed that he faced inevitable ruin if deprived of the lease, even mentioning that he had a wife from a noble family (presumably implying that she had expensive tastes) and eight children to support. By the summer of 1635 he had managed to reduce his share of the penalties to £12,000,[2] which was eventually the total levied on both former partners, Brooke made liable for £5,000 and Mynne for £7,000; both had paid off their share by the start of 1637.[3] Mynne, having sold out of the partnership for £8,000 and further considerations for his share of the stock, probably felt that he had emerged with a balance sheet in his favour.[4] Brooke, though he and Winter were deprived of the lease of the ironworks, avoided the ruin he had prophesied and continued in possession of his estate and works in Shropshire until they were sequestrated to Parliament in the Civil War. A leading Roman Catholic, he then supported the royalist cause,[5] as was the case with both Winter (also a Catholic) and with Mynne;[6] if there was still lingering resentment at their treatment at Gloucester, it had by then been eclipsed by other and more serious considerations. Nor at that time of rapidly-moving events and shifting allegiances is it likely they saw any irony in the fact that Lord Holland, the man who had sat in judgement on them, and Lord Pembroke, who had aided the calling of the eyre, were to be found on the opposing side.

Winter combined his pleas for leniency with an energetic campaign to establish himself in favour as the king's main support in the Forest area.[7] His efforts began to bear fruit when he was appointed secretary to Queen Henrietta Maria in 1637 and culminated in 1640 in a grant of rights in the Forest more extensive in scope than anything enjoyed by a subject before. His total fines at the eyre were reduced to only £4,000, for which he received quittance with a full

---

[1] GA, D 1677/GG 1220, pp. 22–5.

[2] TNA, SP 16/293, no. 69; *Cal. S.P. Dom.* pp. 1635, 250, 253, 262, 276, 308–9.

[3] TNA, E 401/1923, entries for 9, 19 Aug., 2 Dec. 1636; E 401/1924, entry for 27 May 1637.

[4] Ibid. SP 16/293, nos. 68–9.

[5] *VCH Shropshire,* xi. p. 48 ; *ODNB*, vii. p. 871.

[6] *ODNB*, xl. p. 85.

[7] See *Cal. S.P. Dom.* 1636–7, pp. 267–8 (drawing to the king's attention, among other matters, his part in suppressing the 'Skimmington' riots); ibid. 1637, p. 412 (mentioning that he had defeated a prominent opponent of ship money, Sir Robert Cooke of Highnam, in an election for verderer).

pardon for all offences in 1637.[1] John Gibbons secured a comparatively modest reduction to £8,000 in his fine, which he had paid off by 1638.[2] Some of the other offenders, mainly Forest gentry convicted for offences committed on their own lands, gained reductions by direct petition to the chief justice-in-eyre or by other means. Benedict Hall of Highmeadow secured a reduction by half on fines of £300 for each of two iron furnaces he maintained and a reduction to £10 of a £40 fine for converting waste land to arable,[3] but he paid others in full, including £100 for a forge at Lydbrook.[4] Sir Richard Catchmay of Bigsweir had a fine of 100 marks (£66 13s. 4d.) for a furnace reduced to 20 marks and also secured reductions on small fines for felling groves on parochial lands (£3 to 30s. and 10s. to 6s. 8d.).[5] Francis Bridgeman of Blakeney, gentleman, fined £2,400 for felling trees on the demesne, paid only £50,[6] while he and a partner had a fine of £50 for another vert offence reduced to £4.[7] As with the original sums imposed, there seems to have been no consistent plan in the scale of the reductions.[8]

What is not clear is how fully the fines on the numerous humbler offenders were levied, sums of only a pound or two but proportionately of as much or more significance to them as the fines on the gentry and ironmasters. The only clue given by the marginalia added against the swanimote presentments is a note of a reduction from £3 to 10s. that George Bradley, labourer, secured for his cottage built on parochial land at Ruardean.[9] Few such men had the means or knowledge for making a plea for leniency or employing someone to do it for them, but by the same token few had goods or possession of sufficient value to be distrained on for failure to pay, so there must be doubt that much was ever collected.

The eyre led to little improvement in the state of the Forest. The operation of the king's ironworks and the cordwood concession was suspended temporarily but in July 1636 a new lease was granted to a partnership which included Sir Baynham Throckmorton, successful at last in his campaign to acquire a share in the works. The new partners were soon subject to the same

---

[1] GA, D 421/E 4. His quittance recited a fully-itemized list of the fines as first assessed on him at the eyre; well aware of the tendency of the king and his lawyers to dredge up long-forgotten claims, he may have insisted on that degree of clarity.

[2] Hammersley, 'Revival of Forest Laws', p. 96; Cal. S.P. Dom. 1638–9, p. 123.

[3] Below, p. 94 (no. 678); p. 96 (nos. 703–4).

[4] Below, pp. 52–3 (nos. 84, 91, 95); pp. 58–9 (no. 152); pp. 94–5 (nos. 679, 693).

[5] Below, p. 52 (nos. 86, 88); p. 96 (no. 706).

[6] Below, p. 93 (no. 668); the size of the fine originally imposed probably reflected the fact that a forged warrant was involved: see below, pp. 12–13.

[7] Below, p. 44 (no.10).

[8] The fragmentary evidence surviving, almost all of it relating to the major offenders, and the inconsistency shown in such final payments as are recorded make it impossible to give a useful estimate of the total collected in fines following the eyre. Hammersley offered a 'cautious' one of between £26,000 and £30,000 (out of a total of c. £140,000 as originally assessed): 'Revival of Forest Laws', pp.99–100.

[9] Below, p.70 (no.316).

complaints as the old ones.[1] Meanwhile requests to the Crown for land and rights continued,[2] encouraged by the fact that the owners of Cannop and Mailscot had been left in possession of their estates and, more generally, by a process of disafforestation in other royal forests, such as the nearby Malvern Chase.[3] A logical culmination of the king's policy towards Dean was reached in March 1640 with the finalization of the extensive grant he had been for some time negotiating: for £106,000 (to be paid in instalments over six years) and an annual fee-farm of £1,951, Sir John Winter was given 18,000 a., the bulk of the demesne, including the right to the minerals, underwood, and game but reserving ship timber and a quota of cordwood for the lessees of the ironworks. Another 4,000 a. was left open to the commoners; the question of the miners and how their rights were affected was once more left unresolved.[4]

When the war came it was Winter, with the most to lose, who took the lead in the fighting on the Crown's part, engaging in a spirited duel with the parliamentary garrison at Gloucester before leaving the Forest in April 1645 after burning down his manor house at Lydney. Most other leading landowners found themselves on the royalist side or at least suspected later of sympathies. Notable among them was Winter's cousin, the earl (later marquess) of Worcester, the owner of Tidenham, Woolaston and large estates in neighbouring Monmouthshire, while others included Winter's brother-in-law and fellow Catholic Benedict Hall, the Vaughans, and the Throckmortons. In the years following the war, with most of the gentry under sequestration and without influence, the Forest was subjected to the depredations of former army officers who secured control of the ironworks and woodlands. Efforts at reform under the Commonwealth[5] included, paradoxically, recourse to the discredited machinery of the forest eyre: it was convened again at Mitcheldean in 1656 in the name of the Lord Protector and under the presidency of his local 'major-general' John Desborough, who also held the office of constable of St. Briavels.[6] More effectively, Cromwell appointed a new administrator John Wade, who (in spite of his eventual disillusionment with his task) paved the way for a wide-ranging reorganization in the 1670s. Under the direction of Henry Somerset, marquess of Worcester (and later duke of Beaufort), the Crown's chief man in post-Restoration Gloucestershire, the ironworks were discontinued, the remaining squatters expelled, the administration reorganized to include a new class of forest keeper housed in lodges built on the demesne, and an extensive programme of inclosure for navy timber put in hand.[7] Those new measures can be said to mark

---

[1] Hart, *Royal Forest*, pp. 116–18, 123.
[2] *Cal. S.P. Dom.* 1637, p. 205; 1637–8, pp. 254, 531.
[3] B.S. Smith, *A History of Malvern* (1964), pp. 150–5.
[4] GA, D 421/E 5.
[5] *VCH Glos*. v. p. 365.
[6] A copy of the presentments made at the preparatory swanimote survives in GA, D 2026/X14. For Desborough, see A.R. Williams, 'Gloucestershire's Major-General', *Trans. BGAS*. lxxxix. pp. 123–9.
[7] *VCH Glos*. v. pp. 366–7.

the end of the troubled period in which the forest eyre of 1634 was a major landmark. It was in effect the last eyre of Dean, for the proceedings of 1656 were not recognized as valid by the restored royalist government,[1] and recommendations made in 1680 and 1692, that the system be reintroduced with eyres held every six or seven years by the assize judges on their regular circuits, were not adopted.[2]

The inconsistencies in the policy towards the forests followed by Charles I and his ministers at the period of the eyre are clear[3] and in the case of the Forest of Dean particularly apparent. The raising of cash by the lease of the ironworks, the sale of cordwood, and grants to individuals of land and other assets conflicted at every turn with the avowed intention of preserving the woodland for naval and other national needs. Able royal officials at the time urged concentration on the latter purpose,[4] which ostensibly was always kept in mind, by measures intended to preserve the timber trees in the coppices and otherwise regulate the cordwood concession, and by excluding from the various grants the Lea Bailey woodlands, which were then regarded as the best timber in the Forest;[5] but the execution of the policy meant that it was short-term exploitation of its assets for which in Dean those years came to be remembered. The revival of a system, the forest eyre, that had been dormant for centuries would always be controversial, but handled differently it might have weighed in the scale of preservation by correcting and regulating some of the abuses and some of the failures of the local officers. Conducted so transparently as a form of non-parliamentary taxation, the eyre appeared only as part of the exploitation. Charles II and his ministers, with the advantage of a different political and financial climate, showed later what might be done, and their measures did succeed in producing a legacy of fine timber for the navy in the following century. The period of efficient administration that followed their reforms did not, however, long obtain, faltering into a new phase of lax central control and corrupt local officialdom. Governing the Forest of Dean would never be easy.

THE DOCUMENTS; EDITORIAL METHOD

British Library, Harleian MS. 4850. A manuscript volume which includes, of the various documents edited below: the writs summoning the eyre; lists of Forest officers and others attending the eyre in July 1634; presentments at the swanimote held 10 June 1634, with fines noted in the margins; presentment of those keeping unexpeditated dogs; and presentments at swanimotes held between September 1634 and December 1636. The documents are in Latin, but with occasional use of English (e.g. for the occupations of offenders presented) and

---

[1] GA, D 2026/X 20.
[2] Hart, *Royal Forest*, pp. 300, 305.
[3] In this connexion, see Hammersley's pithy summary in 'Revival of Forest Laws', pp. 101–2.
[4] e.g. *Cal. S.P. Dom.* 1633–4, 484; 1634–5, pp. 561, 607; Hart, *Royal Forest*, pp. 276–7.
[5] GA, D 421/E 3, E 5; Hart, *Royal Forest*, p. 274.

sometimes providing an English translation of particular words and phrases. In addition to the above-mentioned documents, the volume includes (bound into the front) a careful index of the persons presented at the post-eyre swanimotes and a list of the 'Articles of the Charge' (i.e. the heads of enquiry put to the jury at a forest eyre); the latter, in pencil and in English, is later in date than the other items and probably doesn't relate specifically to the Dean eyre. The record of the swanimote of June 1634 appears to be fullest that survives, though there is at least one other (in Bodleian MS. Gough, Glouc. 1, ff. 17–68v.) which omits some items and gives the others in a much more summary form. The Harleian volume comprises paper leaves written on both sides and the ink has 'bled' through, making parts difficult to read. On a microfilm the difficulty is compounded, and, though one was used to make the transcript, much was checked back to the original in the British Library. The occasional word or phrase remained indecipherable.

Gloucestershire Archives, D 1677/GG 1220 (in the archives of the Hall and, later, Gage families, owners of the Highmeadow estate): An account of the proceedings at the eyre. The original source has not been discovered. This is an 18th-century copy, evidently acquired in connexion with litigation by the first Lord Gage (d. 1754) against the Forest administration. The document is given as a transcript below but omitting its last five pages which have details of proceedings against Brooke and Mynne following the eyre.

Bodleian Library, Oxford, Gough MS. Glouc. 1, ff. 3–16v.: Notes of the proceedings at the eyre by Sir John Finch, as reported to Charles I. This is one of numerous copies of Finch's statement surviving.[1] The transcript given below has been collated with a copy in GA, D 15/4. (In the Gough MS. this is followed by the abbreviated version of the presentments of June 1634 mentioned above).

The National Archives, C 99/11–20: Claims of rights and privileges entered at the eyre by Forest officers and landowners. In Latin, on parchment rotulets. Another set of the same claims (on separate membranes) is in TNA, C 99/10. The salient details of the claims are presented in this volume as a calendar; an example of an original claim is given in Nicholls, *Forest of Dean*, pp. 261–3.

That the official records produced by the eyre were extensive is suggested by a mention of 'book 7' of the presiding judges.[2] Very probably more remains to come to light.

---

[1] See Hammersley, 'Revival of Forest Laws', 93 and *nn*. In addition to those he cites, other copies are in Lincoln's Inn Library, Maynard MS. 59 (pt. 1), no. 4, and Northants. Record Office, Isham (Lamport) MS. 3006.

[2] Below, p. 45 (no. 13).

Particular aspects of the editing of each document (or section of each) are indicated below in the footnotes. Generally with the swanimote presentments I have reduced unnecessary verbiage and repetition.[1] The original Latin is given in brackets where the terminology is obscure or unusual, and in most cases where the clerk provides his own translation (prefaced by '*anglice*') I have reproduced it, in case it throws light on contemporary usage: the translation he gives in these cases is not always as might be expected. Some obscure terms used once or twice are discussed in footnotes when they occur, while those more generally used (mostly forest terms) will be found in the glossary. Surnames are left as in the original, with varying forms of the same name gathered together in the index. Place-names have been modernized to the forms in common use today (generally following Ordnance Survey maps). Some place-names are identified from older sources, as indicated in the footnotes, but all which are (or appear to be) no longer in use are left in the original form and given in italics. 'The Forest' is used when it is Dean that is being referred to, but the word is given with a lower-case initial letter when the context is royal forests in general.

[Notes on the appended map of *c.* 1680 are given at p. 182 below.]

---

[1] e.g. trees are almost invariably reported as '*succidit et prostravit*', cottages '*erexit et edificavit*'.

THE FOREST OF DEAN EYRE OF 1634

WRITS SUMMONING THE EYRE
(British Library, Harleian MS. 4850, f. 1)

Charles, by God's grace, King of England, Scotland, France, and Ireland, Defender of the Faith, to the sheriff of Gloucestershire, greetings. You are to summon by good men all archbishops, dukes, marquesses, earls, viscounts, bishops, barons, knights, and all free tenants who have lands or tenements within the bounds of our Forest of Dean in your county; and, from each town or township of the same county within the bounds of the said Forest, four men and the reeves of the said towns or townships; and, from each borough within the bounds of the said Forest, 12 good and law-abiding men and the reeves and foresters of the said boroughs; and all others who are accustomed and ought to come before the justices of the pleas of the Forest: that they may be at Mitcheldean, co. Glos., on 10 July next before our well-beloved and most trusty kinsman and counsellor Henry, earl of Holland, warden and chief justice and justice-in-eyre of all and singular our Forests, parks, chases, and warrens on this side of Trent, or his deputy or deputies appointed or to be appointed to exercise the said office, to hear and perform our order concerning those things that appertain to the said pleas. Also, you will cause to come before the said earl or his deputies all the foresters and verderers of the said Forest, and all those who were foresters and verderers of the same in the said county since the last pleas of the said Forest, with all their attachments, both of vert and venison, which have arisen since the last pleas of the Forest and are not yet determined, viz. both those attachments which belong (*manent*) within the bounds of the Forest and those which belong outside it. Also, you will cause to come before the said earl or his deputies, our regarders of the said Forest so that they may hold all their regard there, certified by their seals, and all our agisters of the said Forest with their attachments. And you will have there the summons and this writ.

Witnessed myself at Westminster, 21 March 1634.

The execution of this writ appears in certain schedules annexed to the said writ – Giles Fettiplace, kt., sheriff

Henry, Earl of Holland, knight of the of the noble order of the Garter, chief justice and justice-in-eyre of all the king's Forests, chases, parks, and warrens on this side of Trent, to Philip, earl of Pembroke and Montgomery, chamberlain of the king's household, warden of the king's Forest of Dean, co. Glos., or his deputy in same, greetings.

On the lord king's behalf, I order and firmly enjoin you that you cause to come before me, or my deputy or deputies constituted or to be appointed, on Thursday, 10 July next, at Mitcheldean all foresters, verderers, regarders, woodwards, and all officers of the said Forest who now are, or were since the last pleas of the Forest that were held, and exhibit by all rolls, writings, and muniments the attachments of the Forest, both of vert and venison, that have arisen since the last pleas and are not determined. Also, you will cause to come the regarders of the Forest who now are, and were since the last pleas were held, with all their regards made and enrolled during that time. Furthermore, you will cause to come all agisters of the Forest, who now are, and since that time were, each of them with all their attachments and rolls of agistments, to do right thereby (*ad standum inde recto*) and to do all that each of them is enjoined that he should do according to the forest law. Also, you will cause to come all those who claim to have any liberties, franchises, or privileges within the said Forest, that they may be before me or my deputy or deputies at the same day and place to show in what manner they claim to have those liberties, franchises, or privileges, and by what warrant. And that you, having done other things to this end, will remit this precept, with the names of all the said officers, to me or my deputy or deputies.

Given under my seal at Westminster, 12 May 1634, H. Hollande

The reply of the within-named Philip, earl of Pembroke and Montgomery to this warrant: the execution of this warrant appears in a certain schedule annexed to the same – Pembroke and Montgomery

AN ACCOUNT OF THE PROCEEDINGS AT THE EYRE,
10–18 JULY 1634
(Gloucestershire Archives, D 1677/GG 1220)[1]

The Justice Seat for the Forest of Dean holden at Mitcheldean within the Forest 10 July 1634 and adjourned from thence to Gloucester Castle and there continued until 18 July, and then adjourned several times, [before] Henry, Earl of Holland, Chief Justice and Justice-in-Eyre. Sir William Jones, Kt., one of the Justices of the King's Bench, Sir Thomas Trevor, Kt., one of the Barons of the Exchequer, and Sir John Bridgeman, Kt., Lord Chief Justice of Chester, assisted his lordship by virtue of the king's letters to them directed. Sir John Finch, the king's attorney, and Ralph Whitfield of Grays Inn, Esq., by the king's command signified to him by letter from the Earl of Holland, attended this Justice Seat as of counsel for the king.

It was resolved by his lordship and the three judges, his assistants, that, the court-in-eyre being summoned to be held at Mitcheldean within the Forest, his lordship might make a deputation to call the court at Mitcheldean on 10 July and then adjourn the same, before the charge given or officers or jury called, to the castle of Gloucester in the county of Gloucestershire, being without the Forest. For the Statute 7 Ric. II. cap. 3 is that the jury shall not be driven to travel from the place where their charge is given, which doth not extend to an adjournment before the charge given, and therefore before their charge given they may be adjourned. And according to this resolution the Lord Chief Justice-in-Eyre made a deputation to the three judges assistant, or any of them, to call and adjourn the court. And upon Thursday, 10 July, Justice Bridgeman at Mitcheldean at 8 o'clock in the morning called the court and then adjourned it to the castle of Gloucester to 10 that day, and then he came to Gloucester where the Lord Chief Justice was. And his lordship with the three judges went to the court, which was prepared on a hill[2] adjoining to the castle, and there called the court, so adjourned, his lordship sitting in the court and the three judges assistant sitting by him, bare[-headed].

---

[1] This account is taken from a copy in the Highmeadow estate archives, which is endorsed with the following notes: '10 July 10 Chas. I; earl of Holland, Justice-in-Eyre; the perambulations of the Forest made 12 Hen. III, 10 Edw. I the only good ones and so adjudged by this *Iter*; the manors of Staunton and Bicknor (i.e. those belonging to the owners of Highmeadow) only bailiwicks to the Forest and lords thereof only woodwards there as of those two bailiwicks.' In this transcript the spelling and punctuation have been modernized, occasional insertions made (in square brackets) to help with the sense, and dates, which in the MS. are by regnal year, altered to years of grace.

[2] Evidently the mound known as the Barbican which adjoined the castle on its east side: *VCH Glos.* iv. p. 247.

Then were read the letters patent dated 25 May 1631 by which his lordship was made Chief Justice and Justice-in-Eyre *durante bene placito* (during the [king's] good pleasure) with £100 per annum fee, and 100 marks per annum in lieu of justice acre[1] were granted to him. Then the writ of assistants dated 21 March 1634 was read. [*p. 2*] Then Justice Jones delivered to the clerks of the eyre[2] the letter of assistants written by His Majesty to him dated 16 June 1634, which being read, he put on his hat. Then the like was done by Baron Trevor and Justice Bridgeman, one after the other. Then proclamation was made if any one would be essoined he should enter his essoin.[3] Proclamation was made that no fairs or markets should be kept within the county during the eyre upon pain of seizure. Proclamation also made that all brewers, bakers, ostlers, etc. should keep the assize of bread, beer, oats, etc., according to the law, and that no person should enhance bread, beer, lodging, etc. by reason of this justice seat.

Proclamation [was] also made that the sheriff of the county of Gloucester should return his precept for summoning of the justice seat. Thereupon Sir Giles Fettiplace, kt., sheriff of the county, delivered into court the writ with a schedule of the names of the Constable of the castle of St. Briavels and Warden of the Forest and his deputy, all the foresters and their deputies, verderers, regarders, the woodwards and their deputies, rangers, keepers, bow-bearers, beadle of the castle of St. Briavels and bailiff of the hundred of St. Briavels, and four men of every town[4] within the Forest, and all the freeholders within the Forest. Then all these were called by name.

Philip, earl of Pembroke and Montgomery, Constable and Warden of the Forest, being called, made default, but was not fined but his attendance spared. James Kyrle, esq., his deputy, kneeling on his knee, delivered his horn[5] to the Lord Chief Justice. Sir Baynham Throckmorton, bt., chief forester-in-fee, did the like. Every forester did the like that appeared. But Sir Edward Basse, kt., forester-in-fee, made default and Philip Meek appeared for him as his deputy, but because he had no deputation in writing his default was recorded and he fined £10. Isabel Wise and Susan, the wife of [Anthony][6] Darling, were called as foresters-in-fee and Darling fined £5 for his default, although it was affirmed his wife was in the ward to the king and that he had not sued out her livery.[7] [*p. 3*] John Stayner, a forester-in-fee, made default but John Price, his deputy by deed produced, made oath that he was so old he was not able to travel to the court, and the court thereupon excused his default, Price delivering his horn on his knee to the Lord Chief Justice. John [Worgan],[8] a forester-in-fee, appearing had no horn and therefore was fined £5. As those horns were delivered to the Lord Chief

---

[1] A perquisite of this justice's office, presumably originally in the form of land.

[2] Here and at later occurrences the MS. uses the Latin *iter*, which is anglicised in this transcript.

[3] An excuse for non-attendance.

[4] Used here in the sense of 'township' or 'tithing', a division of a manor or parish.

[5] The official accoutrement of a forester.

[6] *sic* but his forename is given as 'Richard' below: p. 29.

[7] Had not gone through the formal procedure to assume possession of her office and other assets.

[8] MS. has 'Morgan', evidently a scribal error: see below, p. 30.

Justice he delivered them to the Marshal,[1] where they remained until the owners fetched them back, every one paying 6s. 8d.

Every woodward when he was first called delivered his hatchet[2] to the Lord Chief Justice on his knee. Sir Baynham Throckmorton, woodward of Bearse bailiwick, delivered his hatchet, but John Morgan,[3] his deputy, making default was fined 40s. Benedict Hall, esq., woodward of Staunton bailiwick, delivered his hatchet, and, being called again as woodward of Bicknor bailiwick,[4] his appearance for that was recorded without delivering another hatchet.

[Ordered] by the court[5] 'Every ranger ought to bring a bag of hog rings'.[6]

Divers of the four men and reeve made default and were fined 40s. apiece.

Then all the officers and their deputies, reeves and four men of every town which appeared took this oath: 'You shall diligently enquire and true presentment make to the court of all trespasses and other offences, as well of vert as of venison, as of all other offences which shall be given you in charge, which have been committed and done within the precincts of his Majesty's Forest of Dean against the laws and assizes of the Forest which concern this present service and which have not been heretofore presented. So help you God.'

By the court resolved: 'Although by the general summons of the eyre none are bound to attend at the eyre but those that are inhabitants within the Forest, yet when the justice seat was called at Mitcheldean and adjourned to Gloucester Castle before the charge if the gentlemen of the country which are not inhabitants in the Forest be there present the sheriff may return them of the grand inquest for the eyre and they are bound to serve. And it is more fit and agreeable to the course of justice to have them serve than those who are inhabitants within the Forest who are like to be offenders'. And accordingly the sheriff returned divers present who dwelt in several places within the county of Gloucester without the perambulation of the Forest, and they appeared and were sworn of the grand inquest.

Resolved: 'If one be presented and convicted at the swanimote court and that conviction certified to the eyre, though the party convicted appear not in person or by attorney at the eyre, he may be fined, being absent'. And so were many hundreds at this eyre, both for vert and venison. Whitfield said: 'If one be indicted or an information preferred against him in *Banco Regis* (King's Bench) for a nuisance or the like and pleads not guilty and a verdict pass for the king in this case the judges in *Banco Regis* will, and usually do, fine the party in his absence', which Justice Jones affirmed to be so.

[p. 4] Sir John Finch moved that there were no agistors returned by the sheriff nor called but, informed that Sir Richard Catchmay, although no agistor, had

---

[1] Court official (of royal court) appointed to carry out policing and other duties.

[2] The official accoutrement of a woodward (used to mark trees for felling or preservation for the king's use).

[3] Named as Griffin Morgan below (p. 30).

[4] *Bicknall* in MS. The clerk, presumably unfamiliar with the locality, uses obscure spellings for some of the bailiwick names.

[5] Here and usually at later occurrences the MS. uses Latin '*per (totam) curiam*', anglicised in this transcript.

[6] Presumably in Dean their duties had formerly included ringing pigs pastured for pannage in the Forest.

taken upon him to receive the herbage and pannage money and thereby made himself an agistor of his own wrong, therefore desired that he may account as an agistor, which the court ordered. And Justice Jones said it was like an executor in his own wrong. But afterwards Sir Richard Catchmay producing a lease under seal of the herbage and pannage from his Majesty, nothing was done thereupon, but the lease enrolled here.

Whitfield moved that the foresters might make account in writing which venison had been killed since last eyre and by what warrants and that the court might judge whether the warrants were sufficient or not, which was ordered they should do the next morning.

Justice Jones: 'No offence ought to be presented at the swanimote but such as were committed after the last swanimote before; but those offences that were committed before the last swanimote and were not presented may not be presented at this justice seat'.

Littleton, Recorder of London:[1] 'There are divers presentments and convictions at the swanimote which are certified to this eyre against Sir John Winter, Sir Basil Brooke, Mr. Mynne, and the Lady Villiers for cutting of timber and wood within the Forest, which, as he is informed, they were able to justify by letters patent', and therefore [he] desired that they might have copies of those presentments and convictions. But the court denied it, saying it was an unusual course after conviction to deliver copies, but ordered, in respect they made title by letters patent, that they should have notes of the times and places where the timber and woods grew and were cut and the quantities thereof as the same are mentioned in the presentments. Mr. Seys moved the like for Mr. Hacket and had the like order. Upon the motion of Sir John Finch, Sir John Winter and Sir Basil Brooke were enjoined upon a pain not to depart without licence.

Mr. Trotman moved that Mr. Wyrall was at the swanimote convicted for divers several offences done within the Forest and desired notes thereof. But he pretending no discharge nor justification for the same, it was denied him because that everyone might demand the like copies, which was not reasonable.

Sir John Finch moved that Richard Constable, William Cowse, William Rolls, and Francis Bridgeman, who were trusted by the King for the delivery of cordwood and logwood to the farmers,[2] might bring in all the books of account which they had concerning the same upon oath, which was ordered accordingly.

Sir John Finch moved that by virtue of warrants directed to the woodwards of the Forest to survey all trees standing there was one survey made in 1628, another in 1632, and another in 1633, which he desired might be brought in upon oath the next morning by Sir John Winter and Broughton, deputy to Mr. Harboard, the King's surveyor, in whose custody they remained,[3] But Sir John Winter alleging he had only the survey of 1632, which he delivered to Mr. Attorney-General long since, keeping a copy thereof, it was ordered Sir John Winter should bring in that

---

[1] Edward Littleton, later Chief Justice of Common Pleas and Lord Keeper: *ODNB* xxxiv. pp. 29–32.
[2] i.e. the lessees of the king's ironworks.
[3] The 1633 survey, made by John Broughton, recently appointed deputy surveyor for Dean under Charles Harbord, is printed in Hart, *Royal Forest*, pp. 274–7.

copy and Broughton the two surveys of 1628 and 1633 upon oath the next morning.

[*p. 5*] Upon the motion of Sir John Finch [it was] ordered that all the woodwards and their deputies bring in their accounts upon oath next morning. Hill, son and heir of Hill, woodward, deceased, was called to bring in his father's roll,[1] who said he had none. But Sir John Finch said that must not excuse him, for the rolls must be brought in, and in ancient time the heir's lands had been seized and their wives and children put out of possession until the rolls were brought in.

Whitfield moved that William Rolls[2] had sold divers woods and trees out of the Forest on pretence he had warrants so to do from the Lord Treasurer, which if he had yet they were not legal, and desired he might bring in his accounts on oath next morning. Rolls affirmed he had made up his accounts in the Exchequer and had his *quietus est*[3] and desired he might not be driven to account here. Whitfield said: 'As your warrant was illegal so your proceedings have been deceitful, for there is no charge in the Exchequer to draw you to account, but if you have made any account you have made your own charge and accounted on that. But this is the proper court for the King to know how his timber and wood have been disposed of, and therefore you ought to account here', which was ordered accordingly and he bound in a recognizance of £1,000 not to depart without licence of the court. And afterwards Rolls, being fined and committed for another offence, escaped from the Marshal and was called upon his recognizance and made default. His default was recorded and his recognizance ordered to be estreated.[4]

Mr. Kyrle moved that Edward Sargeant who was to put in a claim this eyre could not do it by reason that his evidences were in the Court of Wards [and] that therefore the putting in of his claim might be spared. Justice Bridgeman: 'No man can make a claim but it must be by patent. He might have a copy of the record. If by prescription, he needs no evidences.' And therefore [it was] ordered he should put in his claim at his peril.

John Hamblyn for carrying a gun in the Forest was fined £40, the gun to be seized and the value answered [for] to the King.

Charles Kingston and Thomas Kingston, being presented and convicted at the swanimote divers times for chasing and killing divers deer within the Forest and no mention made to what places those deer were carried, Whitfield moved that the keepers might be called to discover to what places the deer were carried. Whereupon the keepers were called and examined by oath and did discover that some of those deer were carried and eaten at the house of Richard Thomas, gent., and one doe to George Kingston's. Whereupon it was ordered that indictments should [be] presented against Richard Thomas and George Kingston for the same.

---

[1] Richard Hill, who had recently succeeded his father in the Blaize Bailey woodwardship: *VCH Glos*. x. pp. 39–40.

[2] Rolls (Rowles) was appointed in 1621 a commissioner for delivering cordwood to the lessees of the ironworks: Hart, *Royal Forest*, pp. 98, 103.

[3] 'He is quit', i.e. has paid his account and been discharged.

[4] A record of it to be delivered in to the Exchequer.

Sir John Finch [said that] there were divers grounds sowed within the Forest that lay not within any parish, and desired that the jury might enquire who had taken the tithes of those lands and the value of the same, because they belonged to the king. [*p. 6*] Recorder of London said that these things were granted to the bishop of Llandaff by Edward I.[1] Sir John Finch: 'Then the bishop of Llandaff must put in his claim and plead it'. Whitfield: 'If any thing be claimed from the king out of the Forest, though it be but a lease for years, it must appear upon record in this court, or else it is not to be allowed', which was agreed by the court. And [it was] resolved that if the bishop have such a grant he must put in his claim, which he afterwards did.

Richard Howell fined £20 for keeping a gun and a greyhound at his house within the Forest, and the gun to be seized.

Thomas Dawe fined £20 for keeping a gun at his house in the Forest and committed until he paid the £20 and put in sureties to be true to the Forest.

Wiliam Elverton, a freeholder within the Forest, appeared the first day and, being afterwards called and absent, was fined £20 for not attending the court.

William Cornehill, convicted for carrying of a doe out of the Forest upon a horse worth £6, was fined £60, and the horse [ordered] to be seized.

Walter Howell for selling fat venison in the Forest fined £40.

Benedict Hall, esq., fined £10 for hunting foxes in the Forest and committed until he paid it and gave sureties to be true to the Forest.

Richard Collins, a deputy forester-in-fee, fined £10 for not attending the court.

Servis Boys convicted at the swanimote for that he 3 Dec. 1629 had fat venison and four deerskins found at his house within the Forest, for which he was fined £100. He was also convicted for that he had divers times planted sharp stakes and withies to take the deer going out of the Forest, for which he was fined £100.

George Wyrall, Thomas Baynwood, [Christopher][2] Hodges, and Richard Hannis convicted at the swanimote as common misdoers and taking hares and other beasts with hare pipes and other engines, for which they were fined £40 apiece.

A bill of indictment being preferred to the grand jury against John Gibbons, esq., for cutting down 3,000 of the king's timber trees in the Forest, to the value of £4,500, marked for shipping and other uses for His Majesty, and witnesses sworn to give evidence. Sir John Finch moved that he, for the king, might go to the grand jury in private to inform them for the king and to see the witnesses examined. The court agreed that it was very fit and had been often used so to be done. And thereupon Sir John Finch went and gave in evidence accordingly.

[*p. 7*] Philip Tilslow, convicted at the swanimote for building a house and stable with the king's timber and being called to the bar to be fined, Whitfield, for the king, demanded of him whether any of the officers of the Forest had knowledge of the taking of the king's timber or if he had given them any reward for concealing the same, who acknowledged that Anthony Callow, deputy woodward for Nicholas Roberts, esq., for the woodwardship of Mitcheldean, had

---

[1] For this, see below, p. 125 (no. 118).

[2] MS. has *Croser*: see below, p. 104 (no. 799).

taken 10s. of him and suffered him to carry away the said timber, and concealed the same. And Callow, being called, acknowledged it to be true. Whitfield: 'This is a court of record, and here is a deputy officer confessed the taking of a bribe to conceal the carrying of the king's timber and this confession in court is as much as if he had been convicted at the swanimote or by a jury in this court', and therefore [he] prayed that Callow and Tilslow might be fined. And Tilslow was fined 40s. and Callow £100, and both committed. But afterwards, on Callow's submission, his fine was remitted to £10, which he paid in court.

Edward Morse confessed in court that he with four oxen had carried away a ton of the king's timber out of the Forest and employed it to his own use. Whitfield: 'This confession in court is as strong against delinquents as a conviction', and therefore [he] prayed the judgement of the court against Morse, who submitting himself was fined £5, and the four oxen to be seized to the king's use.

Thomas Marsh, deceased, was presented and convicted at the swanimote for erecting a cottage and the cottage ordered to be seized, but no fine because the king had granted away the assart.

It was presented in the swanimote roll that divers men [were] keeping many dogs, mastiffs, etc. not expeditated. This by the court was holden an imperfect presentment, and therefore the (sic)[1] fined £5 apiece upon motion of Sir John Finch and Mr. Whitfield.

It was presented and convicted at the swanimote that Sir John Winter had a park within the Forest and that there were two deer-leaps in the park pale, wherefore Sir John Winter was fined £10 and [ordered] to make up the deer-leaps, and the park seized to the king's use.

Anthony Williams presented and convicted at the swanimote for fishing at Walmore[2] within the Forest and taking two fishes, for which he was fined £5.

John Costlet, [James][3] Oliver, William Murrell, and others were presented and convicted at the swanimote for fishing in the Forest, for which they were severally fined.

William Morgan was presented and convicted at the swanimote for keeping five horses and mares five years within the Forest without warrant, for which he was fined £6 13s. 4d.

And John Wast and divers others were fined for the like offences.

[p. 8] Sir John Winter was presented and convicted at the swanimote for building an iron forge within the Forest within nine years past. Sir John Finch moved that the forge might be pulled down and Sir John Winter fined. Recorder of London, after counsel with Sir John Winter, desired that Sir John might have respite to make answer to this, for he was a stranger to the presentment and knew nothing of it and hoped he should have good matter to free him from the fine by grant from the Crown. Whitfield: 'Sir John Winter cannot excuse himself as ignorant of the presentment, for he is a forester-in-fee and either was or ought to have been at the swanimote when this presentment and conviction was made, and, if he were absent, [that is] no reason he should take benefit of his own

---

[1] 'verderers' apparently omitted here; see below, p. 97 (no. 713).

[2] MS. has *Wadmor*; see below, p. 97 (no. 716).

[3] See below, p. 97 (no. 717).

wrong. And to say he can discharge himself by grant is no cause to respite the proceedings against him. But he ought to be now fined, and if afterwards he show a good warrant for erecting and continuing the forge, upon his claim and allowance therefore, the fine is to be discharged. As at Windsor[1] one, being presented and convicted for waste, he put in a claim to be quit of waste, notwithstanding it was ruled he should be fined for the present and when his claim is allowed that dischargeth the fine', which case the Lord Chief Justice-in-Eyre said he very well remembered. Sir John Finch: 'A furnace is the source and spring of destruction of the Forest, and good reason and authority have been urged why Sir John Winter should be fined presently', and therefore [he] desired no respite might be given. Whereupon he was fined £400 and committed until he paid it, and the forge [ordered] to be pulled down.

Sir John Winter was presented and convicted at the swanimote for erecting a forge and a furnace at Newland within the Forest. For this Sir John Winter showed forth a patent dated 30 June 1618 by which the place where the forge and furnace are erected [was] granted to William Winter and Bell. Justice Jones: 'This is not good unless it be with a *licet sit infra metas foreste*'.[2] Upon reading, it appeared that clause was within the grant, but because there was a clause within the grant that it should be subject to the forest laws Sir John Winter was fined £200 and committed, and the forge and furnace [ordered] to be pulled down.

John Maddocks, clerk of the swanimote court, being called and absent, was fined £40 for not attending. [*p. 9*] Presently, after Maddocks coming, [he] was examined upon oath and confessed he had delivered copies or notes of the presentments at the swanimote court to Sir Basil Brooke, Mr. More, Mr. Vaughan, and Tipper, Sir John Winter's man. And, upon the motion of Sir John Finch, Maddocks was committed close prisoner until he could examine him and an indictment be preferred against him for his offence. And he remained close prisoner two days and within that time was several times examined, and, upon his examination confessing his offence in giving copies and notes of some of the presentments against particular persons in the swanimote roll, he submitted himself and desired mercy. Whereupon he was discharged.

An indictment being found by the grand jury against John Gibbons, esq.,[3] for cutting down 3,000 marked trees within the Forest, William Hamp, his attorney, was called to plead to that indictment. Recorder of London said he was of counsel for Mr. Gibbons, and, although Hamp were attorney for him for such presentments as were against Gibbons at the swanimote, neither he nor Hamp had authority to plead to this indictment, found since the letter of attorney [was] made, and therefore desired it might be respited until Mr. Gibbons were there in person. Whitfield: 'In the eyre of Pickering 17 Edw. I (1288–9) the prioress of Rosedale put in two attorneys *in omnibus placitis et querelis motis et movendis et libertates suas calumpniandas prosequendas et defendendas durante itinere isto*

---

[1] At the eyre recently held for Windsor Forest.

[2] 'It is allowed [although] within the bounds of the Forest', i.e. a clause waiving in that particular case the restrictions of the forest law.

[3] For Gibbons's Cannop estate, above, pp. xi–xii

(in all pleas and suits brought or to be brought and for claiming, prosecuting, and defending her liberties during this eyre). And by virtue of that letter of attorney the attorney did all during the eyre that the prioress should have done. And Mr. Gibbons had made as large a letter of attorney to Hamp in this behalf, and the first day of this eyre the letter of attorney was read and Hamp admitted his attorney according to that letter of attorney, and it was delivered to the clerk of the eyre to be enrolled'. Sir John Finch desired that the indictment and the letter of attorney might be read and, if he would not answer, that the court should proceed against him. The letter of attorney being read, the Recorder of London said [that] he was not acquainted with it before but it was a full authority and Hamp ought to answer. Whereupon Hamp pleaded 'not guilty'. And [it was] agreed by the court that the process in eyre are *de hora in horam* (from hour to hour).

Sir John Winter [was] presented and convicted at the swanimote for building a double forge without the perambulation of the Forest but near adjoining, but because the presentment doth not show that the same was to the prejudice of the Forest, therefore the fining of him was rejected.

Benedict Hall was presented and convicted at the swanimote for building of a furnace upon his own fee within the Forest. His counsel alleged that the same was pardoned by the statute of 21 Jas. (1623–4),[1] which was denied and therefore he was fined £300. [*p. 10*] (Ruled) by Bridgeman: 'All spoils of the king's woods are excepted out of the pardon of 21 Jas., and there has been no pardon these 60 years that pardoned them'.

Sir Edward Villiers and Dame Barbara, his wife,[2] were presented and convicted at the swanimote for cutting down and converting to their own use 1,630 oaks and 7,000 beeches in the Forest, and, Sir Edward Villiers being dead, William, Viscount Grandison, being his son and heir, produced letters patent 28 May 1625,[3] by which his Majesty did grant to Sir Edward Villiers and his Lady the inheritance of divers lands in the Forest in the bailiwick of Bicknor in the said Forest and then sets down the bounds of the said lands and grants to them liberty to cut down all the woods thereon growing. And the said heir alleged that by virtue of that grant the said oaks and beeches were cut down within the said bounds mentioned in the said letters patent. And they found they were cut down within the said bounds. And it was resolved by the whole court that, the said grant being of land expressed by the letters patent to be within the bailiwick of Bicknor and within the Forest and then granting liberty to the grantees to cut down woods growing upon the said lands, the same doth derive a sufficient title and authority to the grantees to cut down the said wood, because the king doth take express notice by his grant that the woods did grow within the said Forest, although these words *nisi sit infra metas foreste*[4] be not contained in the said grant. Bridgeman: 'If the king grant to J. S. to make a park within the Forest this is a good grant although there be no words in the patent *licet sit infra metas*

---

[1] Act for free and general pardon, 21 Jas.I, c.35.

[2] For the Villiers family, above, p. xi.

[3] The date (by regnal year) is incomplete in MS.; for the grant, TNA, C 99/28.

[4] See above, p. 10*n*.

foreste'. And judgement [was] given by the whole court that Sir Edward Villiers and his Lady *exeant sine die* (may depart without a day).[1] In this case it was affirmed by the counsel of the Lord Grandison that when wood is sold or granted the custom of the country is to allow 18 foot to every rood but 16½ when land is sold. But if either wood or land be sold or granted within the Forest then 21 foot measure goeth to the rood, called 'forest measure'. Which being denied by the king's counsel, the regard were charged to enquire of it, who upon their oath said they never heard of any other measure than 18 foot for wood and 16½ for land within the Forest.

John Gibbons and Stephen Vinor were presented and convicted at the swanimote for cutting and converting to their own uses 4,000 oaks and 2,000 beeches, price £6,000. Littleton, Recorder of London, of counsel for them, showed forth a grant whereby the king 15 Sept. 1629 granted the lands whereupon the oaks and beeches grew and all woods thereupon growing to Sir Allen Apsley's trustees in fee and affirmed that Sir Allen and his trustees had conveyed the same to Gibbons in fee, and so no cutting [was done] on the king's soil. [*p. 11*] Sir John Finch and Whitfield: 'Here is no title to Gibbons showed. Admit[ted] that there were a good conveyance and that Gibbons had the same land and wood conveyed to him in fee simple, yet he ought to be fined as for cutting down woods upon his own lands within the Forest', which was agreed by the court, and Gibbon and Vinor were fined £6,000.

Charles Driver was convicted at the swanimote for carrying three tons of the king's crooked timber[2] out of the Forest, who being present confessed the same, and that he bought those three tons and seven tons more of Rolls[3] for £30, which he paid him. And Rolls being present confessed it and alleged that he had a warrant under the Lord Treasurer's hand for the sale of timber within the Forest, and that he sold this to Driver since Michaelmas last, and did intend to account for the same at Michaelmas next. Whitfield: 'The Lord Treasurer's warrant is no legal warrant for felling timber in the Forest, as was ruled in Whitlock's case in the eyre at Windsor. Neither is the same a good warrant for felling the king's timber, which is agreeable to all our books. So here are two offenders: Rolls in felling the king's timber, which he confesses in court, and that is as a strong as a conviction and he the greater offender of the two, and Driver, an offender convicted at the swanimote, and he ought to be punished for felling the same'. Which was agreed by the court. Driver [was] fined 6s. 8d. and Rolls £100 and both committed.

Francis Bridgeman [was] convicted at the swanimote for cutting down divers oaks and beeches in the Forest, to the damage of the king £200, and he being present, showed a warrant from Hankinson, clerk to the farmer[s] of the king's ironworks in the Forest, whereby it appears that those trees were taken for the use of the ironworks, according to a grant which the farmer[s] had. Therefore it was presented. But upon examination it appeared that the oaks and beeches were cut down long since and that this warrant, though it bore date long since, viz. about

---

[1] i.e. without having to return to the court.

[2] i.e. timber suitable for the main struts of navy ships: cf. below, p. 93 (no. 667).

[3] See above, p. 7n.

the time when the oaks and beeches were felled, yet the warrant was lately colourably made to deceive the king and discountenance this conviction. And therefore Bridgeman was fined £2,400 and Hankinson £200 and both committed.

William Kingston, esq., was convicted at the swanimote for cutting down Abbots wood and Flaxley grove, being within his own fee. The Recorder said those woods were out of the regard, and therefore prayed that [he] might be discharged. Sir John Finch: 'The presentment at the swanimote is that it is within the Forest', and therefore prayed Mr. Kingston might be fined, and, if afterwards he should put in a claim for the same and it allowed, his fine should be discharged. Baron Trevor: 'If he had allowance in a former eyre yet he must now put in a claim'. Justice Bridgeman: 'If the wood be within the perambulation and out of the regard Mr Kingston must claim it so, but this is fitter to be disputed when his claim comes in'. And by the court [he was] fined £200 and committed.

[*p. 12*] Sir John Finch: 'There ought to be no alehouses within the Forest, and if there be any they are nuisances and ought to be suppressed and punished'. Whitfield: 'It was so ruled at the eyre at Windsor'.

Sir John Finch showed the antiquity of the Forest, the newest being the New Forest made by William the Conqueror [and] this of Dean being long before; and that the laws, liberties, and bounds were as ancient as the forests; that Henry II, Richard I, and King John did by their prerogatives afforest the lands, woods, and grounds of divers subjects; that the laws Magna Carta and *Charta de Foresta* (the Charter of the Forest) made in 1225,[1] when the king was within age, were for the liberty and benefit of the subject, limiting divers laws which before were at the king's pleasure to a certainty and not to go to life or member; and that lands and woods and grounds afforested by Henry II, Richard I, and King John were then to be disafforested, and, as the king had been careful to preserve the subjects' liberties, so the subjects ought to be careful to do the king right. And then [he] showed that there have been divers perambulations of this Forest of Dean,[2] one 1228 and another 1282, whereby the Forest extends from Gloucester bridge to Monmouth bridge. In 1298 and 1300 there were two other perambulations made, which leave out Purton and divers other towns included within the former perambulations. And in 1301 the king grants and confirms 1300, but it appears by a record in *baga*[3] of the forests of Gloucestershire that the perambulation of 1300 was void and erroneous and that Purton and other towns laid out of the Forest in 1298 and 1300 and laid within the Forest by the 1228 and 1282 [perambulations] were, and time out of mind had been, within the Forest and so perambulated from three years to three years; and part of those were the ancient demesnes of the Crown and so were not to be disafforested, and in 1282 was allowed at a justice seat and offences done within those bounds then presented

---

[1] The Charter of the Forest was acquired by the barons in 1217 to confirm and expand the forest clauses included in Magna Carta two years earlier; Finch refers to a confirmation of both documents made during Henry III's minority.

[2] For the complex story of the Forest's bounds and details of the perambulations and other documents cited here, see Hart, 'Metes and Bounds of Dean', and *VCH Glos.* v. pp. 295–8; see also above, pp. xxi–xxiv.

[3] The bag in which the official records were kept (then in the Tower of London).

and punished; and the large bounds of 1228 continued without contradiction until 1298, which was 76 years; and that of 1228 [was] but three years after *Charta de Foresta* when things were fresh in memory; that subjects were not willing to lose any privilege and therefore likeliest to be truest; and the Statute of 1 Edw. III cap. 1 (1327) was made, by which it is enacted that the *Charta de Foresta* should be kept and the perambulation in Edward I's time should be from thenceforth holden in like form as it was then ridden and bounded. And [he] said that the Statute doth not confirm the 1300 [perambulation] because it was a void perambulation. And so [he] prayed that those towns may be laid into the Forest according to the perambulations of 1228 and 1282.

[*p. 13*] Littleton, Recorder of London, of counsel with the towns[1] agreed the king may make a forest by word, and said that *Charta de Foresta* was intended for the benefit of the subject, which could not be unless it was pursued. And it [is] true Henry III was within age when they were made, whereupon Hugh[2] de Burgo, earl of Kent, chief justice, persuaded him that he was not bound to perform those charters by reason he was under age, which was but a fallacy, for the king in judgement of law is never under age. And [he] said the perambulations of 1298 and 1300, coming after 1228 and 1282, shall be intended to be the truest perambulation, and the rather because the same bounds are set forth by an inquisition in 9 Edw. III (1335–6) remaining in *baga diversarum forestarum in Scaccario* (the Exchequer bag of [records] of various forests). Then the 1300 [perambulation] was confirmed by words of grant and confirmation by the king's charter of 1301 and a Fifteenth[3] was given for that perambulation, so as 1300 was a settled perambulation and such a one as the Statute of 1327 did confirm. And then there had been a long and constant usage according to the 1298 and 1300 and these towns laid out by those perambulations ever taken to be out.

Whitfield: 'The question is which is the true perambulation, the 1228 and 1282 or the 1298 and 1300. And it appeareth manifestly by the records now produced that 1300, which is all of one with 1298, is erroneous and, if that be granted, then the letters patent of 1301, confirming 1300, are void, for if the king will confirm a void lease it doth not make good the lease, and so a confirmation of a void perambulation doth not make it good, as is proved by the earl of Leicester's case, [for which see] Plowden's *Commentaries*,[4] where, upon the same rule and reason, divers cases are put. And the Statute of 1327 was not made for confirmation of this particular perambulation of 1300 but of the perambulations of all the forests of England. And here being several perambulations, that of 1228 and 1282 being true and that of 1298 and 1300 being false, the Statute, being in general words, shall never extend to them, but to the perambulations of 1228 and 1282, which are true for an untrue and void and

---

[1] i.e. pleading on behalf of the townships removed from the Forest by the reduced bounds.

[2] *recte* Hubert (Hubert de Burgh, the Justiciar).

[3] A tax on personal property. Edward I's acceptance of reduced perambulations of the royal forests at this time was made under pressure from his barons and in order to secure their agreement to taxation: M. Powicke, *The Thirteenth* Century (2nd edn. 1962) pp. 682–3, 699–703.

[4] A volume of reports of legal cases published by Edmund Plowden in 1571: *ODNB*, xliv. pp. 596–7.

no perambulation are all one (*sic*). The words of the 1327 are general and so may refer as well to 1228 and 1282, as to 1298 and 1300, and so in case of uncertainty that must be taken which is best for the king, and especially the truth being so. It was never the meaning of the law to undo the *Charta de Foresta* but to confirm it, and to exclude afforestations, whether of the king's demesne lands or of subjects' lands, afforested before Henry II's time, is to undo the *Charta de Foresta*. Base usage *in pais* [?in peacetime] cannot prejudice the king, for *nullum tempus occurrit regi* (no time runs against the king)'.[1]

[*p. 14*] Justice Jones: 'It seems all those lands were afforested before Henry II's time and then are not to be disafforested. By the *Charta de Foresta* lands of the king were not to be disafforested without special words. And if the 1300 be not a true perambulation then the confirmation of 1301 doth not work upon it, because the king is deceived in his grant and it makes not good the perambulation that was void before'. And for that [he] cited the earl of Leicester's case, and [said that] the Statute of 1327 doth not confirm 1300, being a false ground, and spake to the same effect as the king's counsel did. Baron Trevor: 'If the perambulation of 1300 be false then the king's grant and Statute do no way aid it, and the best time to know the true perambulation was the nearest to the Charter of the Forest, which was 1228 and 1282'. Bridgeman, chief justice of Chester: 'No lands were to be disafforested but other men's lands that were afforested by Henry II, Richard I, and King John'. And [he] spoke to the same effect as the other judges did.

Whereupon the grand jury, the regard, officers of the forest, and reeve and four men of every town were by the court directed to set down the metes and bounds of the Forest, and after three days consideration they did all present that the true metes and bounds of the Forest were and ought to be according to the perambulation[s] of 1228 and 1282, but did desire the opinion of the court whether the [confirmation] of 1301 and the 1327 did any way weaken those perambulations or make good the perambulations of 1298 and 1300. Whereupon the three judges delivered their opinions: that the confirmation of 1301 did no way weaken 1228 and 1282 nor strengthen 1300, which was void; and the Statute of 1327 confirmed those perambulations that were true and not those that were false, so that 1228 and 1282 stand as perambulations uncontrolled, and 1300 doth no way bind or hurt the king. And the judges having thus delivered their opinions thereupon, the Lord Chief Justice-in-Eyre did adjudge that the perambulations of 1228 and 1282 were the true perambulations of the metes and bounds of the Forest, and those of 1298 and 1300 false and erroneous. And thereupon the jury, regard, officers, and reeve and four men did all deliver up their verdict in writing under their hands that the perambulations of 1228 and 1282 were the true metes and bounds of the Forest.

[*p. 15*] Daniel Morse and Jasper Leg were convicted at the swanimote for cutting down two oaks, containing three tons of timber, which they employed in repairing the church of Mitcheldean [*Great Deane*). And they were now fined 50s. apiece. Rumsey[2] moved [that] they were churchwardens and what they did

---

[1] i.e. the king's rights can not lapse through non-usage.

[2] Evidently their attorney.

was on the behalf of their parish, and therefore desired they might have an order of contribution against the rest of the inhabitants, which was denied because they are convicted as particular men for a wrong done by themselves and this court will grant no contribution in aid of trespassers.

A.B.,[1] being at the bar, desired that the court would hear him in some things that he would inform them for the service of His Majesty; but Sir John Finch desired that he, being of the king's counsel, might first be acquainted with it, lest the same might otherwise prove prejudicial to His Majesty's service or not be moved seasonably, which the court agreed to, and refused to hear him.

Whitfield moved that divers at this eyre had been fined and many committed until they had paid their fines; that, notwithstanding, the Marshal had suffered several of them to go abroad without paying their fines or putting in bonds for payment of their fines, and desired therefore – and it was ordered accordingly – that the Marshal should forthwith take into his custody all who were fined and committed and detain them until they paid their fines or entered into bond for payment thereof the next term.

Sir Thomas Morgan and Thomas Hacket were prosecuted and convicted at the swanimote for cutting down great quantities of wood in the Forest. And they showed forth a grant made of the same woods to William, earl of Pembroke, deceased, and a letter of attorney from the said earl to them to cut down the same, which they accordingly did. And therefore their grant and letter of attorney was enrolled and they discharged.[2]

Sir Basil Brooke and George Mynne were indicted for cutting down [178,200][3] cords of wood within the Forest within six years last past, of the value of £59,400, to which they pleaded not guilty, pretending that they had power by letters patent to cut down 10,000 cords of wood a year. Whitfield: 'It is true such a grant was made to the earl of Pembroke and by him assigned to them of 10,000 cords a year and officers appointed to deliver the same, and Hankinson received the same of the officers for the farmers'. And therefore [he] moved that Hankinson's book and notes might be seen, to see what quantity they had taken above their 10,000 cords per annum. [p. 16] Sir Basil Brooke affirmed and Hankinson deposed that the books which he kept of the wood, delivered by the officers and received by him, he delivered to Sir Basil Brooke and Mynne upon their last year's account, and that they were now at London. But Hankinson acknowledged that he had notes which he collected out of the same, which Whitfield desired might be brought into court, thereby the better to discover the fraud. Sir Basil Brooke, and Mr. Recorder of his counsel, affirmed they were their evidence and [there was] no reason the king's counsel should see them. Whitfield: 'The books are at London and they properly belong to the farmers,[4] and we desire not a sight of them. But Hankinson was appointed by the farmers to receive 10,000 cords per annum, as the surveyors of the king were appointed

---

[1] Presumably an informer, whose identity was concealed.

[2] Evidently refers to the swanimote presentment no. 19 (below, p. 45) but there Morgan's partner is named as Edward Thomas.

[3] MS. has 17,800 in error: cf. below, p. 24.

[4] i.e. the lessees of the ironworks (Brooke and Mynne).

to deliver the same, so that Hankinson and the surveyors were, or should be, indifferent between the king and the farmers, for by those notes it will appear whether they have received more or less than their 10,000 cords per annum. And therefore [the notes] ought to be showed to the king's counsel, that they might thereby prepare themselves against the trial', which was ordered accordingly and the notes delivered.

And the next day, when the issue, being not guilty, was tried: the king's counsel, having proved the cutting down and taking away the cords of wood mentioned in the judgement, the Recorder of London proved the grant made to the earl of Pembroke, whose assignees Sir Basil Brooke and Mr. Mynne were, for the taking of 10,000 cords of wood a year, affirming they had taken 60,000 cords of wood by virtue of the said grant within six years. But because the wood was to be delivered by three officers of the king by indenture, and no part was delivered by the officers, nor by indenture, but taken by the farmers themselves of their own wrong, therefore Sir John Finch moved they might be allowed no part of their 60,000 cords. And it was agreed by the court that they were trespassers for the whole, because they had not taken it according to the grant. And [it was said] by Justice Bridgeman: 'If the king grant 20 trees to be taken by delivery of his officers and the grantee take them without delivery, he is a trespasser, and by Justice Jones: 'If the king grant to me estovers to be taken by delivery of his officers I cannot take them without delivery'.

And afterwards the jury found Brooke and Mynne guilty [of] 172,800 cords, value £57,939 16s. 8d., and not guilty for the residue. Whereupon judgement was given against them for £57,939 16s. 8d. and either of them fined £100. And the court resolved [p. 17] that the value which is damages must be joint upon them both, but their fine several. And Sir Basil Brooke, being present, was committed for his fine and damage, and afterwards was delivered out upon his entering into a recognizance of £100,000 to appear before the Lord Chief Justice-in-Eyre the 20 October then next coming, and so from time to time until he discharged all fines set upon him in this eyre. And it was agreed by the court that, although Sir Basil Brooke were delivered out of prison upon his said recognizance, yet the king might take him again in execution for his fine and damage. And Bridgeman said: ' If a man be in execution at a common person's suit and let go he cannot be taken in execution again, but in the king's case he may'.

Sir John Winter, being fined about £21,000 and committed for the same, was delivered out of prison upon his recognizance of £40,000 with the like condition.

Richard Hankinson, being fined £200 and committed for the same, was delivered out of prison upon Sir Basil Brooke's recognizance and his own of £400 with the like condition.

William Parlor was convicted at the swanimote for erecting of a watermill, and his counsel alleged that by the Statute of *Charta de Foresta*, cap. 12, a man may erect a watermill upon his own soil, and therefore prayed he may be discharged. [Ordered] by the court [that] the erecting of a watermill upon a man's own fee out of the covert, when *Charta de Foresta* was made, was not punishable, but if the place where the mill was erected then were, or since was, covert then it is punishable and out of the Statute of *Charta de Foresta*. And the regard were charged to enquire whether the place where Parlor's mill is erected were covert in Henry III's time or since, who affirmed that it never was covert. Whereupon, Parlor was discharged.[1] And the same resolution was [made] in [Ketford][2] Brain's case.

Edward Morse was convicted at the swanimote for erecting a windmill upon the fee of Nicholas Roberts. Whitfield: 'Windmills are not within the Statute of *Charta de Foresta* but is a new invention since, and Sir Samson Dayrell at the eyre at Windsor was fined £5 for erecting a windmill upon his own fee within the forest there, and this Statute extends to watermills erected out of the covert'. Which was agreed by the court, and Morse fined £6 13*s*. 4*d*.

[*p. 18*] Robert Treswell [was] fined £20 for building a house and watermill upon the king's soil within the Forest.

[It was] agreed by the court that an heir should be answerable for [vert][3] though not for venison, taken in the Forest by his ancestors, in Sir John Winter's case, and Sir Baynham Throckmorton's case, and Hill's case. Sir Richard Catchmay was convicted at the swanimote for cutting down 60 acres of the king's wood at Whitemead within the Forest, but he produced letters patent whereby the king granted him liberty to cut down all the said wood except 400 marked trees and proved by witnesses, sworn in court, that he did leave 400 marked trees, and thereupon he was discharged. In Sir Richard Catchmay and Benedict Hall's case, Bridgeman said that men may not take upon their own grounds wood for fuel nor timber for reparations for their own use, but by view of the foresters and, if to sell, by licence. It was presented and convicted at the swanimote that Sir William Throckmorton, deceased, had cut down three acres of his own woods without licence, and Sir Baynham Throckmorton, his son and heir, being present in court, was fined for the same 30*s*. and committed until he paid it. And by the court [it was ruled that] the heir should be punished for wood cut down by his ancestors, as well in the lands of a subject as of the king.

The inhabitants of Littledean were presented and convicted at the swanimote for spoiling woods and digging cinders, and for this the town was fined 20*s*.

The miners offered a claim by which they would prescribe that they ought to have free liberty to dig mines in the Forest, paying to the gavellers[4] 1*d*. for every 9*d*. worth of mine[5] and pay 125 turves of coals.[6] Sir John Finch: 'It is impossible that those miners, being no corporation, should make a good claim, and all mines and quarries ought to be seized for the king'; and, [it] being the 8th day of the session and no claim put in, he said he would not suffer the same to be received. Bridgeman: 'All manner of mines in the Forest are the king's and no man may dig any'.

---

[1] Parlor's mill was near Joyford in English Bicknor: below, p. 57 (no. 133).

[2] MS. has *Kefford.* The case was evidently that of another mill, presented as having been built by Thomas Brain (Brayne) of Littledean, whose heir was Ketford Brain: below, p. 55 (no. 110); *VCH Glos.* v. p. 164.

[3] MS. has *rent*, in the context an obvious misreading.

[4] Officials appointed to collect the king's revenues from mining in the Forest.

[5] Iron ore.

[6] The reference (in the context) appears to be to mineral coal but the use of the term turves is unusual and possibly a misreading.

[*p. 19*] Whitfield [said] that no woollen cardmakers[1], trencher makers, joiners, coopers, saddle-tree makers, brewers, bakers, nor whittawers are to be permitted to be within the Forest, but are to be removed. Which was agreed by the court, and [that] they may be fined for using their trades in the Forest.

In Humphrey Blunt and Bridget Wyrrall's case it was resolved that if a stranger erect a cottage upon the soil which another hath for life or in fee, in this case the owner of the soil, as well as the erector, shall be punished, and if the owner died and his reversioner or heir receive rent for this cottage or do any other act that amounts to a continuance he shall be punished.

It was often resolved that if one be convicted at the swanimote as *communis* (a common) malefactor in vert or venison it is good, and so it was now resolved in Downing's case, who was indicted by the space of six years last past, and that his was a good indictment. Had it been that he had been a common malefactor without [?transgressing][2] in vert or venison it had been naught.

Sir Basil Brooke and George Mynne, being at the justice seat indicted for cutting down great quantities of the king's woods in this Forest, to which indictment they pleaded not guilty, being found guilty were adjudged to pay the value thereof and such damages as are before mentioned. And John Gibbons, being also indicted and found guilty upon his own traverse[3] for the like offence, judgement was thereupon given against him. And Sir John Winter, being also indicted at this justice seat for the like offence, confessed the indictment and thereupon judgement was given against him. But this justice seat being ended and the King's Majesty giving directions that these three judgements should not be estreated into the Exchequer, the great question was by what court, and how, all these great sums of money judged to the king upon these three indictments should be levied. Which by His Majesty's command and in Michaelmas term 1634 was referred to the consideration of Sir Thomas Richardson, Lord Chief Justice of the King's Bench, Sir John Finch, who that term was made Lord Chief Justice of the court of Common Pleas, Sir George Crook, and Sir Robert Berkeley, justices of the court of King's Bench. And by them all it was agreed that by process in the court of justice seat Sir Basil Brooke and the rest might be sued to the outlawry. And it was doubted by some of them whether that court might award execution against their bodies, goods, and lands; but they all agreed that *certiorari*[4] might be granted out of the Chancery, directed to the Lord Chief Justice-in-Eyre, [*p. 20*] requiring him to certify the same indictments and proceedings thereupon. Which being done, the same might be sent into the court of King's Bench, and then that court award a *scire facias*[5] against Sir Basil Brooke and the rest to show cause why the king should not have execution upon

[1] Makers of 'cards' (teasels or iron wire set in a frame for raising the nap of woollen cloth) are not otherwise mentioned among the despoilers of the Dean woodlands, and possibly there is confusion here with makers of 'cardboard' (thin board or planking).

[2] MS. has *expressing*.

[3] A formal denial of the facts alleged in a plea: *OED*.

[4] A writ directed by a higher court to a lower court asking for a record of the proceedings in a particular case: *OED*.

[5] A writ requiring a defendant to appear and show cause why a court should not execute an order made against him: *OED*.

these judgements given at the justice seat. Which resolution of the justices His Majesty commanded should be followed.

(*The remainder of the account (pp. 20–25) describes subsequent proceedings against Brooke and Mynne in Chancery and King's Bench, adding little detail to that given above*)

NOTES OF THE PROCEEDINGS BY SIR JOHN FINCH
(Bodleian Library, MS. Gough, Glouc.1)[1]

[*f. 3*] **The Proceedings at the Justice Seat held for the Forest of Dean at Gloucester Castle the 10th of July 1634 before the Right Honourable Henry, Earl of Holland, Lord Chief Justice-in-Eyre, assisted by Justice Jones, Baron Trevor, and Sir John Bridgeman, Justice of Chester, as it was delivered to the King by Sir John Finch**

On Saturday, 12 July 1634, in the presence of the grand jury, being 15, the 12 regarders, all the officers of the Forest, and the four men and reeve of the several townships within the Forest, the matter concerning the perambulation of the Forest was solemnly debated.[2]

[*f. 3v.*] The king's counsel [i.e. Finch] produced two ancient perambulations, one in 1228 and the other in 1282, both agreeing that the bounds of the Forest began at Gloucester bridge and so went to Monmouth bridge and came round again by the Severn to Gloucester, taking in those 17 towns.[3]

The counsel for the towns produced a perambulation of 1298 and another of 1300, both agreeing that the 17 towns were not anciently [forest] but were afforested by King John, and so by the Statute of *Charta de Foresta* (the Charter of the Forest) ought to be disafforested, and produced also letters [*f. 4*] patent in [1301][4] whereby that perambulation of 1300 was confirmed, and lastly insisted upon an Act of Parliament in [1327][5] whereby the perambulations made in the time of Edward I were confirmed. And they urged also the long and constant usage ever since, agreeing with that perambulation of 1300, concluding that by the law the metes and bounds ought not to be questioned contrary to that perambulation confirmed by letters patent and by an Act of Parliament.

The king's counsel replied that the perambulation of 1300 and so consequently that of 1301 were false and erroneous perambulations, prejudicial to the [*f. 4v.*] king and contrary to the Charter of the Forest, and whereas by the Charter of the Forest no disafforestation should be of any lands that were afforested before Henry II's time, nor of any of the king's demesne lands[6] though

---

[1] This is one of many copies of the document surviving; this copy has been checked against another, in GA, D 15/4. In this transcript spelling and punctuation have been modernized, occasional insertions (given in square brackets) made to help with the sense, and dates, which are by regnal year, altered to years of grace.

[2] For the background to the discussion of the Forest bounds and the documents cited here, see above, pp. 13–15, and *nn*.

[3] i.e. the townships which under the reduced bounds (by the perambulations of 1298 and 1300) were removed from the Forest.

[4] MS. here gives the date of this document as *24 Henry III*, but later correctly as *29 Edward I*.

[5] MS. consistently gives the date of this as *10 Edward III*, in error for *1 Edward III*; cf. above, p. 14.

[6] In this context, the reference is to 'ancient demesne', manorial lands held by the Crown at the time of Domesday Book.

afforested after the beginning of the reign of Henry II, yet this perambulation did disafforest those 17 towns afforested by King John, whereas the truth was they were afforested long before and divers of them were of the king's own demesne lands. And for that cause the perambulation of 1300 was afterwards revoked as a void and erroneous perambulation. And to prove it [he] produced an old record in [*f. 5*] the Tower[1], which hath no date but by the body of the record it appeareth to be after 1300, reciting it as a void and revoked thing. For the long usage, it was answered that no eyre had been there since 1282 and so no man could say what was the usage. But divers of those towns had since claimed common in the Forest, which showed they took themselves to be [of] the forest and not [of] the purlieu[2], because by *Ordinationes Foreste* (the Ordinances of the Forests) in 1305 no purlieu man can have common within the forest. For the confirmation in 1301, it was answered that the perambulation being void and erroneous the said letters patent confirming it were void, the king doing it upon false [*f. 5v.*] information. And for the Act of Parliament in 1327, that did not confirm the perambulation of 1300 by name but the perambulations throughout England of all forests made in the [reign of] Edward I generally. And, therefore, that of 1300 being a void perambulation, [the Act of Parliament wrought not upon that but had his operation upon the perambulation][3] of 1282 which was within the words of that Act as well as the 1300, and was within the meaning, being a true perambulation. And [he] demanded judgement of the court whether this question of the bounds were not, for all the reasons aforesaid, agreeable at law.

To which the judges assistant answered that it was legal and not contrary to the Act of Parliament in 1327 and left it to the country[4] to consider of the record [*f. 6*] in the Tower produced by the king's counsel as an evidence to overthrow the perambulations of 1300 and 1298. And if those perambulations were void it must follow that the perambulations of 1228 [and 1282][5] were the true ones.

The grand jury and the rest went together and in the afternoon of that day, being called but not agreed, they desired further time of the court as a matter of great weight, which was granted. On Monday the grand jury and the rest brought in their verdict touching the perambulation, which was to this effect: 'We agree that the metes and bounds of the Forest of Dean ought to be according to the perambulations made in 1228 and 1282, but, because we find the perambulation of 1300 to be granted by a patent [*f. 6v.*] of 1301 and because of that Act of Parliament of 1327 and possession of three hundred years and odd concurring therewith, we therefore refer it to the judgement of this honourable court whether the perambulation of 1300 ought to stand in force. Whereupon the king's counsel moved the judges to deliver their opinions for the matter in law, which they all agreed in as before. And then the king's counsel moved the jury, since when their doubt in law was satisfied by the judges, that they would agree to leave out the latter part of their verdict and let the first part only stand for their verdict, viz. 'We

---

[1] The Tower of London, where the archives of national government were then housed.

[2] Areas once within a forest, since disafforested.

[3] The bracketed wording, omitted from the Gough MS., is restored from GA, D 15/4, p. 5.

[4] i.e. left it to a jury from the locality.

[5] Restored from GA, D 15/4, p. 6.

agree that the metes and bounds of the Forest [*f. 7*] of Dean ought to be according to the perambulations made in 1228 and 1282'. To which the grand jury, the 12 regarders, the officers of the Forest, and the four men and reeves subscribed their names thereunto.

By this the king hath much enlarged the Forest of Dean, and all in the 17 towns were fearful they should have been questioned for many things done contrary to the forest law. But the king's counsel, in regard they were but now brought in and long usage, thought it not fit to proceed with any of them at that justice seat.

On Monday after dinner a presentment and conviction of the swanimote court was read against Mr. Gibbons,[1] by which he was convicted for cutting [*f. 7v.*] down 4,000 oaks and 2,000 beeches worth 20*s.* apiece between 31 March 1629 and 30 April 1634, and for spoiling certain coppices to the damage of £22,000, and for enclosing 940 acres valued at £113 13*s.* 4*d.* per annum with a wall *ultra assisa foresta* (contrary to the assize of the forest). At the same time an indictment found by the grand jury was read against the said Mr. Gibbons for cutting down divers goodly timber trees, marked by the king's officers for shipping and other uses for his Majesty.

To this indictment one Mr. Hampe on the behalf of Mr. Gibbons [*f. 8*] pleaded to that indictment '*non culpabilis* (not guilty)'. Whereupon trial was had upon evidence, witnesses being heard in open court in Mr. Gibbons's case, as well concerning the presentment as the indictment *super totam materiam* (on the whole matter), set out to be thus:

King James had at his great cost and charge enclosed with a pale two several parcels of land for coppices, of which Mr. Gibbons afterwards got a lease for 41 years by name of 574 acres more or less under the yearly rent of £28 14*s.*, which came to so much after the rate of 12*d.* per acre, which was the constant rent to the king used to be reserved, and for a fine of £280, all timber trees and wood being thereby [*f. 8v.*] especially reserved to the king. Whilst this lease was obtained and before it was passed Mr. Gibbons set some on work to join in one inclosure those two parcels severally enclosed, and by that means drew into the inclosure so much more not intended him as made the 574 acres to be between 1,000 and 1,100. And therein the king was deceived of 500 a. or thereabouts, which at 12*d.* an acre comes to £25 per annum or thereabouts, and the true value of what he had is now £200 per annum at the least, and will be worth twice as much more within a few years. After this lease thus obtained, Sir Allen Apsley having a patent to pass off divers lands in fee [*f. 9*] farm from the king, Mr. Gibbons procures this to be inserted in that patent, by particular names of lands containing by estimation 574 a. more or less in the possession of John Gibbons, and in that patent there being a general clause whereby all timber trees and woods growing upon any [of] the said manors or lands passed to Sir Allen Apsley was granted. Mr Gibbons under Sir Allen Apsley's title claimed the fee farm of the land, but no conveyance was produced to that purpose, though the king's counsel much urged to have a sight of it. What Mr. Gibbons really paid for this did not plainly appear. It was alleged very near £1,000. [*f. 9v.*] Since Mr. Gibbons's purchase,

[1] For John Gibbons, above, pp. xi–xii.

and not long before the justice seat, it was affirmed that he had sold the land to Sir Robert Bannister, for which it is said Sir Robert paid £3,000. But Sir Robert, although he was at Gloucester, did not appear in it, neither was there any proof in it. The timber trees growing upon the said lands were as goodly trees as any in the Forest and a great number of them marked for the king, all which were cut down by Mr. Gibbons.

In all this the court, finding the king deceived in the quantity of acres to the number of 500 or thereabouts, [and finding] that Mr. Gibbons under the title of Sir Allen Apsley had [f. 10] no power to cut down any timber or wood, because being a forest the grant of woods gives no power to cut them unless there be special words for the purpose, and finding, as well by the reservation in the lease as by the marking of the trees for the king, that the king never intended that Mr. Gibbons should fell the timber trees, it was thought fit to repair the king's losses procured by the undue ways aforesaid with fining Mr. Gibbons £6,000, according to the value of the trees found upon oath. And for his offence in that, and the cutting down marked trees, destruction of coppices, and inclosing with a wall contrary to the [f. 10v.] forest laws, as much more, as in all, with the former £6,000, came to about £9,000, the court conceiving the king had lost so much by Mr. Gibbons's means.

Sir Basil Brooke and Mr. Mynne,[1] as assignees of the earl of Pembroke, have a grant from the king for divers years yet to come of 10,000 cords of complement wood[2] yearly and the windfalls and offals,[3] and logwood for maintenance of the ironworks in Dean Forest, paying to the king 6s. 8d. a cord for the complement wood and 3s. 4d. a cord for the logwood, windfalls, and offals, those to be delivered by the officers of the king, appointed for that purpose, or in case of neglect [f. 11] upon request, to make proclamation in the parish church of Mitcheldean (*Great Deane*), and so take them. The swanimote court presented and convicted them for felling divers great quantities of wood, but because the swanimote court had not presented all and to the end [that] all the particular abuses and deceits might justly appear upon oath when they might have liberty to make their defence, when at the swanimote court they did not, being absent, it was thought fit by the king's counsel that an indictment should be preferred against them, to the which they might plead and upon their traverse[4] might be admitted to examine what witnesses they would for the clearing of themselves. [f. 11v.] Accordingly, an indictment was preferred, charging them to have taken off the king's wood within six years last past (they coming by assignment from the earl of Pembroke in June 1628) to the number of 178,200 cords of wood to the value of £59,400. This indictment being found upon evidence to the grand jury in open court, they had time given them by the court to plead to it, and after had Wednesday morning, 16 July, assigned for trial. At which time, a jury of the best rank and quality there being sworn, the matter was at large heard by

---

[1] For Brooke and Mynne, above, p. xi.
[2] Evidently a phrase used to designate wood granted as part of the ironworks concession.
[3] Refuse, waste, or fallen pieces of wood: *OED*.
[4] A formal denial of the facts of a case: *OED*.

counsel as well on their behalf as for the king, and seven hours spent in hearing the cause.

[*f. 12*] The king's counsel charged them with two things, viz. the number of cords, and the abuses in taking them. For the number of cords of wood, there were produced divers witnesses, who deposed that, the farmers having four furnaces for making of raw iron and five forges, whereof three are double forges, for making of bar iron, those furnaces and forges would not (being always set on work) spend less than that quantity of wood wherewith they were charged, as they demonstrated by the several quantities of raw iron made in every furnace and of bar iron made in every [*f. 12v.*] forge, by the quantity of coals that served for the making of that iron, and by the quantity of cordwood that must needs be spent in making those coals. This being but a probable argument, the king's counsel rested not there but by several witnesses made it clear to the court what number of acres had been felled by them, how many trees were in every acre, how much cordwood those trees would make, and so punctually charged them with the quantities in the indictment.

For the abuses in taking the cordwood, the king's counsel urged many particulars, and fully proved all, [*f. 13*] as namely:

1. That they caused great quantities of cordwood to be wheeled into their pits without delivery of the king's officers, and so of all them the king was deceived.

2. That where cordwood was delivered by tale, they found 23 for the most part instead of 20.

3. That by the bargain with the king the cord wood being agreed to be of a certain size, they had exceeded the size, and therein also much abused the king.

4. That they had invented a way of making half cordwood instead of whole, and by that had so increased the size that in every two whole cords they [*f. 13v.*] gained a fourth part, it being proved that three half [cords] went as far as two whole cords.

5. That they had taken great quantities of the best timber trees, fit for the complement wood, for which they were to pay 6*s*. 8*d*. a cord, and reckoned it for the logwood and for windfalls and offals, for which they paid but 3*s*. 4*d*. a cord, and so deceived the king half in half.

6. That they had by cutting glades and destroying the shelter of great timber trees left them open for the wind upon sides of hills and in wet ground, so as when winter came the wind having power upon them blew down a great number of goodly timber trees, a thousand in one [*f. 14*] night, many of them marked for the king, and those they took as windfalls.

7. That they had felled some young springs, good for nothing, to the destruction of the Forest in the future.

8. That, having by bargain from some other patentees divers roots and stools, they had caused excellent timber trees to be felled and mingled amongst them, of all which the king was deceived and no *accompt* (account) made.

9. That contrary to express agreement, they had felled divers marked timber trees which were reserved for the king's store, and with which they ought not to have meddled.

10. That they had destroyed woods [*f. 14v.*] in which were eyries of hawks, contrary to express direction.[1]

11. That, notwithstanding a restraint by the now Lord Treasurer of which they had notice, that since that restraint and in contempt of it felled timber and wood to as great or a greater proportion than before the restraint.

12. That they had suffered and brought in others to cut down wood and to make coals of it, and to serve them coals at a price.

13. That they had brought in multitudes of cottagers and cabiners, who all made their cottages and cabins of the king's wood and lived upon spoil of the woods.

14. That they had threatened officers to have them turned out of their [*f. 15*] office if they pried too narrowly into their accounts, whence it came that the officers were for the most part combiners and confederates with them to deceive and abuse the king.

Their counsel by way of defence brought in some of their agents to depose what quantity of iron was made by them in the several furnaces and forges, and so for the quantity of coals that served the making of that iron, and of the wood that served the making of those coals, whose testimony the court did not much weigh, in regard they would not produce their original books of *accompt* (account), which they [*f. 15v.*] were before commanded by the court to do, but deposed out of notes and abstracts to serve their turns. And for the justification of the quantity they read the grant to the earl of Pembroke under the claim of 10,000 cords a year, for which they had accounted in the Exchequer and paid the king.

But the king's counsel pressing them to prove delivery by the king's officers according to the words of the patents, they answered they could not, and thereupon took occasion to desert the defence and proceeded no further but left themselves *in misericordia regis.*[2] Upon which the king's counsel took occasion to let the court and auditory know how just [*f. 16*] it was not to allow them more than was delivered by the officers of the king, because, had the king's officers delivered all the cordwood as was agreed and directed by the patent, the farmers could not have put the deceits and abuses above mentioned upon the king, and therefore it was no reason they should take advantage of their own wrongs. They thus giving over the cause, the judges directed the court they had failed of their justification.

After dinner, viz. about 5 o'clock, they coming on purpose to receive the verdict, the jury found them guilty to the value of £57,939 16s. 8d., whereupon the court gave judgement against them. And the Lord Chief Justice set [*f. 16v.*] the fine only proportionably to the value found by the jury and not according to the forest laws, being twelve times more the value.

---

[1] GA D9125/12937 f. 37v. adds that they built charcoal pits below the eyries, so that the smoke drove the birds away.

[2] 'In the king's mercy', i.e. submitted themselves to be penalized at the court's discretion.

Sir John Winter[1] had by grant as assignee of the earl of Pembroke 2,500 cords of wood a year at 6*s*. 8*d*. the cord. Sir John Winter was presented and convicted for cutting down and taking within six years last past 60,700 cords of wood to the value of £2,050. Sir John Winter was also indicted for the same quantity, and on Tuesday, [15] July, pleaded '*non culpabilis* (not guilty)'. When the king's counsel was prepared for trial, Sir John Winter, conceiving his case to be like Sir Basil Brooke's and Mr. Mynnes's, in open court, *relict. verificare*,[2] he confessed the indictment. So the court gave judgement against him according to his confession [and fined him] £20,230.

---

[1] For Winter, above, p. xi.
[2] Presumably a legal phrase for abandoning the attempt to prove a case.

LISTS OF FOREST OFFICERS AND OTHERS ATTENDING
(British Library, Harleian MS. 4850)

[f. 2]

The Eyre of the king's Forest of Dean begun at Mitcheldean, in Gloucestershire, on Thursday, 10 July 1634, before John Bridgeman, knight, justice of Chester and deputy to Henry, earl of Holland, knight of the most noble order of the Garter, chief justice and justice-in-eyre in all the lord king's forests, chases, parks, and warrens on this side of the Trent; and there immediately adjourned by the said John Bridgeman to Gloucester castle, in Gloucestershire; and held at the said castle on the same Thursday before the said Henry, earl of Holland, chief justice and justice-in-eyre aforesaid.

The Names of those who are Foresters, Verderers, Woodwards, and other Officers of the Forest of Dean

Philip, earl of Pembroke and Montgomery, the king's constable of the manor and castle of St. Briavels, and warden of the said Forest (by James Kyrle, his deputy)

James Kyrle, esq., deputy of the said warden (sworn)

FORESTERS

Baynham Throckmorton, bt., chief forester-in-fee (sworn)

George Hamblyn, gent., his deputy (sworn)

Hugh Dowle, gent., forester-in-fee (sworn)

Geoffrey Lippiat, his deputy (he gave 8*s.*)

William Graye, forester-in-fee (sworn)

Richard Collyns, his deputy (sworn; he gave a fine of £10)

John Hannys, forester-in-fee (sworn; he produced his horn)[1]

John Wintour, forester-in-fee (sworn)

Richard Dorsett, his deputy (sworn)

Edward Bashe, forester-in-fee (£10 for absence)

Philip Meeke, his deputy (sworn)

Isabel Wye, spinster, and Susan, now the wife of Richard Durlinge, gent., coheirs of Anthony Wye, esq., deceased (fine £5)

John Baker, their deputy (40*s.*)

---

[1] i.e. the official accoutrement of a forester.

29

[*f. 2v.*]

John Steyner, forester-in-fee (infirm, by oath of John Preece)

John Preece, his deputy (sworn)

John Worgan, forester-in-fee (he gave £5 for default of his horn)

John Jefferys, his deputy (sworn)

VERDERERS
Charles Bridgman, esq. (sworn)
Warren Goughe, gent. (sworn)
John Berrowe, gent. (sworn)

REGARDERS

Warren Goughe, esq. (sworn)
George Wyrrall, esq. (sworn)
Anthony Arnold, gent. (sworn)
John A Deane, gent. (sworn)
Anthony Bower, gent. (sworn)
George Bond, gent. (sworn)

William Wargent, gent. (sworn)
John Jane, gent. (sworn)
Nicholas Morse, gent. (sworn)
Thomas Arram, gent. (sworn)
Edmund Browne, gent. (sworn)
Richard Byrkyn, gent. (sworn)

WOODWARDS

Bayneham Throckmorton, bt., woodward of Bearse (*Beers*) bailiwick[1]

Griffin Morgan, his deputy (40*s.*)

Benedict Hall, esq., woodward of Staunton bailiwick (sworn)

Richard Smythe, his deputy (sworn)

The same Benedict, woodward of English Bicknor bailiwick

Thomas Harsfield, gent., his deputy (sworn)

Joan Vaughan, widow, woodward of Ruardean bailiwick

Henry Bridge (sworn)

The same Joan, woodward of Abenhall bailiwick

Walter Bower, her deputy

[*f. 3*]

The same Joan, woodward of Badcocks Bailey, alias Littledean, bailiwick

Thomas Lokyer, alias Sparks, her deputy (sworn)

Edmund Berrowe, esq., woodward of Blakeney (*Backney*) (sworn)

John Fryer (sworn) and William Treganoe, gent. (sworn), his deputies

Nicholas Roberts, esq., woodward of Mitcheldean bailiwick (sworn; £20)

Anthony Callowe, gent., his deputy (sworn)

The same Nicholas, woodward of Lea (*Lacu*) bailiwick

Robert Meeke, his deputy (sworn)

---

[1] The bailiwick, which lay at the western edge of the royal demesne with Bearse common near St. Briavels its main surviving part by this date, was held with Clearwell manor: *VCH Glos.* v. 197, pp. 210, 357–8.

Richard Hill, gent., woodward of Blaize Bailey (*Bleiths Bayly*) bailiwick[1]
    (sworn; 40*s.* for default of the hatchet; fine pardoned by the court)[2]

RANGERS (*reingers*) BY LETTERS PATENT

John Arthur, gent. (fine £20 for absence)

George Southe, gent.

John Lewis, his deputy (sworn)

KEEPERS (*custodes anglice the keepers*)

Thomas Cheyney, gent. (sworn)   William Brethers, gent (sworn)
Henry Gaynsford, gent. (sworn)   Richard Jelfe, gent.
William Foxe, gent. (sworn)   Addams, gent.

OTHER OFFICERS OF THE FOREST

Richard Powell, gent., bowbearer of the warden of the Forest (sworn)
Richard Whittington, gent., bowbearer of the chief forester of the Forest (sworn)
Thomas Smith, gent., beadle of the king's castle of St. Briavels (40*s.*)
Walter Heane, gent., bailiff of the hundred of St. Briavels (sworn)

[*f. 3v.*]

The Names of the Four Men and Reeves of all the Towns and Townships within the Forest of Dean[3]

ST. BRIAVELS	William Davis, constable (sworn)
	John Worgan (sworn)
	John Jane (sworn)
	John Braban (sworn)
	William Tyler (sworn)
MITCHELDEAN (*Deane Magna*)	Thomas Workman, constable (sworn)
	Mose, gent. (sworn)
	Robert Kirke (sworn)
	John Nashe (sworn)
	Daniel Morse (sworn)
LEA	Thomas Wirrall, constable (sworn)
	Robert Phillips (sworn)
	William Lovell (sworn)
	John Lloyd (sworn)
	Thomas Rudge (sworn)

[1] The bailiwick, which lay at the eastern edge of the royal demesne, its name still used for woodland adjoining Newnham parish, was held with Blythes Court manor in Newnham: *VCH Glos.* v. 357; x. pp. 39–40.

[2] The hatchet, official accoutrement of the woodward, was used for marking trees within his bailiwick for felling or preservation for the king's use.

[3] For the constituents of this list of townships and the list of free tenants following, see above, p. xxiii. In this list the first (unheaded) section comprises parishes and tithings in the hundred of St. Briavels.

LITTLEDEAN (*Deane Parva*)	William Nicholls, constable (40*s*.; sworn later) Anthony Stratford, gent. (sworn) Thomas Morse, the elder (40*s*., pardoned by court; sworn later) Thomas Lovell (40*s*., pardoned by court; sworn later) Christopher Tucker (sworn)
STAUNTON (*Stantone*)	David Powell, constable (40*s*. pardoned by court) Henry Dowle (sworn) Robert Griffith (40*s*., pardoned by court) Edward Smyth (sworn) James Keere (sworn)
ABENHALL	Thomas Morgan (sworn) James Heynes (sworn) William Vaughan (sworn) John Meeke (sworn) Walter Mowsell (sworn)
ENGLISH BICKNOR (*Bicknor Anglicanorum*)	William Godwyn, constable (sworn) Benedict Jorden (sworn) Roger Lewys (sworn) Richard Vaughan (sworn) Matthew Ambrose (sworn)
BLAKENEY	John Tyler, constable (40*s*., pardoned by court; sworn later) John Wyntle (sworn) Andrew Horne (sworn) Francis Bridgman (40*s*.) Gough Chyn (sworn)
COLEFORD BEAME[1]	Richard Higgins, constable (40*s*., pardoned by court) William Dowle (sworn) William Yem (sworn) Sturley Kedgwyn (sworn) Henry Marshe (sworn)
CLEARWELL (*Clower Wall*)	Hugh Dowle, constable (sworn) Thomas Kedgwyn (sworn) Thomas Keare (sworn) Thomas Howper the elder (sworn) Thomas Skyn (sworn)
FLAXLEY	Edmund Mills, constable (40s; sworn later) George Mills (sworn) John Nelme (sworn) John Hayle (sworn) Richard Nelme (sworn)

---

[1] 'Beam', a local equivalent of 'tithing', was used for the divisions of Newland parish, of which Coleford then formed part: *VCH Glos*. v. p. 222.

RUARDEAN   Thomas Smart, constable (sworn)
                        Henry Rudge (sworn)
                        Thomas Rudge (sworn)
                        Thomas Martyn (infirm)
                        John Dowle (sworn)

[*f. 4*]   LIBERTY OF THE DUCHY OF LANCASTER[1]

RODLEY   Griffin Challenger, constable (sworn)
  AND BOLLOW (*Bully*)[2] Robert Newton (sworn)
                        John Wyntle (sworn)
                        Richard Stevens (sworn)
                        John Stevens (sworn)

NEWNHAM   John Aram, mayor (sworn)
                        Thomas Kirke (sworn)
                        Thomas Chyn (sworn)
                        Thomas Hodges (sworn)
                        John Jeffreys (sworn)

BULLEY   Thomas Drewe, constable (40*s*., pardoned by court;
                          sworn later)
                        John Yonge (sworn)
                        Henry Ravenhall (sworn)
                        John Holder (sworn)
                        William Brushe (40*s*.)

TAYNTON   Thomas Drewe, constable (40*s*., pardoned by court;
                          sworn later)
                        Richard Ayleway, gent. (40*s*.; sworn later)
                        Roger Nelme (40*s*., pardoned by court; sworn later)
                        John Culverhouse (40*s*.; sworn later)
                        Anthony Creese (40*s*.; sworn later)

                        HUNDRED OF BLEDISLOE

AWRE   Richard Browne, constable (sworn)
                        John Warren (40s, pardoned by court; sworn later)
                        Richard Driver (sworn)

ETLOE[3]   Richard Hodges of Etloe (pardoned by court)
                        Thomas Awre (sworn)

                                        Giles Fettyplace, kt., sheriff

[1] Duchy of Lancaster hundred, comprising manors that had passed to the Crown as possessions of that dukedom.
[2] Tithings of Westbury-on-Severn parish.
[3] A tithing of Awre parish.

[*f. 4v.*]

The Names of all the Free Tenants within the Forest of Dean

HUNDRED OF ST. BRIAVELS

ST. BRIAVELS
Richard Catchmay, kt.
Warren Gough, esq.
William Wargent, gent.
Edward Adale
John Worgan
John Jane
John Braban
William Cole
Christopher Worgan
Arthur Mallett, esq. (20*s.*)
Alexander Thorne (20*s.*, pardoned by court)
George Reeve (20*s.*)
William Davis (20*s.*)
Francis Carpenter (20*s.*, pardoned by court)
Thomas Veale
Francis Grissett (20*s.*)

HEWELSFIELD
  AND BROCKWEIR
John Jane, gent.
Thomas Hopkins the elder (20*s.*, pardoned by court)
Edward White, gent. (20*s.*, pardoned by court)
Thomas Browne (20*s.*, pardoned by court)
William Wigfall (20*s.*, pardoned by court)
William Welford (20*s.*, pardoned by court)
Richard Williams (20*s.*, pardoned by court)
William Smith (20*s.*, pardoned by court)
William Williams (20*s.*, pardoned by court)
Richard Higgens (20*s.*, pardoned by court)
Thomas Matthews (20*s.*)
Thomas Hopkins the younger (20*s.*, pardoned by court)

MITCHELDEAN
Edward Morse, gent.
Anthony Bower, gent.
Edward Serjeant, gent.
Thomas Woode, gent.
Anthony Callewe, gent.
John Partridge, gent. (20*s.*)
Nicholas Morse, gent.
Daniel Morse, gent.
Robert Kirke
John Lane
John Nashe
Thomas Weale
William Davis (20*s.*)
John Wood

Edward Jennings (20*s.*)
Edward Partridge (20*s.*)
Edward Hathaway (20*s.*)
William Vaughan

LEA — Robert Phillippes
Henry Phillippes
William Phillippes
Thomas Wirrall
Richard Dorsett
William Lovell
John Baddam
John Floyde
John Rudge of the Rudge
John Hannis
Thomas Rudge

[*f. 5*]
LITTLEDEAN — Edward Bash, kt. (20*s.*)
Charles Bridgman, esq.
John Winsere, esq. (20*s.*, pardoned by court)
Ketford Brayne, gent.
James Heane, gent. (20*s.*)
Henry Heane (20*s.*)
Anthony Stratford, gent.
Thomas Morse the elder (20*s.*)
Thomas Lovell (20*s.*)
Christopher Tucker
Richard Brayne, gent. (20*s.*)

STAUNTON — Richard Smith
Christopher Stephens (20*s.,* pardoned by court)
Thomas Wysom (20*s.*, pardoned by court)
John Hoskins
Henry S [*sic*]
Arthur Payne
Robert Griffith (20*s.*, pardoned by court)
James Keare

ABENHALL — James Haynes
William Vaughan
John Meeke
Walter Mowsall

ENGLISH BICKNOR — George Worrall, gent. (20*s.*)
William Munmothe the younger, gent. (20*s.*, pardoned by
court)
Benedict Jordan
John Batchelor (20*s.*, pardoned by court)

William Parlor
William Cr [*sic*] (20*s.*, pardoned by court)
John Gardner (20*s.*)
Richard Terret (20*s.*, pardoned by court)
Roger Lewis
Richard Vaughan
Thomas Mowsall (20*s.*, pardoned by court)
John Fisher
Matthew Ambrose
Edmund Browne

BLAKENEY

Chyn, gent.
John Berrowe, gent.
Francis Bridgman gent. (20*s.*)
William Vertue (20*s.*)
John Wintle
John Bucke (20*s.*)
Andrew Horne
Robert Frier
Richard White (20*s.*)

COLEFORD BEAME

William Carpenter, gent.
William Dowle
Robert Jordan (20*s.*, pardoned by court)
John Yerroth
William Ymme
Sturly Kedgwin
Henry Morebold
Stephen Gagge
Henry Marshe
Richard Moreton

CLEARWELL

Baynham Throckmorton, kt. and bt.
Thomas Kedgwin
Thomas Keare
Thomas Hooper the elder
Kedgwin Hoskins
Hugh Dowle
William Skynn

[*f. 5v.*]

Henry Worgan
John Symonds
Edward Palmere
Richard Howell (20*s.*)
Thomas Hooper the younger
Edward Wheeler alias Partridge (dead)

HIGHMEADOW[1] (*Highmeade*)	Benedict Hall, esq.
NEWLAND	George Bond, gent. William Ricketts (20*s*.) John Court William Tyler (20*s*.)
REDBROOK[2]	Athanasius Elly, gent.
BLACKMORE'S HALE[3]	Tanner Morse Anthony Arnold of the Grange, gent.
FLAXLEY	William Kingston, esq. (20*s*.) Edmund Milles (20*s*.) George Milles John Nelme John Hayle Richard Nelme
RUARDEAN	Baynham Vaughan, esq. (20*s*.) John Bufford (20*s*.) Thomas Smart Richard Imme (20*s*.) Henry Rudge Henry Rudge the younger Thomas Rudge Thomas Marten (infirm) William Imme John Dowle John Knight George Harris

THE EARL OF WORCESTER'S HUNDRED[4]

BEACHLEY[5]	William Higgins William Philpott John Hopkins Thomas Luellyn (20*s*.)
WOOLASTON	Henry Morris, gent.

---

[1] A hamlet straddling the boundary between Newland and Staunton parishes, by this date all in the ownership of the Hall family and largely depopulated: *VCH Glos*. v. pp. 275–7.

[2] A tithing of Newland parish.

[3] A hamlet partly in Westbury-on-Severn parish, and partly in the royal demesne at Pope's Hill.

[4] A southern, detached part of Westbury hundred, comprising manors then owned by Henry Somerset, earl of Worcester.

[5] A tithing of Tidenham parish.

Charles Gough of Plusterwine (*Plasterwyne*)
William Gough, gent
Richard Tippett (20*s.*, pardoned by court)
Edward Sheare (20*s.*)
Edward Worgan
George Maddockes (20*s.*)
James Woodrooffe, gent.
John Smarte
William Hughes
John Imme (20*s.*)
William Welford (20*s.*)
William Clarke, gent.

[*f. 6*]
TIDENHAM

William Hopkins, gent.
William Catchmay, gent. (20*s.*)
John a Wirwood
Stephen Dapwell
John Smart (infirm, old, etc.)
John Hopkins, gent.
John Williams (20*s.*)
William Philpott
John Maddocke (20*s.*)
Christopher Shipman
William Webly
John Stephens of Lancaut[1]
William Warwood
John Collins
William Stephens
John Horne (20*s.*)
John Stephens the younger (20*s.*)
William Reynolds
Arthur Philpott (20*s.*, pardoned by court)
Richard Darling, gent.

LIBERTY OF THE DUCHY OF LANCASTER

RODLEY AND
 BOLLOW (*Bully*)

Thomas Wintle, gent. (20*s.*)
William Wintle
Thomas Lovell (20*s.*)
Robert Bayse
John Manson (20*s.*)
Griffin Challiner
Thomas Bullocke (20*s.*)
Jerome (*Jeromias*) Batherne (20*s.*)

---

[1] Lancaut was a small depopulated parish by the river Wye that came to be regarded as part of Tidenham.

Roger Taylor, gent.
Thomas Maldson
Robert Crumpe (20*s.*)
Zacharias Crumpe, gent.
Robert Newton
Richard Maldson of *Netherend* (20*s.*)
John Wintle of the same
John Wintle of Cowley's Elm (20*s.*)
Richard Stephens
John Stephens
John Morwent (20*s.*)
Robert Maynard
Thomas Bellamy (20*s.*)

BULLEY

John Holder (20*s.*)
John Yonge
William Brushe (20*s.*)
Henry Ravenhill
Henry Crumpe (20*s.*, pardoned by court)

CHAXHILL (*Caxhill*)[1]

Ralph Drewe (20*s.*)
Henry Carpenter
Henry Maynard (20*s.*)
William Bayse, gent. (20*s.*)
John Callowe
Robert Crumpe
Thomas Younge, gent. (20*s.*)

[*f. 6v.*]
CLEEVE[2]

Richard Batherne (20*s.*)
Samuel Moore
Robert Custance
Joseph Bellamy
Thomas Maldson
Thomas Rushe
Richard Nurth

HUNTLEY

William Keyse (20*s.*, pardoned by court)
William White (20*s.*)
Joseph White (20*s.*)
William White (20*s.*)
Thomas Weke (20*s.*)
Thomas Draper (20*s.*)

LONGHOPE

John Nurse, gent. (20*s.*)
William Dobbes (20*s.*)
Thomas Okey

[1] A tithing of Westbury-on-Severn parish.
[2] Ditto.

Edward Fowle (20s.)
William Hodges (20s.)
Thomas Hobbes (20s.; dead)
Thomas Dawe
Simon Powell

ELTON[1]
William Aylebertone, gent. (£20 for non-attendance)
William Carpenter, gent. (20s.)
Christopher Cowles (dead)
Thomas Launder (20s.)
John Braban
John Rider
Henry Cowles
John Hampton
John Hampton [sic]

TIBBERTON
John Perry the elder (20s., pardoned by court)
Thomas Handman
John Reeve (20s., pardoned by court)
John Sandford (20s., pardoned by court)
Walter Branch (20s., pardoned by court)

MINSTERWORTH
Richard Watts (20s.)
Thomas Addams (20s.)
Richard Bosby (20s.; dead)
William Barret of *Knightsend* (20s.; dead)
Robert Lowe (20s.)
Arthur Callowe (20s.; dead)
William Arnold (20s.; dead)
John Pearton (20s.)
Richard Fewterer (20s.)

[f. 7]

HUNDRED OF BLEDISLOE

LYDNEY
Walter Webley, gent. (20s., pardoned by court)
Thomas Kempe, gent. (20s., pardoned by court)
Thomas Bucke (20s.)
Anthony Hamond (20s., pardoned by court)
Edmund Berrowe (20s.)
William Duning, gent.
George Duning, gent.
William Jones of Nass (*Nashe*), gent. (20s.)

AWRE
John Birkin, gent.
John Warren (20s.)
Richard Hooper (20s.)
Richard Driver

[1] A tithing of Westbury-on-Severn parish.

ETLOE[1]	James Robbins, gent. (20*s.*)
	Richard Hodges (20*s.*)
	John Adeane, gent.
	Matthew Adeane
HAGLOE[2]	Richard Birkin, gent.
	Thomas Morgan of Hurst, esq. [3]
	Charles Trippett, gent.
	Richard Browne of Kettles
	Richard Driver
	John Heman
	John Bayley (20*s.*)
	Richard Browne
	John Browne
	Thomas Awre (20*s.*)
	Richard Hooper (20*s.*)
	John Awre
	John Robbins (20*s.*)
	Caleb Huling (20*s.*)
	Richard Hopkins
BLAKENEY	Thomas Sallence
	John Tyler (20*s.*)
	Robert Fryer
	John Preece
	Matthew White (20*s.*)
	Richard Browne of Kettles
	John Worgan (20*s.*)
	Richard Vertue (20*s.*)
	Edward Butler (20*s.*)
	Morgan Griffin
	George Birkin
	Robert Yonge

[*f. 7v.*]

HUNDRED OF WESTBURY

NEWNHAM	John Arram, gent.
	Thomas Chyn, gent.
	Thomas Kirke
	Richard Hill, gent. (20*s.*)
	John Ayleberton, gent.
	John Trigge, gent. (20*s.*, pardoned by court)
	John Morse (20*s.*)
	John Jefferies

[1] A tithing of Awre parish.
[2] Ditto.
[3] Hurst Farm was in Lydney parish.

	Thomas Hodges
BLAISDON	Henry Gynnell (20*s.*)
	Peter Ayleway, gent. (20*s.*)
	Richard Robbins (20*s.*)
	William Boulton
	John Robbins
	William Trigge
	John Hooper (20*s.*)
	John Bullocke the younger (20*s.*)
CHURCHAM	Edmund Wicke (20*s.*; dead)
	John Hopkins (20*s.*)
	William Cokle (20*s.*)
	William Hyett (20*s.*)
	John Smyth (20*s.*)
RUDDLE [1]	John Witt, gent.
	William Arram
WESTBURY	Nicholas Roberts, esq.
	Joseph Wintle
	Charles Driver, gent. (20*s.*)
	Joseph Morwent
	Thomas Osborne (20*s.*)
	William Bellamy (20*s.*)
	John Yonge of Lower Ley (*Netherly*) gent. (20*s.*)
	William Tilton (20*s.*)
	John Phillippes
	George Wintle of Ardens, gent. (20*s.*)
	Joseph Holsteede (20*s.*)
	John Cadle (20*s.*)
	William Ayleberton of Alvington, gent. (20*s.*)

Giles Fettyplace, kt., sheriff

[*f. 8*]

Jury to Enquire for the Lord King

William Masters, kt. (sworn)   William Osborne, gent. (sworn)
Thomas Ri [*sic*], esq. (sworn)   John Barnard, gent. (sworn)
Thomas Morgan, esq. (sworn)   Francis Izod, gent. (sworn)
William Carpenter, gent. (sworn)   George Morse, gent. (sworn)
Edward Adale, gent. (sworn)   John Sloper, gent. (sworn)
Thomas Tayloe, gent. (sworn)   Thomas Yonge, gent. (sworn)
Edward Hooke, gent. (sworn)   John Wyde, gent. (sworn)
John Keyse, gent. (sworn)

Giles Fettyplace, kt., sheriff

---

[1] A tithing of Newnham parish.

PRESENTMENTS AT THE SWANIMOTE JUNE 1634
with the Fines Imposed at the Eyre
(British Library, Harleian MS. 4850)

[*f. 10*]

Gloucestershire, Forest of Dean: **Court of Swanimote of our lord King Charles, by the Grace of God King of England, Scotland, France, and Ireland, Defender of the Faith, etc., held at Mitcheldean in the said Forest on 10 June 1634, before Charles Bridgman, esq., Warren Gough, esq., and John Berrowe, gent., verderers of the said Forest**[1]

It is presented by the foresters, regarders, and 12 jurymen, and convicted by the verderers that:

1 Edward Villiers (*Villars*),[2] late of London, kt., who died before the regard, and Lady Barbara Villars, his widow, at various times between 31 January 1620 and 30 April 1634 felled 1,634 oaks and 7,066 beeches, each worth 20*s.*, in places within the demesne land of the king's Forest called Coverham, *Stoneheald, Brookshill, Luteshill, Branyroft*, and Mailscot; and they converted the timber and wood from the same and the underwood growing there to their own use.

2 Lady Barbara Villiers, widow, Thomas Tylman, and John Wright, late of Mailscot in the Forest, gent., between 1 June 1630 and 30 April 1634 in several places within the metes and bounds of the Forest encroached on the following parcels of land of the king's soil of the Forest: 30 a. at Coverham worth 45*s.* 2*d.* a year; 120 a. called *Stoneheald* worth £7 10*s.* a year; 80 a. called *Brookshill* worth £6 a year; 100 a. called *Luteshill* worth £7 10*s.*a year; 50 a. called *Branyrofte* worth £3 15*s.* a year; 50 a. called Mailscot worth 35s a year; and they took the receipts and profits to their own use and retain them.

3 John Gibbons,[3] late of London., esq., and Stephen Veynor of the same, gent., at various times between 31 March 1629 and 30 April 1634 in several places in the Forest called Mirystock, *Dowleys Chamber, Buckholde Barne*, Buckholt (*Buckholde*), Beechenhurst (*Burching Hurst*), and Cannop felled 4,000 oaks and 2,000 beech, each worth 20*s.*, and converted the timber and wood to their own use. (fine £6,000)

4 John Gibbons between 1 April 1633 and 30 April 1634 encroached on the following parcels of land of the king's soil of the Forest: 40 a. called Mirystock worth £5 a year; 100 a. called *Dowleys Chamber* worth £15 a year; 120 a. called Buckholt (*le Buckholde*) worth £13 13*s.* 4*d.* a year; 80 a. called *le Barne Buckholde* worth £5 a year; 300 a. called Beechenhurst worth £35 a year; 300 a. called Cannop worth £40 a year; those parcels of land, contrary to the assize of the Forest, are enclosed by a wall; and he took the receipts

---

[1] In translating the following presentments unnecessary and repetitive wording in the original has been omitted or paraphrased. The record of the fine and other notes, given here in brackets at the end of the items, is in the original MS. a marginal addition. Figures for tonnage of timber, acreage of land, etc. are in the original usually followed by the phrase *per estimationem*.

[2] See pp. xi, xviii–xix.

[3] See pp. xi–xii, xix.

43

and profits to his own use and retains them. (fine £500) [*fine crossed through, and note added:* prostern'[1] according to the assize of the Forest]

[*f. 10v.*]

5   John Gibbons and Stephen Veynor within the same period despoiled the coppice (*subboscum anglice the coppice*) at Mirystock, with loss to the king £200 and harm to his Forest. (fine £500)

6   Robert Treswell,[2] late of Cannop in the Forest, on 29 February 1632 built a water mill and a malthouse (*domum brasilem anglice a malt howse*) at Cannop, for building which he took 30 tons of timber (*dolia maeremii anglice tonns of timber*) of the king's wood of the Forest, worth 6*s*. 8*d*. a ton. (fine £20)

7   Stephen Veynor and Robert Treswell within the same time despoiled the coppices at Buckholt in the Forest, containing 100 a., with loss to the king £100 and harm to his Forest (fine £10 each)

8   John Gibbons and Stephen Veynor on 29 February 1632 built a house called a *Sopehouse* at Cannop, for building which they took 20 tons of timber of the king's woodland of the Forest, worth 6s. 8d. a ton. (fine £50 for the house and £80 for the timber)

9   John Wintour,[3] late of Lydney, kt., between 1 May 1631 and 30 April 1634 felled divers oaks and beeches in a parcel of woodland in the Forest called Haywood (*Eywood*)[4] in which parcel are 1,549 cords of wood (*cordas bosci anglice cords of wood*), each worth 6*s*. 8*d*., which cords exceed the common fixed standard (*assisam communem*) by four inches in length and four inches in width, with loss to the king £10. (fine £3,000)

[*f. 11*]

10   William Rowles of Cockshoot, in Newnham, gent.,[5] and Francis Bridgeman, late of Blakeney, gent., on 1 August 1633 took 20 tons from the woodland at Haywood within the king's demesne of the Forest, each ton worth 6*s*. 8*d*., and converted the timber and wood to their own use. (fine £50 each; Bridgeman's fine, by petition, £4)

11   Edward Wintour, late of Lydney, kt., deceased, between 1 August 1603 and 31 August 1614 felled beeches in the places in the king's demesne of the Forest called *le Copes*, Bradley, *Penny Well*, and *Piggslade*, near Blakeney,[6] containing 300 a., with loss to the king and harm to his Forest £300. (fine £1,800)

12   Philip Harris of Truro, co. Devon (*sic*), gent., and Richard Challinor of Bristol, merchant,[7] between 31 August 1618 and 30 June 1630 felled oaks and beeches in a parcel called the Snead in the king's demesne of the Forest containing 100 a., with loss to the king £200 and harm to his Forest. (fine £1,000 each)

[1] Presumably 'it (i.e. the wall) is to be thrown down'.
[2] For Treswell, see below, p. 49*n*.
[3] See pp. xi, xx, xxxiv–xxxv.
[4] For this form of the name, see TNA, F 17/7.
[5] For the Cockshoot estate in Newnham, see *VCH Glos*. x. p. 40.
[6] Sir Edward, who died in 1619, held a lease of these coppices under the Crown from 1610: B.L. Lansdowne MS. 166, ff. 348–56.
[7] Harris and Challinor were the lessees of the king's ironworks from 1621: Hart, *Ind. Hist. of Dean*, p. 12.

13   Basil Brooke, late of Shropshire, kt., and George Mynne, late of London, gent.,[1] between 1 April 1633 and 30 April 1634 felled divers oaks and beeches to make into charcoal (*ad carbonandum*) in a parcel called Staple Edge, containing 200 a., within the king's demesne of the Forest, in which parcel there are now 7,500 half-cords of wood, worth 3*s*. 4*d*. each, and 2,000 stools (*de cippis anglice stowles*). (fine £6,000; the record and the whole process is entered in book 7 of the presiding judges (*presidentium*) at f. 2)

14   Edward Osbourne, late of Flaxley, yeoman, took and carried off two small pieces of beech timber, containing ½ ton, in the demesne of the king's Forest; he carried them with oxen and a cart worth £6. (fine £14, and £6 for the oxen)

15   There are 34 tons of unsquared timber (*inquadrata anglice . . . unsquared timber*) and four tons of cut and squared timber now lying in Haywood in the Forest, reserved for the king for the use of his officers. (for the lord king's service)

16   Basil Brooke and George Mynne between 1 May 1620 and 31 March 1630 felled beeches to make charcoal in a place within the king's demesne of the Forest called Blaize Bailey (*Bleythes Baly*), containing 50 a, where there are 6,000 stumps and stools (*trunci anglice stumps and stowles*); with loss to the king £200 and harm to his Forest. (fine £2,400 and the value)

[*f. 11v.*]

17   John Wintour, kt., between 1 May 1622 and 6 May 1633 felled oaks and beeches to make charcoal in a parcel within the king's demesne of the Forest called Edge hills (*Negge hills*), containing 300 a; with loss to the king £200 and harm to his Forest. (fine £2,400 and the value)

18   Richard Challinor and Philip Harris between 6 June 1618 and 31 March 1630 felled oaks and beeches to make charcoal in a parcel within the demesne of the king's Forest called Moorwood, containing 200 a., with loss to the king £300 and harm to his Forest. (fine £1,500 each)

19   Thomas Morgan, late of Ruperra (*Ruperry*) (Glam.), kt., and Edward Thomas of (*?Wealto*) (Glam.), esq., between 1 August 1603 and 31 March 1630 felled oaks and beeches in several places in the demesne of the Forest called Worral hill (*Wyrall hill*), Great Bourts, Little Bourts, and Bourts Edge, containing 600 a., with loss to the king £1,000 and harm to his Forest. (fine £1,000 each, which is pardoned by virtue of a lease of the late King James)

20   Richard Brayne, late of Littledean, gent., by his agents, associates, and workmen, felled and entirely laid waste a parcel of wood or underwood in the Forest called Chestnuts,[2] containing 300 a., which now lies open; the trunks and roots were grubbed up, so that they [i.e. the foresters, etc. making the presentment] can not count the trees and timber which grew there; with loss to the king £200. (fine £2,600)

21   Thomas Tayler, late of Etloe, in Awre parish, labourer, between 1 April 1632 and 30 April 1634 felled 16 beeches, each worth 6*s*. 8*d*., within the king's demesne of the Forest at Middleridge, and converted the timber and wood from the same to the use of the king's farmer. (fine £64 and the value)

22   William Wyrrall and John Pychard, late of Mitcheldean, between 1 March 1631 and 1 April 1634 felled divers oaks in a parcel of the Forest called Lea Bailey (*le Lea Bayly*) containing 15 tons of timber, worth 6*s*. 8*d*. a ton. (fine £100 each and the value)

---

[1] For Brooke and Mynne, see pp. xi, xix, xxxiii–xxxiv.
[2] Brayne had a lease of the Chestnuts from the Crown in 1624: GA, D 421/E 5.

[*f. 12*]

23   William Baddam, late of Mitcheldean, within the same period felled and 'girded' (*circumcidivit anglice girded*)[1] oaks and beeches growing in Lea Bailey, containing 9½ tons of timber, which he took and carried away and converted to his own use. (fine £100)

24   William Dyke, late of Mitcheldean, and John Evans of Lea Bailey between 1 April 1631 and 30 April 1634 felled four oaks lately growing in Lea Bailey, containing three tons of timber, which they took and carried away and converted to their own use. (fine £20 each)

25   Matthew Morse of Mitcheldean during the same period felled two oaks growing in Lea Bailey, containing 1½ tons of timber, which he took, etc. (fine £30)

26   The aforesaid Tanner[2] Morse during the same period felled two oaks growing in a parcel of the Forest called Edge hills, containing 2½ tons of timber, which he took, etc. (fine £50)

27   Richard Vaughan, late of Abenhall, yeoman, between 1 April 1629 and 6 May 1634 felled an oak growing in Lea Bailey, containing one ton of timber, which he took, etc. (fine 20 marks)

28   John Godenough of Elton within the same period felled an oak in a parcel of the Forest called Edge hills, containing one ton of timber, which he took, etc. (fine 20 marks)

29   William Lovel of Lea Bailey Side[3] within the same period felled an oak growing in Lea Bayley, containing 1½ tons of timber, which he took, etc. (fine 20 marks)

[*f. 12v.*]

30   John Hopkins of Mitcheldean within the same period felled a beech growing in a parcel of the Forest and holly and hazel (*vert . . . anglice holy and hasull*) growing in Edge hills, with loss to the king 12*d.* (fine 20*s.*)

31   Edward Morgan of Mitcheldean within the same period felled a beech growing in a parcel called Middleridge, containing two tons of timber, which he took, etc., with loss to the king 13*s.* 4*d.* (fine £20)

32   John Kirle, late of Much Marcle (Herefs.), kt. and bt., or his servants between 1 April 1625 and 30 April 1634 felled eight oaks growing in Lea Bailey in the Forest, containing eight tons of timber worth 6*s.* 8*d.* a ton, which he took, etc. (fine £40 and the value)

33   John Kirle or his servants within the same period felled eight beeches growing in Lea Bailey, containing six tons of timber, worth 6*s.* 8*d.* a ton. (fine £30 and the value)

34   Thomas Wylde of Mitcheldean within the same period felled nine oaks growing in Lea Bailey, containing 12 tons of timber worth 6*s.* 8*d.* a ton, which Philip Tilsley,[4] late of Gloucester city, took and converted to his own use. (fine £100 each, and the value)

---

[1] The meaning of this term, much used in these presentments, is not clear but it possibly describes the practice of cutting the bark all around the trunk of a timber tree, causing it to die, to be later removed by theft or under a right to estovers: cf. Hart, *Royal Forest*, p. 312.

[2] Evidently an alternative forename of Matthew. An earlier family member, 'Thomas Morse alias Tanner', had it as an alternative surname: TNA E134/36 Hil. no. 21.

[3] Adjoining the west side of Lea Bailey woods, this was one of the detached parts of Newland that formed Lea Bailey tithing: *VCH Glos.* v. pp. 196, 314.

[4] See below, p. 71*n.*

35   Daniel Morse and Jasper Lugg, late churchwardens (*procuratores*) of Mitcheldean, within the same period felled two oaks growing in part of the Forest called Lea Bailey, containing three tons of timber, which they took and converted for the repair of the parish church of Mitcheldean and not for any other use. (fine £5 each)[1]

36   Edward Morse of Mitcheldean within the same period felled an oak growing in Lea Bailey, containing one ton to timber, which he took, etc. (fine £20 and the value)

[*f. 13*]

37   Thomas Wade, late of Mitcheldean, gent., within the same period felled an oak growing in Lea Bailey, containing a ton of timber, worth 6*s*. 8*d*., which he took, etc. (fine £4 and the value)

38   Robert Kirke of Mitcheldean, mercer, within the same period felled a beech growing in Haywood (*Eywod*), a parcel of the Forest, containing two tons of timber and wood worth 6*s*. 8*d*. a ton, which he took, etc. (fine £20 and the value)

39   John Lane of Mitcheldean within the same period felled an oak growing in Lea Bailey, containing two tons of timber worth 6*s*. 8*d*. a ton, which he took, etc. (fine £20 and the value)

40   Arthur How of Hope Mansell (Herefs.) within the same period felled an oak growing in Lea Bailey, containing three tons of timber worth 6*s*. 8*d*. a ton, which he took, etc. (fine £30 and the value)

41   William Blast of Hope Mansell within the same period felled or uprooted one oak growing in Lea Bailey, containing two tons of timber worth 6*s*. 8*d*. a ton, which he took, etc. (fine £20 and the value)

42   John Rudge of Rudge[2] within the same period felled two oaks and one beech growing in Lea Bailey, containing 2½ tons of timber worth 16*s*., which he took, etc. (fine £20 and the value)

43   John Norton, late of Lea Bailey Side, within the same period cut the top branches of an oak growing in Lea Bailey, containing three horse-loads (*zeam'*) of wood worth 6*s*., which he converted to his own use. (fine 13*s*. 4*d*. and the value)

43[*number repeated*] John Rudge of Pontshill Marsh (Herefs.) within the same period felled two oaks growing in Lea Bailey, containing three loads of timber, worth 6*s*. 8*d*. a ton, which he took, etc. (fine £30 and the value)

44   Thomas Rudge of Lea (*le Lea*) between 1 April 1625 and [*date incomplete*] felled an oak in Lea Bailey within the perambulation of the Forest, containing 1½ tons of timber, which he took, etc., with loss to the king 6*s*.8*d*. a ton. (fine £5 13*s*. 4*d*. and the value)

[*f. 13v.*]

45   John Rudge of Lea within the same period felled an oak growing in Lea Bailey, containing two tons of timber worth 13*s*. 4*d*., which he took, etc. (fine 20 nobles and the value)

46   Robert Rudge of *Walton'* (Herefs.) within the same period felled an oak in Lea Bailey, containing 1½ tons of timber worth 10*s*., which he took, etc. (fine £13 6*s*. 8*d*. and the value)

---

[1] For this case, see above, pp. 15–16 (where Jasper's surname is given as Leg).
[2] In Weston under Penyard parish.

47   Edward Bower of Lea within the same period felled two oaks growing in Lea Bailey, containing three tons of timber worth 20*s.*, which he took, etc. (fine 20 marks and the value)

48   Robert Rudge of Carnage (*Cawnedge*), in Lea parish, within the same period felled two oaks growing in the king's wood, containing two tons of timber worth 13*s.* 4*d.*, which he took, etc. (fine 20 marks and the value)

49   Alexander *alias* Saunders Morgan of Ruardean within the same period felled a beech, containing four tons worth 26*s.* 8*d.*, growing in Moorwood in the Forest, which he took, etc. (fine £30 and the value)

50   John Knight of the same place within the same period cut timber containing one ton worth 6*s.* 8*d.*, in the Forest, which he took, etc. (fine £10 and the value)

51   John Gwillim of the same place within the same period felled an oak, containing two tons worth 13*s.* 4*d.*, growing in the Forest, which he took, etc. (fine 20 marks and the value)

52   James Madocke of Longhope (*Hope Longa*) within the same period felled an oak, containing one ton of timber worth 6*s.* 8*d.*, growing in Lea Bailey, which he took, etc. (fine £10 and the value)

53   Philip Harris and Richard Challenor, their agents, and workmen, between 1 April 1617 and [*date incomplete*] felled divers parcels of great wood in the Forest called *Godingescott, Hedgeley*, Ruardean's Eaves, part of Astonbridge (*Assenbridge*), and part of Brierley (*Bryery*), containing 1,000 a. of woodland, which wood or timber, having been grubbed up by the roots, they [i.e. the foresters, etc. presenting] can not now enumerate; with loss to the king £1,000. (fine £6,000, viz. £3,000 each)

[*f. 14*]

54   Basil Brooke, kt., George Mynne, esq., and Thomas Hackett, gent., their agents, or workmen, within the same period felled divers parcels of wood and great timber in a certain place in the Forest lying between *Samforde* and Serridge (*Sheredge*), and in another parcel of land (*fundi*) called *Cadmead* and Mirystock (*Moyristock*), and on a hill or parcel of great wood called the Berry, containing in all 400 a. of woodland, in all of which places the trunks and roots were grubbed up, so that they can not count the trees or the wood; with loss to the king £400. (fine £1,600 each, and the value)

54 (*number repeated*) Basil Brooke and George Mynne, their agents, and workmen, within the same period felled divers great groves called Serridge, *Dunellmoore*, and Birch wood in Serridge, where a goshawk (*una esprier' anglice goshawke*) nested, the whole containing 1,000 a. of woodland, which, as the trunks and roots were grubbed up, they can not enumerate; with loss to the king £1,000. (fine £20,000 each, and the value)

55   Basil Brooke and George Mynne or their workmen between 1 April 1608[1] and 1 April 1634 felled a great parcel of beeches within the king's demesne of the Forest called Blakeney's Eaves,[2] containing 200 a.; they can not count the trees formerly growing there, as the trunks and roots were completely destroyed; with loss to the king £300. (fine £1,000 each, and the value)

56   John Wintour, kt., or his workmen between 28 February 1627 and 30 April 1634 felled three parcels of woodland within the king's demesne of the Forest called *Thorney*

---

[1] *sic* (6 James) but perhaps a scribal error for '6 Charles'.
[2] The old name for the Blakeney hill area: TNA, F 17/7.

Hills, Bramiscu[mbe], and Blakeney bailiwick, containing in all 200 a. of woodland; but what trees were there before the felling they can not enquire into, as they were grubbed up; with loss to the king £200. (fine £1,200 and the value)

57   Robert Treswell, late of London, gent., and the said William Rowles, or their workmen, between 1 March 1622 and 1 April 1634 took and converted to charcoal the greater part of the felled or dead wood of the Forest, for which wood and charcoal they took divers sums of money from the farmers of the king's ironworks (*operariorum ferrariorum anglice iron works*),[1] viz. worth 500 (*sic*). (fine £500 each, and the value)

58   Henry Bush, the servant and agent of John Duncumb, gent.,[2] between 28 February 1626 and 30 June 1633 felled eight oaks in a place called *le Fayre tree hill* within the perambulation of the Forest, all of which he barked (*excoriavit anglice barked*); within the same period Henry barked other oaks growing on the king's soil, worth 20*s.* each, and he sold the bark from all the trees to Thomas Hall of Littledean, a currier. (fine £100)

[*f. 14v.*]

59   Richard Catchmay, kt.,[3] his servants, or workmen within the last two years felled an inclosed parcel of timber and wood within the king's demesne, growing in a place called Whitemead park, containing 60 a., which he converted to charcoal; the number of trees formerly growing there can not be counted, the trunks and roots having been completely grubbed up; with loss to the king £50. (fine pardoned by virtue of letters patent, as enrolled)

60   Richard Pullen, late of Lydney parish, at divers times between 1 August 1631 and 1 June 1634 made treenails (*clavos ligneos…anglice trundells pinnes*) in a place in the Forest called Oakwood; over a long period he made 7,000 of them, worth 6*s.* 8*d.* per thousand. (fine 20 marks)

61   Benedict Hall, esq., within the last five years built a great and spacious mansion[4] at a place called Highmeadow, in Staunton parish within the metes and bounds of the Forest, containing many rooms (*structuras anglice roomes*) and much timber; but they do not know what quantity of timber was used to build it. (fine £500) [*item crossed through, and notes added:* fine afterwards, by warrant of the chief justice, £400; he paid £5 and afterwards 10*s.*; paid to Thomas Leake, esq., the receiver]

62   Basil Brooke and George Mynne, by their servants or workmen, between 1 February 1631 and 30 June 1634 felled a parcel of wood called Wet wood within the king's demesne of the Forest, containing 200 a. of woodland, including much oak timber which

---

[1] Treswell and Rowles were appointed from 1621 as overseers to deliver cordwood to the lessees of the ironworks (Treswell is usually described as 'the younger' to distinguish him from a namesake, presumably a relative, who was surveyor-general of the forests south of the Trent at the same period): Hart, *Royal Forest*, pp. 86, 98, 103, 126; *Cal. S.P. Dom.* 1628–9, p. 509.

[2] Duncombe had a grant in 1630 of the bark from the trees felled under the current cordwood concession: *Cal. S.P. Dom.* 1629–31, p. 277.

[3] Whitemead park, held by the constables of St. Briavels as an adjunct of Newland manor and St. Briavels castle, had been sub-let to Catchmay: *VCH Glos.* v. p. 209–10.

[4] This presentment confirms that the Halls' large new mansion at Highmeadow dated from the early 1630s, and not from c. 1670, as is suggested in *VCH Glos.* v. 278, which dismissed as a probable misreading a statement in Bigland (*Collections Relative to the County of Gloucester*, ii. pp. 258–9) that it bore the date 1633. From its appearance in surviving illustrations it is clear, however, that the new mansion (since demolished) was extensively refashioned at some time in the late 17th century: *VCH Glos.* v. plate 5. The presentment locates the new house very exactly as 'in Staunton', whereas the Halls' old house, immediately adjoining, was just over the parish boundary in Newland.

they converted into charcoal; there are 6,700 half-cords of wood there worth £1,000, and, contrary to the assize of the Forest, they are oversized by two inches in height and three inches in length; with loss to the king 20 marks. (fine £3,300 each, and the value)

63   Basil Brooke and George Mynne, their servants, or workmen, within the same period felled a parcel of oak timber called *Cissetree hill* within the king's demesne of the Forest, containing 150 a., in which there are now 2,589 half-cords of wood worth £400. (fine £1,000 each)

64   Basil Brooke and George Mynne, or their servants or workmen, during the last 15 years felled a parcel of timber and wood called *Braderuge ruff* within the king's demesne of the Forest, containing 500 a. of woodland; they can not specify for certain the number of trees, the trunks and roots being almost destroyed; with loss to the king £100. (fine £300 each)

65   The said Basil and George, or their servants or workmen, between 3 March 1625 and 3 March 1634 felled a parcel of timber and wood in places in the Forest called Bromley (*Bramley*) and Ellwood, containing in all 150 a. of woodland; the trunks and roots of the trees were grubbed up, so that they know nothing of the trees growing there; with loss to the king £300. (fine £900 each, and the value)

[*f. 15*]

66   The said Basil and George, their servants, or workmen, between 1 March 1625 and 31 March 1634 felled and destroyed other parcels of timber and wood in the places in the Forest called Cleave hill, *Delves*, and *Quisclade*, containing in all 100 a. of woodland, with loss to the king £200. (fine £200)

67   The said Basil and George, their servants, or workmen, during the last 11 years felled and destroyed another parcel of woodland called *Fayre tree hill* and *Humbers Beech*, containing 160 a. of woodland, with loss to the king £350. (fine £1,050 and the value)

68   Thomas Hackett, late of Tintern (Mon.), gent.,[1] his companions, servants, or workmen, during the last 20 years felled and entirely destroyed a parcel of woodland in the Forest and the king's demesne called *Brodewell hill*, containing 100 a., with loss to the king £150. (fine pardoned by virtue of letters patent, and thus enrolled)

69   Philip Harris and Richard Challinor, late the farmers of the king's Forest, their servants, or workmen, within the last 20 years felled a parcel of timber and woodland commonly called *Rushie Fellet,* adjoining the upper part of the wood called Moseley within the king's demesne, containing 100 a.; they can not enumerate the exact number of trees growing there, as the trunks and roots were entirely destroyed; with loss to the king £200. (fine £1,000 each)

70   John Wintour, kt, his servants, or workmen, within the last 10 years felled and destroyed a parcel of young beeches in a place in the king's demesne, called Yorkley Well, containing 60 a. of woodland, in which part of the woodland a goshawk (*phasumgerum anglice goshawke*) was accustomed to nest; with loss to the king £80. (fine £500 and the value)

71   John Wintour, his servants, or workmen, within the same period felled and entirely destroyed another parcel of woodland within the king's demesne, called Bream's Eaves (*Breene Eves*), containing 100 a., with loss to the king £150. (fine £900)

---

[1] See p. xi.

72   John Wintour , his servants, or workmen, within the last three years felled another parcel of timber and wood within the king's demesne, called Oakwood, containing 100 a. of woodland, with loss to the king £200; in it there is, or was, much timber that was converted to charcoal (*in carbonibus anglice charcoales*), and 4,170 half-cords of wood, which exceed the assize of the Forest in both height and length by four inches, with loss to the king £10. (fine £1,200)

[*f. 15v.*]

73   And, further (they say), in the same parcel are now, or were, 131 pieces of round and squared timber, amounting to 220 tons worth 6*s*. 8*d*. per ton. (to be disposed of for the king's use)

74   Thomas Phillipps the younger, of Parkend (*le parkend*) in the Forest, labourer, within the last 10 years near to a place called Bromley (*Bramley*) in the Forest felled timber assigned and reserved for the king's use, containing six tons of timber worth 6*s*. per ton. (fine £50 and the value)

75   Christopher Clerke and James Fox of Coleford, carpenters, within the last 10 years felled four oaks assigned to the king's use in a place in the Forest next to the Park furnace, containing 15 tons of timber worth 5*s*. per ton. (fine £80 each, and the value)

76   Richard Bleeke of Ivy Moor Head,[1] next to Parkend in the Forest, labourer, within the last 10 years felled an oak growing next to Moseley in the Forest, containing three tons, which he took and converted to his own use, with loss to the king 15*s*. (fine £20)

77   John Dirram, servant of John Duncum of London, gent.,[2] John Dobbes of Whitemead park in the Forest, and Dobbes's servants, barked (*excoriaverunt anglice barked*) 100 oaks now lying in Wet wood in the Forest, containing in all 200 tons; if they had been allowed to grow for a longer time, they would have become full-sized timber trees (*integra maeremia*); with loss to the king £50. (fine £100 each).

Woodlands outside the King's Demesne

It is presented by the foresters, regarders, and the jury of 12, and convicted by the verderers that:

78   William Perkins of Pilstone (Mon.), gent., on 1 June 1627 felled a wood, underwood, or grove in St. Briavels parish within the perambulation of the Forest, of which William Throckmorton, kt. and bt., deceased, was seized, containing 4 a. and worth £2. (fine 20 nobles)

[*f. 16*]

79   Arthur Mallett of St. Briavels, esq., between 1 June 1603 and 1 June 1634 felled two groves in St. Briavels parish within the Forest perambulation, of which he is now or late seized as his demesne, containing 4 a. of land and worth £2. (fine 20 nobles)

80   William Griffiths of Mitchel Troy (Mon.) within the same period felled a little grove lying next to Mork, in St. Briavels parish within the Forest perambulation, on the free tenement belonging to him and his wife Tacy, containing 1 a. of woodland worth 10*s*. (fine 40 marks)

---

[1] East of Parkend: TNA, F 17/7; Atkinson, *Plan of Forest of Dean.*
[2] See above, p. 49*n*.

81   John Gonning the elder, late of Bristol, merchant,[1] between 4 May 1630 and (*date incomplete*) felled two little groves on his free tenement in St. Briavels parish within the Forest perambulation, containing 3 a. of woodland worth 30*s.* (fine 20 nobles)

82   Walter[2] Gough of Willsbury, in St. Briavels parish, gent., between 1 May 1629 and 1 May 1634 felled a little grove of his free tenement, lying near Willsbury, containing 1 a. worth 10*s.* (fine 50*s.*)

83   William Catchmay of Tintern (Mon.), gent., between 1 April 1620 and 1 April 1634 felled four groves, containing 10 a. of woodland worth £5, on the free tenement belonging to him and his wife Tacy, near the river Wye in Newland parish within the Forest perambulation. (fine £20) [*item crossed through and note added*: fine, reduced to £5, paid to Thomas Leake, esq., the receiver]

84   Richard Catchmay of Bigswear (*Bicksweare*), kt.,[3] and Benedict Hall of Highmeadow, in Newland parish, esq., between 30 April 1631 and 30 April 1634 felled a grove called *Churchgrove* on their free tenement lying in Newland parish, within the Forest perambulation, containing 4 a. of woodland worth £2. (fine 40*s.* each) [*item crossed through and note added*: fines paid to Thomas Leake, esq., the receiver]

85   Richard Howell of Clearwell, yeoman, between 1 April 1622 and 1 April 1634 felled a little grove of his free tenement at Coxbury, in Newland parish within the Forest perambulation, containing 1 a. of woodland worth 10*s.* (fine 20*s.*)

[*f. 16v.*]

86   Richard Catchmay, kt., between 1 April 1616 and 31 May 1634 felled three groves commonly called *Bowryes grove*, *le Picke*, and *Okengrove*, containing in all 6 a. and worth £3, on his free tenement (fine £3, reduced by petition to 30*s.*) [*item crossed through and note added*: fine paid to Thomas Leake, esq., the receiver]

87   William Perkins of Pilstone (Mon.), gent., between 3 April 1614 and [*date incomplete*] felled a grove of his free tenement in Newland parish, containing 6 a. of woodland worth £3. (fine £5)

88   Richard Catchmay, kt., between 30 April 1632 and 31 January 1634 felled a grove of his free tenement next to Redbrook, in Newland parish, within the Forest perambulation, containing 1 a. of woodland worth 10*s.* (fine 10*s.*) [*item crossed through and note added*: fine, reduced by petition to 6*s.* 8*d.*, paid to Thomas Leake, esq., the receiver]

89   William Catchmay during the same period felled a grove called *le forge grove* of his free tenement in Newland parish, containing 3 a. of woodland worth 30*s.* (fine £3) [*item crossed through and note added*: fine, reduced to 33*s.* 4*d.*, paid to Thomas Leake, esq., the receiver]

90   Christopher Dubberley and Christopher Rive, of Redbrook, yeomen, between 2 April 1622 and 2 April 1634 felled a grove called *Worgans grove* on George Wyrrall's free tenement at Redbrook, containing 3 a. worth 30*s.* (fine 40*s.* each)

91   Benedict Hall between 30 April 1631 and 3 April 1634 felled a grove called *le forge grove* in Newland parish, containing 4 a. of woodland worth £2. (fine £10) [*item

---

[1] For Gonning's estate, *VCH Glos.* v. p. 262.

[2] *sic*, but possibly a scribal error for 'Warren', as Warren Gough was the owner of the Willsbury estate at that time: *VCH Glos.* v. p. 261.

[3] For the Catchmays, owners of the Bigswear estate in St. Briavels, ibid.

crossed through and note added: afterwards, by warrant of the justices-in-eyre, fine £6, paid to Thomas Leake, esq., the receiver]

92   Lewis (*Leodivicus*) Evans of Redbrook, yeoman, between 3 April 1623 and 3 April 1634 felled three groves on the free tenement of William Jones, of *Treowen* (Mon.), in Newland parish within the perambulation, containing 3 a. of woodland worth 30*s.* (fine 20 nobles)

[*f. 17*]

93   Richard Bond of Redbrook, gent., deceased, between 3 March 1615 and 2 March 1634 felled 4 a. of woodland of his free tenement in Newland parish within the perambulation, containing 5 a. of woodland worth 50*s.* (fine 40*s.*) [*item crossed through and note added*: fine paid to Thomas Leake, esq., the receiver]

94   Athanasius Elly of Redbrook, gent., during the same period felled two groves of his free tenement in Newland parish within the perambulation, containing 2 a. of woodland worth 20*s.* (fine £3)

95   Benedict Hall during the same period felled three groves within the lordship of Staunton (*Staundon*) called Bunjups (*Bungops*) grove, *Clares grove*, and *Clift grove,* containing 10 a. of woodland worth £5. (fine £30) [*item crossed through and note added*: fine paid to Thos Leake, the receiver]

96   William Throckmorton, kt. and bt., deceased, between 31 March 1622 and I April 1634 felled woodlands or underwoods of the free tenement of Baynham Throckmorton, kt. and bt., his son and heir, lying dispersed in Noxon park within the Forest perambulation,[1] containing 3 a. of woodland worth 30*s.* (fine 30*s.*)

97   Andrew Horne of Blakeney, yeoman, between 1 March 1616 and 30 April 1634 felled a grove of his free tenement in Awre parish, containing ½ a. and worth 10*s.* (fine 20*s.*)

98   John Dryver, late of Hagloe (*Haglow*), during the same period felled a grove in (*incomplete*), containing ½ a. and worth 10*s.* (fine 20*s.*)

99   Edward Wyntour, kt., within the same period felled a little grove of the free tenement now of John Wyntour, kt., his son and heir, containing ½ a. worth 10*s.* (fine 5*s.*)

Hawks (*De Accipitribus*)

99 (*number repeated*) It was presented by the foresters, regarders, and jury of 12, and convicted by the verderers, that:

There was within the last three years a goshawks' eyrie (*ayeria phasianophorum anglice an ayrey of goshawkes*) in a parcel of the king's demesne of the Forest called Lea Bailey (*le Lee Baylie*); and there was another within the last 12 years in a parcel of the king's demesne of the Forest called *le Lute*, which Edward Villers, kt., cut down entirely and laid waste, as a result of which the goshawks left the place. There was another on a hill in the king's demesne of the Forest called *Buckhill*, now or late enclosed within Cannop Vallets, and others in the places in the Forest called Serridge (*Sheredge*),

---

[1] For the Throckmortons' Clearwell estate, to which Sir Baynham had succeeded on Sir William's death in 1628, see *VCH Glos*. v. p. 211.

Wayneway,[1] and *Whachershill*, all of which eyries left the places where they used to be built because the trees and wood that grew there has been clear felled and laid waste.

[*f. 17v.*]

And there was a goshawks' eyrie built in a parcel of the Forest called Middleridge which left there after, it is said, the eggs were taken; of it only one (?)tercel (*sodalis anglice the tassel*) now remains; others say that Henry Watkins, living near Middleridge, was suspected.

Waste in the Woods

100   It was presented that John Peckover, late of Clearwell, collier, within the last seven years cut down trunks and stumps, amounting to two cords and worth 3*s.* 4*d.* the cord, in the king's woodland of the demesne of his Forest; he made the wood into charcoal and sold the charcoal at a price of 18*d.* the wagon load to the king's farmers in the Forest and to other persons who worked the furnace at Bishopswood, but they do not know by what warrant. He carried the charcoal by eight horses, each worth 40*s.*, and kept those horses grazing on the king's soil within the Forest demesne for the greater part of the winter. (fine £20 and the value)

Ports

It was presented that:

101   John Purnell of Lydney on 1 June 1634 built a bark or pinnace (*unum navigiolum anglice a bark or pinnace*) at Purton by the river Severn, outside the Forest perambulation, for which, they estimate, [he used] 30 tons of timber worth 6*s.* 8*d.* a ton.[2] (fine 40*s.*)

102   Thomas Colly, late of Purton, on 1 June 1634 took timber growing in the Forest to make barrel staves (*ad cados faciendos anglice to make barrell staves*), containing around 3 or 4,000 staves worth £5. (fine 40*s.* and the value)

Ships and barks are based at other ports on the Severn, viz. Gatcombe and Newnham within the Forest perambulation, but no timber or wood belonging to the king has been discovered there.

[*f. 18*]

103   M (*sic*) Kenn and Walter (*sic*), late of Upleadon (*Leadon*), coopers, acting by their servant Thomas Colly, within the last seven years felled and took away 120 complete great oaks and beeches, growing in a place within the Forest perambulation called Blakeney bailiwick, to make barrel staves, worth £60. (fine £1,000 and the value)

Purprestures within the Forest

It is presented by the foresters, regarders, and jury of 12, and convicted by the verderers, that:

---

[1] A plan of *c.* 1680 marks *Wainway hill* in the area between Yorkley and Moseley Green: TNA, F 17/7. The name possibly referred to the old timber-carrying road leading from Parkend via Viney Hill to Purton and Gatcombe on the Severn: *VCH Glos.* v. p. 289.
[2] The deputy surveyor for Dean had reported this matter to the government in November 1633, stating that Purnell had taken a 60-ft. beech tree to make the ship's keel: *Cal. S.P. Dom.* 1633–4, p. 292.

104   John Taylor, late of Awre, within the last 30 years built a cottage or tenement at Etloe, within the Forest perambulation, on the soil of Thomas Windam, kt.[1] (fine 20*s.*)

105   Thomas James of the same, labourer, within the last 12 years built a cottage at Etloe on Thomas Windam's waste ground, within the bounds of the Forest. (fine 20*s.*)

106   James Rashford, late of the same, labourer, within the last 30 years built a cottage, now or late in the occupation of Thomas Benfield, at Etloe on Thomas Leighton's soil within the Forest. (fine 20*s.*)

107   John Bucke the elder, late of Blakeney, deceased, within the last 20 years built a house or barn near the covert (*latibulum anglice covert*) of the deer, now or late in the fee of John Bucke, his son and heir. (fine 40*s.*, rent 6*d.*) [*item crossed through and note added:* fine paid to Thomas Leake, esq., the receiver)

108   John Wintle, late of Blakeney, yeoman, deceased, within the last 30 years built a tenement or dwelling house, within the regard and next to the covert of the Forest, now in the fee of John Wintle, his son and heir. (fine £5)

109   William Collier, late of Littledean, labourer, within the last six years built a cottage, now or late in his occupation, on the king's waste soil, and enclosed in its garden a little piece of waste land around it. (fine £5)

110   Thomas Brayne, late of Littledean, gent., deceased, within the last 50 years built a water mill on the king's waste soil, now in the fee of his heir and now or late in the occupation of John Gwillim. (fine £100)

111   The same John Gwillim, late of Littledean, miller, within the last 10 years enclosed a parcel of the king's waste soil adjoining the same mill, containing 'six parts of an acre'. (fine 20*s.*)

112   Furthermore, the same John within the same period enclosed another little piece of the king's waste ground, containing two perches. (fine 10*s.*)

[*f. 18v.*]

113   The same John within the last 10 years built a sheepcote (*ovile anglice shepecoat*) and a barn on the king's waste soil near the same mill, where he keeps goats, sheep, and pigs, with loss to the king 20*s.* (fine 20 marks)

114   John Wyntour of Lydney, kt., by himself or his workmen, dug a coal mine (*carbonicum minerum anglice coale myne*) in a place on the king's soil called the Snead, but they have no knowledge of what rents or other dues he pays for it. (fine £5)

115   Samuel Magor, late of Bream, labourer, within the last three years dug three stone quarries in a place in the king's demesne woodland in the highway leading from Coleford to Mitcheldean; those quarries or mines lie unfilled, by which the king's subjects pass there in great danger, and scarcely [? *da' ferunt*] there; with loss to the king 10*s.* (fine £10; the pits to be filled)

116   Richard Jones and William Rogers, of Coleford, labourers, within the last 10 years dug a quarry or mine of tiles (*quarreram aut mineram tegularum anglice tyle quarry*) in a place within the demesne woodlands in the Forest perambulation called Bicknor's Eaves; it lies open, to the harm of the king's deer 2*s.* (fine £10; to be filled up)

117   Basil Brooke and George Mynne, or their workmen, between 1 March 1627 and 30 April 1634 dug iron cinders (*scorias ferreas anglice cynders*), worth £100 a year, in the

[1] Windam's estate was Etloe Duchy manor in Awre: *VCH Glos.* v. p. 26.

king's demesne of the Forest, with which they fuelled the ironworks (*opera ferraria anglice the furnace*); this was to the great danger of the king's subjects and deer because the places that were dug were left unfilled, so that the way over Cinderford (*Synderford*) bridge, leading from Gloucester city towards Monmouth and from South Wales towards London, is obstructed and destroyed. (fine £5 each, and they are to make good and fill up the pits)

118   Thomas Jones, late of the Forest, labourer, within the last 30 years built a cottage and enclosed two gardens adjoining it, containing a full ¼ a. of the vert, next Broadwell (*Brodwlde*) within the king's demesne of the Forest. (fine £3)

119   William Gylbert alias Nashe, late of the Forest, labourer, within the last 30 years built a cottage and enclosed a garden, containing ¼ a., in Gorsty Knoll within the demesne woodlands of the Forest (fine 20*s.*; rent 2*d.*)

120   Henry Elly, late of the Forest, labourer, within the last 30 years built a cottage in a place called Ellwood and enclosed a little garden adjoining to it within the king's demesne woodlands. (fine 2*s.*)

[*f. 19*]

121   Richard Hankinson, late of Parkend, gent., a clerk of Basil Brooke, the farmer, within the last 14 years built a dwelling house at Whitemead park within the king's demesne and adjoining to the covert of the king's deer, and within the same period built a stable and barn on the king's soil near the same house; by pretext of those buildings and, claiming no right of common, he pastures his pigs and other animals on the king's soil, disturbing the deer from the pasture and covert, to the serious oppression of those living in the Forest (fine £20) [note: ?*bis script' quia inde*)

122   The same Richard keeps a dairy herd (*vaccarialam anglice daerie*) pasturing there, viz. 10 milk cows, to the king's loss. [*no fine given*]

123   Godfrey Parlor of Parkend, labourer, within the last 15 years built a dwelling house at Whitemead park within the Forest perambulation adjoining the covert of king's deer, where he pastures pigs and other animals, by which the deer are frightened away (?)from their resting-place (*depossima*). (fine 40*s.*)

124   John Jeffreys of the same, labourer, within the last 12 years built a dwelling house in Whitemead park within the demesne woodlands adjoining the covert of the king's deer, from where, by the pasturing of pigs and the feeding of other animals, the deer flee away. (fine £5)

125   Humphrey Mason of the same, labourer, within the last 15 years built a dwelling house in Whitemead park, similarly adjoining the deer covert, where he pastures pigs and other beasts on the king's soil, causing the banishment and grave oppression of the king's deer. (fine £5)

126   Anne Gibbins of the same, widow, within the last 10 years built a cottage or dwelling house in Whitemead park adjoining the covert of the king's deer, as a result of which the deer scarcely come to that place; the common pasture is overburdened by her pigs and other animals. (fine £5)

127   John West of the same, coal carrier, within the last 12 years built a cottage in the same park near the deer covert, where he keeps six horses freely pasturing on the king's soil, to the grave damage of the soil and the terror of the deer. (fine 40*s.*)

128   Robert Frogshell of the same within the last 10 years built a cottage in the same park adjoining the deer covert, where he feeds pigs and other animals to the grave damage of the king's soil and the terror of the deer. (fine £4)

[*f. 19v.*]

129   George Moore, late of the same, deceased, within the last 20 years built a large house at Cannop in the king's demesne of his Forest[1]. (fine £50)

130   John Dobbes of Parkend, in the Forest, labourer, built a cottage in Whitemead park near the deer covert, where he pastures pigs and other animals to the grave oppression of the soil and terror of the deer. (fine 20*s.*)

All of those cottages are built with the king's timber, cut and taken in the Forest, and the occupants burn daily the king's wood, gathered for their fires, to the grave loss of the king of 40*s.* a year by each of them.

130 (*number repeated*) William Latham, of Soudley in the Forest, took and enclosed three parcels of land or pasture from the king's soil next to Bradley forge in the Forest, containing 9 a. and worth 30*s.* a year. (fine £40; (?) *bis script' c' inde*)

131   George Wyrrall, late of Eastbach, esq., built a spacious house, a barn, and many other buildings in Edward Machen's free land at Hoarthorns (*Whorethornes*)[2] within the Forest perambulation. (fine £20; rent 5*s.*)

132   The said George within the last 30 years built a little tenement or cottage at Hoarthorns on Edward Machen's free land. (fine 40*s.*; rent 6*d.*)

133   William Parlor, late of Joyford, in [English] Bicknor parish, yeoman, deceased, built a water mill, a barn, and other buildings at Joyford within Bicknor and Newland parishes,[3] now in the tenure of William Parlor of Joyford, yeoman; and he made a little pond to supply the mill with water (fine £20) [*fine crossed out and note added*: he petitions]

134   William Wigfall alias Godfrey, of Hewelsfield, labourer, within the last 20 years built a cottage near a place called *le Clayes*, within the metes and bounds of the Forest but outside the king's demesne; he holds it as his own fee (*in proprio dominicio*). (fine 10*s.*)

[*f. 20*]

135   Tristram Tristed of Ellwood, in Newland parish, within the last 12 years built a cottage at Ellwood grounds within the metes and bounds of the Forest and in Thomas Sillance's free land. (fine 10*s.*)

136   Richard Baker, late of Chestnuts in the Forest, labourer, within the last nine years built a cottage on the king's soil in Chestnuts. (fine 40*s.*)

---

[1] The house was built shortly before 1618, at a cost of £200, by Moore and a partner, then lessees of the king's ironworks at Cannop and Lydbrook; it was later used for some years by the forest officers as a 'speech house' for holding the courts: B.L. Lansdowne MS. 166, f. 380; TNA, E 178/5304, m. 13; *VCH Glos*. v. pp. 324, 340.

[2] Edward Machen owned the Eastbach estate in English Bicknor but its house, and evidently some of the land, was occupied by his brother-in-law George Wyrrall: *VCH Glos*. v. p. 109. Hoarthorns lay south of Bicknor parish in a detached part of Newland parish.

[3] Joyford lay on the south boundary of Bicknor, partly in the detached part of Newland. For this mill, see *VCH Glos*. v. p. 112.

137 Anne Palmer of Blackmore's Hale (*Blackemoresale*) took a parcel of land from the king's soil called Chestnuts, containing ¼ a., now enclosed, and converted it to her own use. (fine 10*s.*)

[*unnumbered*] George Sinderby of the same took and enclosed another small parcel of land from the king's soil called Chestnuts, which he converted to his own use. (fine 10*s.*)

137(*number repeated*) Giles Pope of the same built a cottage and made a garden adjoining it on the same soil, which he converted it to his own use. (fine 20*s.*)

138 Thomas Davis, late of the same, built a cottage on the same soil, which he converted to his own use. (fine 20*s.*)

139 Robert Conway of the same built a house and enclosed a garden on the same soil called Chestnuts. (fine 10*s.*)

140 Thomas Jenyngs built a cottage and enclosed a garden adjoining it on the same demesne soil of the king. (fine 10*s.*)

141 Susan Godcheap, late of the same, built a cottage on the same soil. (fine 10*s.*)

142 Henry Fowle of the same encroached and enclosed two gardens and built two sheepcotes (*ovilia anglice sheepecoats*), containing ½ a., on the same soil. (fine 20*s.*)

143 John Cooke, clerk, enclosed and formed (*fundavit*) a garden on the same soil. (fine 10*s.*) [*item crossed through and note added*: fine paid to Thomas Leake, esq., the receiver]

144 William Harris of the same built a cottage and enclosed a garden adjoining it on the same soil. (fine 10*s.*)

145 Lancelot Higgs of the same built a cottage and formed a goat-pen (*hircionam haram anglice a goat pen*) and garden on the same soil. (fine £5)

[*f. 20v.*]

146 Elizabeth Hayes of the same built a cottage and formed a garden on the same soil. (fine 10*s.*)

147 Philip Bullocke of the same built a cottage and formed a garden adjoining it on the same soil. (fine 10*s.*)

148 William Langston, late of Flaxley, claims to hold in fee a cottage or house standing within the same demesne soil of the king, now or late in Richard (?Harell)'s tenure. (fine 10*s.*)

149 Gabriel Packer and Thomas Packer, of Littledean, weavers, encroached part of the same demesne soil, containing ½ a. (fine 10*s.* each)

150 John Cowstans, late of Mitcheldean, built a little cottage and formed a garden on the same soil. (fine 5s)

151 Edward Morse of Mitcheldean, gent., within the last three years built a windmill (*molendinum ventilarium anglice a windmill*) on the free tenement of Nicholas Roberts, esq. within the Forest perambulation. (fine 20 nobles)[1]

152 Richard Wensley alias Wenland of Stowfield, in [English] Bicknor parish, built a new house and barn at Stowfield on land of Benedict Hall, esq. (fine 40*s.*, rent 4d) [*item*

[1] For this case, see also above, p. 18; and for Roberts's Mitcheldean manor estate, *VCH Glos.* v. p. 180.

crossed through and note added: fine paid by Benedict Hall to Thos Leake, esq., the receiver]

153 Richard Catchmay, late of Bigswear (*Bicksweare*), kt., encroached on the king's soil called Hudnalls, lying next to the river Wye in St. Briavels parish, containing 1 a. (fine 20s., rent 6d) [*item crossed through and note added*: fine paid to Thomas Leake, esq., the receiver]

154 Philip Tilsley[1] of Gloucester city built and enlarged a dwelling house at Mitcheldean, within the Forest perambulation, in his own fee. (twice before (*bis antea*))

154 (*number repeated*) Christopher Hollydaye of Abenhall enlarged a house near Mitcheldean, within the Forest perambulation, in his own fee. (fine 20s.)

155 The inhabitants of Littledean made a purpresture near Littledean by digging and getting iron cinders (*scorias ferreas anglice cynders*). (fine 20s.)

[*f. 21*]

156 William Rowles of Cockshoot[2] made a purpresture near Blaize Bailey within the Forest perambulation, by digging and getting stone to build a wall and setting a hawthorn hedge (*virgulto spinoso anglice quicke conferendo*) under the wall, by which the king's deer are entirely excluded from the demesne soil lying near the Forest, where they used to graze, with loss to the king. (fine £3 6s. 8d.)

157 Rowland Millard built a cottage at a place called Viney (*le Vyney*), near Blakeney within the Forest (fine 10s.)

158 Another cottage, in which Thomas Parry lives, was built near Cinderford bridge within the Forest perambulation. (fine 10s.)

158 (*number repeated*) William Bridge built a cottage and enclosed an orchard on the king's soil called Chestnuts. (fine 2s.)

159 Thomas Bridge built a cottage on the king's soil. (fine 5s.) [*item crossed through and note added*: fine paid to Thomas Leake, esq. the receiver]

160 A new tenement was built on land of William Kingston, esq., near Littledean, by Francis Aram, who lives in it. (fine 40s.)

161 Thomas Godwyn, late of Huntsham (*Hunsome*), in Goodrich parish (Herefs.), Dr. of Theology,[3] by his servants, viz. William Hugh, late of Welsh Newton (Mon.), labourer, John Colsey, late of Huntsham, labourer, John Thomas of the same, labourer, and John Wansley, late of the same, labourer, enclosed a great part, amounting to 200 a., of the Forest waste land near Mailscot with a dyke, 4½ ft. high, 3 ft. deep, and 98 ft. long, to the king's loss £10 a year and to the harm of his subjects. (he is pardoned under Lady Villiers's patent[4] (?)*m' si' intr'*)

162 Walter Smith, late of Chestnuts, labourer, built a cottage and enclosed a garden adjoining to it in the king's demesne in Chestnuts. (fine 40s.)

163 John Knight of Chestnuts built a cottage and enclosed a garden adjoining it on the king's soil called Chestnuts. (fine 40s.)

---

[1] See below, p. 71*n.*

[2] For Rowles, see above, p. 44*n.*

[3] Godwyn, a son of the bishop of Hereford, was vicar of Goodrich from 1629: Foster, *Alumni Oxonienses, 1500–1714*, p. 586; *VCH Glos.* v. p. 115.

[4] Presumably he occupied part of the Mailscot estate granted to the Villiers family in 1625.

164   Michael Martin of the same built a cottage and surrounded it with a garden on the king's soil there. (fine 40s.)

165   Thomas Goodman and Francis Tyler, late of Cannop, had in their possession a house and stable next to Cannop in the Forest, to which adjoin two gardens containing 1 a. (fine 20s. each) [*item crossed through and note added*: fine paid to Thomas Leake, esq.)

166   Lewis (*Lodvicus*) Awrey of Cannop holds a cottage and has enclosed a garden adjoining it on the king's soil. (fine 40s.)

167   John Morgan of Cannop holds a cottage there. (fine 40s.)

[*f. 21v.*]

168   Edward Jones of the same built a messuage, with a garden enclosed adjoining it, in Bream's Eaves in the king's demesne. (fine £3)

169   Edward Leeke of Staple Edge in the Forest built a cabin (*cabinum anglice cabine*) at Staple Edge in the king's demesne. (fine 5s.)

170   Thomas Payne and George Rudge, of Huntley, husbandmen, within the last three years felled a grove called *Lane grove* within the Forest perambulation, part of the lordship of Nicholas Roberts, esq.,[1] containing 10 a. (fine 50s. each)

171   the same Thomas and George within the last two years [felled] a grove called *le Harpe grove* within the Forest perambulation, part of Nicholas Roberts's free tenement, containing 3 a. and worth 30s. (fine 50s. each)

172   William Callow of Mitcheldean, gent., deceased, within the last seven years felled a grove or underwood called *Bakers land* within the Forest perambulation, part of the free tenement of Edward Sergeant, gent., containing 2 a. and worth 20s. (fine 20s.)

173   Robert Pyrke, late of the same, gent., deceased, within the last 20 years felled a grove or underwood called Abenhall grove within the Forest perambulation, part of the free tenement of Joan Vaughan, widow,[2] containing 60 a. and worth £30. (fine 20 marks)

174   Edward Morse of the same, gent., within the last six years felled a grove or underwood called *Pippins hill* within the Forest perambulation, part of the free tenement of Edward Partridge, clothier, containing 2 a. and worth 20s. (fine 10s.)

175   Thomas Weale of the same, gent., within the last seven years cut down a grove called *Sternes grove* within the Forest perambulation, part of the free tenement of Nicholas Roberts, esq., containing 4 a. and worth £2. (fine 20s.)

176   The same Robert Pirke within the last 20 years built a new house in Mitcheldean within the regard of the Forest, now part of the free tenement of Robert Pirke, his son and heir. (fine, as before)

177   Richard Parsons and John Pullen, of Ruardean, labourers, within the last 30 years felled a grove called *Wilkland grove* within the Forest perambulation, part of the free tenement of Joan Vaughan, widow, containing 6 a. and worth £3. (fine 10s. each)

178   Thomas Sherewood and Thomas Gardener, now or late of Mitcheldean, within the last seven years felled a grove or underwood called *Cromwell's grove*, now part of the free tenement of William Stevington, esq., containing 4 a. and worth £2. (fine 10s. each)

[1] See above, p. 58*n.*
[2] Owner of estates in Abenhall and Ruardean: *VCH Glos.* v. pp. 236–7.

[f. 22]

179   Anthony Bridgeman of Mitcheldean, esq., within the last 10 years felled a grove called *Bartons hills grove*, part of his free tenement, within the Forest regard, containing 2 a. and worth 20*s.* (fine 6*s.* 8*d.*)

180   Edmund Berrow of Quedgeley, esq., within the last 20 years felled a grove called Hayes grove within the Forest perambulation, part of his free tenement,[1] containing 30 a. and worth £15. (fine 20 nobles)

181   Anne Swanley of Awre, widow, within the last 10 years felled a grove, part of Richard Hooper's free tenement, within the Forest perambulation, containing ½ a. and worth 5*s.* (fine 5*s.*)

New Assarts

It was presented by the foresters, regarders, and jury of 12, and convicted by the verderers, that:

182   John Kirle of Much Marcle (Herefs.), kt. and bt., between 1 April 1622 and 1 April 1634 felled, lopped (*truncavit*), and destroyed a grove or underwood called le *Powles*, growing in Abenhall, part of the free tenement of Joan Vaughan, widow, now in John Meeke's tenure, containing 3 a. of which 1 a. is now planted with divers species, and worth 10*s.* (fine £5)

Timber of the King's Woods

It was presented, as above, that:

183   George Partridge, late of Bristol, by himself or his workmen, felled, or caused to be felled, three young oaks, containing four tons of timber worth 20*s.*, which William Cowse sold to him. (fine £10 each, and ?Cowse £50; fine (*apparently meaning Cowse's*), paid to Thomas Leake, esq.)

184   Robert Treswell[2] caused 20 oaks to be felled, containing 100 tons of timber worth 5*s.* per ton; he claims this was to repair Bristol castle, but they do not know by what warrant. (fine £50)

185   The same Robert caused four oaks to be felled, containing 12 tons of timber worth 5*s.* a ton; he claims this was to repair Chepstow bridge. (fine £40)

186   A little boy (*puerulus*), Robert Corsley of Aylburton, cut green oak branches within the Forest, containing two horse-loads of wood worth 4*d.* (fine 2*s*)

[f. 22v.]

Cottages Built on the King's Soil of the Forest[3]

It was presented that:

187   William Dowler, late of Whitecroft (*Wheatcroft*) in the Forest, labourer, on 1 May 1630 encroached on a parcel of the king's soil of the Forest at Whitecroft, worth 12*d.*,

---

[1] Berrow (Barrow) held Blakeney manor with the house there called the Hayes; his address as given here presumably relates to his estate of Field Court, in Hardwicke parish but immediately adjoining Quedgeley: *VCH Glos.* v. p. 28.

[2] Probably this is the elder Robert, deputy surveyor of the southern forests: TNA, C 99/26; cf. above, p. 49*n.*

[3] For the demesne settlements recorded in this section, see pp. xxvii–xxxi.

and built a cottage on it,[1] and took the issues and profits from it for his own use and takes them to this time. (fine £5)

188   William Perrgrove, late of the same, labourer, on the same day built a cottage at Whitecroft, and took, etc. (fine £3)

189   John Hilly of the same, labourer, on the same day built a cottage at Whitecroft, and took, etc. (fine £5)

190   Samuel Dowler, late of the same, labourer, on the same day built a cottage at Whitecroft, and took, etc. (fine £5)

191   Anthony Rede, late of the same, gent., on the same day built a cottage at Whitecroft, and took, etc. (fine £5)

192   Richard Mynshawe, late of the same, labourer, on the same day built a cottage near the new forge at Whitecroft, and took, etc. (fine £5)

193   Roger Dowler, late of Whitecroft, labourer, on 31 August 1628 built a cottage at *Waynewaye*[2] in the Forest, and took, etc. (fine £5)

194   John Davys, late of Whitecroft, labourer, on 30 June 1630 built a cottage at *Waynewaye*, and took, etc. (fine £5)

195   Lewis (*Lodovicus*) Watkins, late of Whitecroft, labourer, on the same day built a cottage at Wet wood in the Forest, and took, etc. (fine £5)

196   James Addams, late of Wet wood, collier, on the same day built four cottages at Wet wood, and took, etc. (fine £20)

[*f. 23*]

197   Thomas Howell, late of Wet wood, labourer, on the same day built a cottage at Wet wood, and took, etc. (fine £5)

198   John Snappe, late of Wet wood, labourer, on the same day built a cottage at Wet wood, and took, etc. (fine £5)

199   Thomas Hannishe, late of Wet wood, labourer, on the same day built a cottage at Wet wood, and took, etc. (fine £5)

200   Thomas Waker, late of Wet wood, labourer, on the same day built a cottage at Wet wood, and took, etc. (fine £5)

201   Thomas Sagdon, late of Wet wood, labourer, on the same day built a cottage at Wet wood, and took, etc. (fine £5)

202   Richard Janson, late of Cannop in the Forest, on the same day built a cottage at Cannop, and took, etc. (fine £5)

203   George Tayler, late of Cannop, labourer, on the same day built a cottage at Cannop, and took, etc. (fine £5)

204   John Williams, late of Cannop, labourer, on the same day built a cottage at Cannop, and took, etc. (fine £5)

---

[1] The entries in this section are made to read as if the offenders built (*erexit*) their cottages on the day cited, whereas that is evidently the date when the forest officers in the course of their rounds discovered the offence; a more appropriate rendering might be '… on [1 May 1630] was found to have built a cottage'.

[2] For the place, see above, p. 54*n*.

205 Richard Clifton, late of Cannop, labourer, on the same day built a cottage at Cannop, and took, etc. (fine £5)

206 John Phillippes of *Quiceslade*[1] built a cottage (*no location given*), and took, etc. (fine £5)

207 Thomas Phillippes, late of the same, labourer, on the same day built a cottage at *Quiceslade*, and took, etc. (fine £5)

208 Thomas Phillippes the elder, late of the same, labourer, on the same day built a cottage at *Quiceslade*, and took, etc.; and at the same time he kept a horse or mare pasturing on the king's demesne land of the Forest without any warrant. (fine 20*s.*)

[*f. 23v.*]

209 William Rosser of the same, labourer, on the same day built a cottage at *Quiceslade*, and took, etc. (fine £5)

210 Henry Morgan, late of the same, labourer, on the same day built a cottage at *Quiceslade*, and took, etc. (fine £5)

211 John Williams of the same, labourer, on the same day built a cottage at *Quiceslade*, and took, etc. (fine £5)

212 Thomas Jones of the same, labourer, on the same day built a cottage at *Quiceslade*, and took, etc. (fine £5)

213 Llewellin Thomas, late of the same, labourer, on the same day built a cottage at *Quiceslade*, and took, etc. (fine £5)

214 Henry Llewellin of the same, labourer, on the same day built a cottage at *Quiceslade*, and took, etc. (fine £5)

215 Richard Davys, late of Parkend within the Forest, labourer, on the same day built a cottage at Parkend, and took, etc. (fine £5)

216 Jenkins George, late of Parkend, labourer, on the same day built a cottage at Parkend, and took, etc. (fine £5)

217 John Edwards of the same, labourer, on the same day built a cottage at Parkend, and took, etc.; and at the same time he kept two cows pasturing on the king's demesne land of his Forest without any warrant. (fine £6)

218 Thomas Turner of the same, labourer, on the same day built a cottage at Parkend, and took, etc. (fine £5)

219 Richard Millard of the same, labourer, on the same day built a cottage at Parkend, and took, etc.; and he kept two horses pasturing on the king's demesne land of his Forest without any warrant. (fine £10)

[*f.24*]

220 William Wayte, of the same, labourer, on the same day built a cottage at Parkend, and took, etc. (fine £5)

221 Grace Embury of the same, on the same day built a cottage at Parkend, and took, etc. (fine £5)

---

[1] Identified ('*Quisc Slade*') on a plan of *c.* 1680 as the valley west of Parkend now traversed by the Parkend–Coleford road: TNA, F 17/7.

[*the number* **222** *is added here, apparently after mis-numbering was noticed, but with no entry attached*]

223 Anthony Mole of the same, labourer, on the same day built a cottage at Parkend, and took, etc. (fine £5)

224 Rother(*sic*) Davis of the same, labourer, on the same day built a cottage at Parkend, and took, etc. (fine £5)

225 Nicholas Hoseyour of the same, labourer, on the same day built a cottage at Parkend, and took, etc. (fine £5)

226 Roger Robins of the same, labourer, on the same day built a cottage at Parkend, and took, etc. (fine £5)

227 Richard Thomas of the Park forge, near to Parkend, labourer, on the same day built a cottage at the Park forge, and took, etc. (fine £5)

228 Thomas Smith of the same, labourer, on the same day built a cottage at the Park forge, and took, etc. (fine £5)

229 Llewellin Edwards of the same, labourer, on the same day built a cottage at the Park forge, and took, etc. (fine £5)

230 John Weaver of the same, labourer, on the same day built a cottage at the Park forge, and took, etc.; and he kept two mares (*equas anglice mares*) pasturing on the king's demesne of his Forest without any warrant. (fine £10)

231 Francis Coslet of the same, labourer, on the same day built a cottage at the Park forge, and took, etc. (fine £5)

232 Walter Weaver of the same, labourer, on the same day built a cottage at the Park forge, and took, etc.; and he kept three mares or horses pasturing on the king's demesne of his Forest without any warrant (fine £12)

[*f. 24v.*]

233 Charles Thomas, late of *Little Hocke* in the Forest, labourer, on the same day built a cottage at *Little Hocke*, near [*blank*], and took, etc. (fine £5)

234 Thomas Jones, late of Poolway (*Pulwey*) Lane End, labourer, on the same day built a cottage at Poolway, and encroached for its garden a parcel of the land of the king's soil of his Forest, worth 2*s.* a year, and took, etc. (fine £5)

235 John Nicholls of Coleford, in Newland parish, labourer, on the same day built a cottage at Coleford, and encroached for its garden a parcel of the land of the king's soil of his Forest, worth 2*s.* a year, and took, etc. (fine £5)

236 Walter Jones, late of Coleford, labourer, on the same day built a cottage at Coleford, and encroached for its garden a parcel of the land of the king's soil of his Forest, worth 2*s.* a year, and took, etc. (fine £5)

237 Thomas Marke, late of Coleford, labourer, on the same day built a cottage at Coleford in the Forest, and took, etc. (fine £5)

238 William Nashe alias Gilbard, late of Milkwall (*Micklewall*) in the Forest, labourer, on the same day built a cottage at Milkwall, and took, etc. (fine £5)

239 Morgan David of *Denalmore*, labourer, on the same day built a cottage at *Denalmore* in the Forest, and took, etc. (fine £5)

240   William Phillipps, late of Cannop, labourer, on the same day built a cottage at [*blank*] near Cannop, and took, etc. (fine £5)

[*f. 25*]

241   James Thomas, late of Cannop, labourer, on the same day built a cottage at Cannop, and took, etc. (fine £5)

242   Jenkins Jones, late of Cannop, labourer, on the same day built a cottage at Cannop, and took, etc. (fine £5)

243   John Archer, late of Cannop, labourer, on the same day built a cottage at Cannop, and took, etc. (fine £5)

244   John Norbury, late of Parkend (*le parke end*), labourer, on the same day built a cottage near the forge of the park, and took, etc. (fine £5)

245   John Rees, late of Parkend, labourer, on the same day built a cottage at Parkend, and took, etc. (fine £5)

246   Leonard Merricke, late of Parkend, labourer, on the same day built a cottage at Parkend, and took, etc.; and he kept a horse pasturing on the king's demesne of his Forest without any warrant. (fine £6)

247   Peter Halle, late of the Park forge, labourer, on the same day built a cottage at the Park forge, and took, etc. (fine £5)

248   Joan Munday of the Lea (Glos.), spinster, and Margery Evans of the same, spinster, on 1 December 1632 encroached ½ a. of the king's soil of his Forest at Lea, worth 12*d.* a year, and built two cottages on it, and took, etc. (fine £5 each)

249   Joan Baddam, late of the Lea, widow, on 6 January 1633 built a cottage near Lea Bailey in the Forest, and took, etc. (fine £5)

250   George Skinner, late of Hangerberry (*Hangerbury*) near Lydbrook, lived in a cottage lately built at Hangerberry in the Forest, and occupied a parcel of the king's soil, worth 2*s.*, lately encroached for its garden, and took, etc. (fine £5)

[*f. 25v.*]

251   Mary Adams, late of Ruardean,, widow, in 1630–1[1] built a cottage near Ruardean on the king's demesne of his Forest, and took, etc. (fine £5)

252   Peter Mutley, late of Ruardean, labourer, on 31 August 1614 built a cottage near Ruardean on the king's soil of his Forest, and took, etc. (fine £5)

253   Philip Ellys, late of Whitecroft, labourer, on 1 May 1630 encroached ¼ a. of land of the king's soil of his Forest at Whitecroft, and took, etc. (fine £5)

Each of the occupiers of the said cottages consumes each year, since the time they built them, 40*s.* worth of the king's woodland of the Forest

254   Richard Williams, late of Bream, labourer, on 5 June 1629 built a cottage on the king's soil of his Forest at Oakwood near Bream, and took, etc. (fine £5)

255   John Hatherley, late of Bream, labourer, on the same day built a cottage at Oakwood on the king's soil, and took, etc. (fine £5)

256   John Jenkins, late of Parkend, labourer, on the same day built a cottage on the king's soil at Oakwood, and took, etc. (fine £5)

[1] MS. gives only the regnal year (6 Chas. I).

257 Philip James, late of the same, labourer, on the same day built a cottage on the king's soil at Oakwood, and took, etc. (fine £5)

258 Peter Beeche, late of the same, labourer, on the same day built a cottage on the king's soil at Oakwood, and took, etc. (fine £5)

[*f. 26*]

259 William (?)Prater of the same, labourer, on the same day built a cottage on the king's soil at Oakwood, and took, etc. (fine £5)

260 Henry Lewys, late of Bream's Eaves, labourer, on the same day built a cottage on the king's soil of his Forest at a place called Bream's Eaves, and took, etc. (fine £5)

261 Richard Bayly, late of the same, labourer, on the same day built a cottage on the king's soil of his Forest at Bream's Eaves, and took, etc. (fine £5)

262 Richard Davys, late of the same, labourer, on the same day built a cottage on the king's soil at Bream's Eaves, and took, etc. (fine £5)

263 Thomas Jones, late of Bream, labourer, on the same day built a cottage on the king's soil at Bream's Eaves, and took, etc. (fine £5)

264 William Howell, late of the same, labourer, on the same day built a cottage on the king's soil at Bream's Eaves, and took, etc. (fine £5)

265 Walter Howell, late of the same, labourer, on the same day built a cottage on the king's soil of his Forest at Bream's Eaves, and took, etc. (fine £5)

266 William Fowle of the same, labourer, on the same day built a cottage on the king's soil at Bream's Eaves, and took, etc. (fine £4)

267 Thomas Cropper, late of Bream's Eaves, labourer, on the same day encroached a garden, worth 6*d.* a year, on the king's soil at Bream's Eaves, and took, etc. (fine 40*s.*)

268 Thomas Rosser, late of the same, labourer, on the same day built a cottage on the king's soil at Bream's Eaves, and took, etc. (fine £5)

[*f. 26v.*]

269 Morgan Thomas, late of the same, labourer, on the same day built a cottage on the king's soil at Bream's Eaves, and took, etc. (fine £5); furthermore, at the same time and place he encroached a garden, worth 6*d.*, for himself from the king's soil, and took, etc. (fine 40*s.*)

270 Thomas Williams, late of the same, labourer, on the same day built a cottage on the king's soil of his Forest at Bream's Eaves, and took, etc. (fine £5)

271 Edward Jones, late of Bream, labourer, on the same day built a cottage on the king's soil at Bream's Eaves, and took, etc. (fine £5)

272 Edward Mothway, late of Bream, labourer, on the same day encroached a garden for himself on the king's soil at Bream's Eaves, and took, etc. (fine 20*s.*)

273 William Allen, late of Soudley, labourer, on 10 June 1626 built a cottage in the Forest at a place called Soudley, and took, etc. (fine £5)

274 John Goslyn, late of Staple Edge in the Forest, on 1 November 1633 built a cottage on the king's soil of his Forest and destroyed one ton of the king's timber, worth 3*s.* 4*d.*; also, within the last two years he has destroyed wood worth 10*s.* (fine £6 13*s.* 4*d.*)

275   Joan Jones, late of Staple Edge, on the same day built a cottage on the king's soil of the Forest at Staple Edge and destroyed one wagon-load of the king's wood, worth 10*s.* (fine £5)

276   Geoffrey (*Jeffridus*) Mason, late of Staple Edge, 'wood wheeler', on the same day built a cottage on the king's soil and destroyed 10 horse-loads (*zeam*') of wood, worth 10*s.*; and furthermore, during the last four years he has destroyed 20s.-worth of the king's woodland. (fine £5)

277   Edward Hope, late of Staple Edge, woodcutter, on the same day built a cottage on the king's soil and in building it destroyed one wagon-load of wood, worth 12*d.*; and furthermore, during the last half year he has destroyed 5*s.*-worth of the king's woodland. (fine 40*s.*)

[*f. 27*]

278   George Nashe, late of Staple Edge, woodcutter, on the same day built a cottage on the king's soil and destroyed the king's timber, worth 3*s.* 4*d.*; and furthermore, during the last year he has destroyed 5*s.*-worth of the king's woodland. (fine £6 13*s.* 4*d.*)

279   Ambrose Goslyn, late of Staple Edge, woodcutter, on the same day built a cottage on the king's soil and in building it destroyed one wagon-load of wood, worth 1*s.*; and furthermore, during the last two years he has destroyed 10*s.*-worth of the king's woodland. (fine £6 13*s.*4*d.*)

280   Francis Mason, late of Staple Edge, corder, on the same day built a cottage on the king's soil and in building it destroyed one ton of timber, worth 3*s.*; and furthermore, during the last two years he has destroyed 20*s.*-worth of the king's woodland. (fine £6 13*s.*4*d.*)

281   John Tompkins of Staple Edge, woodcutter, on the same day built a cottage on the king's soil and in building it destroyed 10 horse-loads of wood, worth 10*d.*; and furthermore, during the last half year he has destroyed 5*s.*-worth of the king's woodland. (fine £6 13*s.* 4*d.*)

282   William Beard of Staple Edge, woodcutter, on the same day built a cottage on the king's soil and in building it destroyed eight horse-loads of wood, worth 8*d.*; and furthermore, during the last half year he has destroyed 5*s.*-worth of the king's woodland. (fine £6 13*s.*4*d.*)

283   Richard Younge of Staple Edge, woodcutter, on the same day built a cottage on the king's soil and in building it destroyed one wagon-load of wood, worth 1*s.*; and furthermore, during the last half year he has destroyed 5s.-worth of the king's woodland. (fine £6 13*s.* 4*d.*)

284   William Pearce of Staple Edge, woodcutter, on the same day built a cottage on the king's soil and in building it destroyed three wagon-loads of the king's wood, worth 3*s.*; and furthermore, during the last four years he has destroyed 40*s.*-worth of the king's woodland. (fine £10)

285   Thomas Chapman of Staple Edge, woodcutter, on the same day built a cottage on the king's soil and in building it destroyed one wagon-load of the king's wood, worth 1*s.*; and furthermore, during the last half year he has destroyed 5s.-worth of the king's woodland. (fine £6 13*s.* 4*d.*)

286   John Poulter of *Syndry hill*, collier, on the same day built a cottage on the king's soil of the Forest and in building it destroyed one wagon-load of the king's wood, worth

1s.; and furthermore, during the last half year he has destroyed 5s.-worth of the king's woodland. (fine £6 13s. 4d.)

[f. 27v.]

287   William Llewellin of *Thornenyhills*, [1] collier, on the same day built a cottage on the king's soil of the Forest and in building it destroyed six horse-loads of the king's wood, worth 6d. (fine £6 13s. 4d.)

288   John Springe of *Thornenyhills*, collier, on the same day built a cottage on the king's soil of the Forest and in building it destroyed two tons of the king's timber, worth 6s 8d.; and furthermore, during the last five years he has destroyed 50s.-worth of the king's woodland. (fine £10 6s.)

289   John Langley of *le Hayend*, collier, on the same day built a cottage on the king's soil of the Forest and in building it destroyed 10 horse-loads of the king's wood, worth 6d. (fine £6 13s. 4d.)

290   William Davys of Blakeney bailiwick (*le Bayly de Blackeney*), woodcutter, on the same day built a cottage on the king's soil of the Forest and in building it destroyed one wagon-load of the king's wood, worth 1s.; and furthermore, during the last three years he has destroyed 30s.-worth of the king's woodland. (fine £10)

291   Morgan James of Blakeney bailiwick, woodcutter, on the same day built a cottage on the king's soil of the Forest and in building it destroyed six horse-loads of the king's wood, worth 6d.; and furthermore, during the last two years he has destroyed 10s.-worth of the king's woodland. (fine £6 13s. 4d.)

292   Henry Watkins of Staple Edge, master collier, on the same day built a cottage on the king's soil of the Forest and in building it destroyed four tons of of the king's timber, worth 6s. 8d. a ton; and, furthermore, during the last half year he has destroyed 3s. 4d.-worth of the king's woodland. (fine £20)

293   Richard Boutlin of Staple Edge, collier, on the same day built a cottage on the king's soil and in building it destroyed 10 horse-loads of the king's wood, worth 10d. (fine £6 13s. 4d.)

294   Thomas Hather of Staple Edge, collier, on the same day built a cottage on the king's soil and destroyed six horse-loads of wood from the king's woodland (fine £6 13s. 4d.)

295   William Sergeant, late of the same, collier, on the same day built a cottage in the Forest at Staple Edge and destroyed six horse-loads of wood from the king's woodland, worth 12d. (fine £6 13s. 4d.)

[f. 28]

296   Eleanor Darley, late of the same, widow, on the same day built a cottage on the king's soil at Staple Edge with 10d.-worth of the king's wood. (fine £6 13s. 4d.)

297   Thomas Sanders, late of the same, collier, on the same day built a cottage on the king's soil at Staple Edge with 15d.-worth of the king's wood. (fine £6 13s. 4d.)

298   David Phillipps, late of the same, collier, on the same day built a cottage on the king's soil at Staple Edge and destroyed two wagon-loads of the king's timber, worth 3s. 4d. a wagon-load; and within the last four years he has consumed 40s.-worth of the king's wood; also, he kept five horses pasturing in the Forest. (fine £40)

---

[1] Identified *c.* 1680 as on the east side of the Blackpool brook valley, near Blackpool bridge: TNA, F 17/7.

299   Richard Whittorne, late of *Thornenyhills*, coal carrier, on the same day built a cottage on the king's soil of the Forest and in building it destroyed one ton of timber, worth 3*s.* 4*d.*; and within the last two years he has destroyed 10*s.*-worth of the king's wood; and he kept five horses pasturing in the Forest. (fine £40)

300   Richard Howford, late of Soudley, coal carrier, on the same day built a cottage on the king's soil of the Forest and in building it destroyed 20*d.*-worth of the king's wood; and within the last two years he has consumed 10s.-worth of the king's woodland; and he kept two horses pasturing in the Forest. (fine £20)

301   John Yeame, late of Blakeney's Eaves,[1] on the same day built a cottage on the king's soil of the Forest and destroyed 12*d.*-worth of the king's wood. (fine £5)

302   John Sugar, late of the same, collier, on the same day built a cottage on the king's soil of the Forest and destroyed six horse-loads of wood of the king's woodland, worth 12*d.* (fine £5)

303   Charles Thomas, late of the Forest, labourer, now lives in a cottage at a certain place in the Forest called *Tellhoockhead,* which was built within the last two years on the king's soil and demesne and is worth 10s. a year. (fine £20)

304   Isaac Coorsom, late of the Forest, collier, now lives in a cottage at a place in the Forest called Mirystock (*Moyryestock*), which was built within the last two years on the king's soil and demesne and is worth 5s. a year. (fine £10)

[*f. 28v.*]

305   Thomas Rawnell, late of the Forest, labourer, now lives in a cottage at a place called Howbrook, which was built within the last four years on the king's soil and demesne; furthermore there is a garden encroaching on the king's demesne; the cottage and garden are worth 20*s.* a year. (fine 40 marks)

306   John Jones of the Forest, labourer, now lives in a cottage at a place called Howbrook*,* which was built within the last four years on the king's soil and demesne; furthermore there is a garden encroaching on the demesne; the cottage and garden are worth 12*s.* a year. (fine £20)

307   William Davis, late of *Brookehill in* the Forest, collier, lives in a cottage[2] built at *Brookehill* on the king's soil, and he occupies a parcel of land of the king's soil lately encroached to the cottage, worth 2*s.* a year. (fine £20)

The several persons written above in this roll have converted, and continue to convert, the issues and profits of their cottages and gardens to their own uses; and, since they were built, each of the occupants of the cottages expends 40*s.*-worth of the king's woodland annually.

Cottages in the Fees of Other [Landowners]

308   Humphrey Blunt, late of English Bicknor, labourer, on 20 August 1614 built a cottage at English Bicknor within the bounds of the Forest on land in the fee of Bridget Wyrrall, widow,[3] and took the issues and profits to his own use and still takes them. (fine £6 13*s.* 4*d.*)

---

[1] In the area of the later Blakeney Hill settlement: TNA, F 17/7.

[2] In MS. *cottagium* replaces *messuagium*.

[3] For this case, see above, p. 19; and for the Wyrralls' Bicknor Court estate, *VCH Glos.* v. p. 108.

309 William Jolly of English Bicknor, labourer, the same day built a cottage at Bicknor on land in the fee of the same Bridget, and took, etc. (fine £3)

310 Thomas Trigge, late of English Bicknor, labourer, the same day built a cottage at Bicknor on land in the fee of the same Bridget, and took, etc. (fine £3)

311 William Hamon the elder, late of English Bicknor, labourer, the same day built a cottage at Bicknor on land in the fee of the same Bridget, and took, etc. (fine £3)

312 John Symons, late of English Bicknor, labourer, the same day built a cottage at Bicknor on land in the fee of the same Bridget, and took, etc. (fine £3)

313 John Thomas of English Bicknor, labourer, the same day built a cottage at Bicknor on land in the fee of the same Bridget, and took, etc. (fine £3)

314 Thomas Gwyn, late of English Bicknor, labourer, the same day built a cottage at Bicknor on land in the fee of the same Bridget, and took, etc. (fine £3)

[*f. 29*]

315 William Crowse, late of English Bicknor, labourer, the same day built a cottage on his own fee at Bicknor, and took, etc. (fine 10*s*., rent 6*d*.) [*item crossed through and note added*: fine paid to Thomas Leake, esq., the receiver]

316 George Bradley, late of Ruardean within the bounds of the Forest, labourer, the same day built a cottage at Ruardean, and took, etc. (fine £3) [*item crossed through and note added*: fine, reduced by petition to 10*s*., paid to Thomas Leake, esq., the receiver]

317 George Dyer, late of Ruardean, labourer, the same day built a cottage at Ruardean on land in a fee, [the owner of] which is unknown to them, and took, etc. (fine 40*s*.)

318 Roger Dyer, late of Ruardean, labourer, the same day built a cottage at Ruardean on land in an unknown fee, and took, etc. (fine 40*s*.)

319 Richard Bradley, late of Ruardean, labourer, the same day built a cottage at Ruardean on land in an unknown fee, and took, etc. (fine 40*s*.)

320 John Chapman of Ruardean, labourer, the same day built a cottage at Ruardean on land in an unknown fee, and took, etc. (fine 40*s*.)

321 Richard Yearsley of Ruardean, labourer, the same day built a cottage at Ruardean on land in an unknown fee, and took, etc. (fine 40*s*.)

322 John Lewes, late of Ruardean, labourer, the same day built a cottage at Ruardean on land in an unknown fee, and took, etc. (fine 40*s*.)

323 Thomas Moore, late of Ruardean, labourer, the same day built a cottage at Ruardean, and took, etc. (fine 40*s*.)

324 Thomas Sterry, late of Ruardean, labourer, the same day built a cottage at Ruardean on land in the fee of Joan Vaughan, and took, etc. (fine 40s.)

325 Robert Trewell, late of Ruardean, labourer, the same day built a cottage at Ruardean on land in an unknown fee, and took, etc. (fine 40*s*.)

326 Thomas Hobbs, late of Ruardean, labourer, the same day built a cottage at Ruardean in an unknown fee, and took, etc. (fine 40*s*.)

326 (*number repeated*) Edward Gaman, late of Ruardean, the same day, built a cottage at Ruardean. (fine 40*s*.)

[*f. 29v.*]

327   Thomas Lloyde, late of Ruardean, labourer, on 31 August 1614 built a cottage at Ruardean near the covert (*coopertum anglice the covert*) of the Forest on land in an unknown fee, and took, etc. (fine 40*s.*)

328   Joan Edith, late of Ruardean, widow, same day built a cottage at Ruardean near the covert on land in an unknown fee, and took, etc. (fine 40*s.*)

329   John Morse, late of Ruardean, labourer, the same day built a cottage at Ruardean near the covert on land in an unknown fee, and took, etc. (fine 40*s.*)

330   Thomas Smart, late of Ruardean, labourer, the same day built a barn at Ruardean near the covert on land in an unknown fee, and took, etc, (fine 20*s.*)

331   Henry Morse, late of Ruardean, labourer, the same day built a cottage at Ruardean near the covert on land in an unknown fee, and took, etc. (fine 40*s.*)

332   Francis Gwilliam of Ruardean, husbandman, the same day built a cottage at Ruardean near the covert on land in an unknown fee, and took, etc. (fine 40*s.*)

333   Richard Marten, late of Ruardean, labourer, the same day (*blank*) at Ruardean near the covert on land in an unknown fee, and took, etc. (fine *blank*)

334   Walter Meeke, late of Ruardean, labourer, the same day built a cottage at Ruardean near the king's covert on land in an unknown fee, and took, etc. (fine £3)

335   Richard Jelfe, late of Ruardean, one of the [keepers][1] of the Forest, lives in a cottage at Ruardean near the covert, which was built 40 years ago or thereabouts and is on the fee of Richard Birke, gent. (fine 40*s.*)

336   Anthony Stratford of Littledean, gent., on 31 August 1633 built a dwelling house at Littledean on land in an unknown fee, and took, etc. (fine £6 13*s.* 4*d.*, rent 6*d.*)

[*f. 30*]

Cottages and Encroachments

337   Anne Palmere, late of Blackmore's Hale, widow, on 1 July 1630 encroached a little parcel of land, worth 6*d.* a year, on the king's soil in the Forest at Blackmore's Hale, and took the issues and profits from it to her own use, and still takes them. (fine 40*s.*)

338   George Sinderby, late of the same, the same day encroached a little parcel of land of the king's soil, worth 6*d.* a year, in the Forest at Blackmore's Hale, and took, etc. (fine 40*s.*)

339   Gabriel Packer, late of Littledean, labourer, and Thomas Packer, late of the same, his son, on I February 1634 encroached ¼ a. of land, worth 6*d.* a year, from the king's soil of the forest in a place called Chestnuts, and took, etc. (fine 40*s.*)

340   Richard Nelme, late of Flaxley, husbandman, the same day encroached land, worth 6d. a year, from the king's soil of the Forest at a place called Badcocks Bailey, and took, etc. (fine 20*s.*)

341   Philip Tillslowe, late of the city of Gloucester, pinmaker,[2] on 20 June 1630 built part of a new house and a stable in Mitcheldean parish within the perambulation of the Forest, and took, etc. (fine 40*s.*, rent 6*d.*)

---

[1]   MS. *unius rangiorum*; but strictly his office was that of a keeper rather than a ranger: see above, p. 31.
[2]   Philip Tillslowe (or Tilsley) was evidently related to John Tilsley who set up a pin-making business at Gloucester in 1627: *VCH Glos.* iv. p. 76.

342   William Kingston the same day built a cottage at Flaxley, and took, etc. (fine 40*s*.)

343   John Hill, late of the same [*presumably Flaxley*], labourer, on 20 July 1631 built a cottage at Flaxley, and took, etc. (fine 20*s*.)

344   Henry Bullocke, late of the same, labourer, on 20 May 1612 built a cottage at Flaxley, and took, etc. (fine 40s.)

345   Robert Goslinge, late of Flaxley, collier, the same day built a cottage at Flaxley, and took, etc. (fine 40*s*.)

346   William Kingston on 1 August 1626 built a cottage at Flaxley, and took, etc. (fine 40*s*.)

347   William Boughton, late of Blaisdon, collier, the same day built a cottage at Flaxley in the Forest, and took, etc. (fine 40*s*.)

348   John Fowle, late of the same, labourer, on 10 September 1612 built a cottage or dwelling house in Flaxley, and took, etc. (fine 20*s*.)

[*f. 30v.*]

349   Edmund Cowlstance, late of the same, tailor, on 3 March 1615 built a cottage or dwelling house in Flaxley, and took, etc. (fine 40*s*.)

350   John Phips, late of St. Briavels parish, shipwright, on 10 May 1633 encroached a garden, containing ¼ a. and worth 2*s*. a year, from the king's soil in a place called *le Lower Meade*[1] near St. Briavels within the Forest perambulation, and took, etc. (fine 40*s*.)

351   Goughe Chin, lateof Blakeney, yeoman, on 10 July 1630 newly built a dwelling house, together with another house as an outhouse (*unacum alio domo anglice an outhowse*), at Blakeney within the regard of the Forest; the dwelling house adjoins the covert; for building it he took three tons of timber from the king's woodland. (fine £50)

352   Rowland Millard, late of Awre, collier, on 31 August 1631 built a dwelling house and a stable at Awre within the Forest perambulation and near the king's covert; for building it he took two tons of timber from the king's woodland and encroached two feet, worth [*blank*] a year, on the king's soil, and took, etc. (fine £20)

353   Rowland Ferrice, late of Newnham, glassmaker, deceased, on 10 July 1613 built a glasshouse (*domum vitreum anglice a glassehouse*) at Newnham within the Forest perambulation, and Robert Mansell, kt.,[2] took the issues and profits to his own use and still takes them. (fine £10)

354   Stephen Wilcocks, late of Newnham, yeoman,[3] on 10 June 1628 built a warehouse (*repositorium anglice one warehouse or storehouse*) at Newnham within the Forest perambulation, and John Dalby took the issues and profits for his own use and still takes them. (fine £5)

---

[1] Probably the place called Lower Meend, formerly a detached part of the extraparochial demesne, adjoining St. Briavels village: *VCH Glos*. v. p. 248.

[2] Apparently one of the earliest references to Newnham's glass-making industry. Sir Robert Mansell held a monopoly right to glass production in England from 1615 to 1642: *ODNB*, xxxvi. pp. 537–40.

[3] The Wilcox family were later glass-makers at Newnham and Stephen's warehouse was perhaps connected with that industry: *VCH Glos*. x. p. 43.

[*f. 31*]

355   James Robins, late of Newnham, on 1 July 1632 newly built a house in the street of Newnham, within the Forest perambulation, for the use of Henry Stafford. (fine 40*s*.)

356   John Swanley, late of *Esserton* (Glos.), gent., the same day newly built a house at Newnham within the perambulation, and took the issues and profits to his own use and still takes them. (fine 40s.)

357   Thomas Hames the elder, late of Abenhall, the same day built a cottage at Abenhall on the king's soil of the Forest, and took, etc. (fine 40*s*., rent 6*d*.)

358   William Collys, late of *le Mynde*, near Littledean, the same day encroached on the king's soil at *le Mynde* by building a sheepcot (*ovile anglice one sheepecott*), worth [*blank*] a year, and took, etc. (fine 20s.) [*item crossed through and note added*: fine paid to Thomas Leake, esq., the receiver]

359   Francis Acton, late of Littledean, labourer, the same day encroached on the king's soil of the Forest at Littledean by building a sheepcot and an outhouse, worth [*blank*] a year, and took, etc. (fine 20*s*.)

360   Thomas Marshe, late of Littledean, labourer, deceased, on 1 June 1625 built a cottage on lands of David Heane in Littledean parish in the Forest, and took, etc. (fine 20s.)

361   John Yeam of the same the same day built a cottage in Littledean parish on lands of the said David Heane, and took, etc. (fine 20*s*.)

362   John Powell of the same, labourer, on 10 June 1632 built a cottage at Littledean within the Forest, and took, etc. (fine 20*s*.)

363   David Heane, late of Littledean, yeoman, deceased, on 20 June 1618 built a cottage or *heyhouse* in Littledean parish within the Forest, and took, etc. (fine 10*s*.)

364   Robert Grundon, late of Hope Mansell (Herefs.), glover, on 10 May 1632 built a cottage in a street (*in platea quadam anglice a certaine streete*) in Mitcheldean within the Forest, and took, etc. (fine £3)

365   Robert Pyrke, late of Mitcheldean, gent., deceased, on 1 May 1625 built a dwelling house in Mitcheldean parish within the Forest, and took, etc. (fine £10)

366   Thomas Soult, late of Mitcheldean, labourer, the same day built a new cottage in Mitcheldean parish in the Forest, and took, etc. (fine 40*s*.)

[*f. 31v.*]

367   Katherine Morse, late of Mitcheldean, widow, the same day built a cottage near Abenhall (*Abinghall*) on the king's demesne of his Forest, and took, etc. (fine £5)

368   John Lewys, late of Abenhall, feltmaker, the same day built a cottage near Abenhall on the king's soil of his Forest, and encroached one-twelfth of an acre of land of the king's soil, worth 6*d*. a year. (fine £5)

369   Edward Powell, late of the same, labourer, the same day built a cottage at Abenhall in the Forest and encroached one-eighth of an acre of the king's soil, worth 6*d*. a year, and took, etc. (fine £5)

370   Alice Floyde, late of the same, widow, the same day built a cottage near Abenhall within the Forest perambulation on the king's soil, and encroached one-tenth of an acre, worth 4*d*. a year, and took, etc. (fine £5)

371   William Gunn the elder, late of Mitcheldean, gent., deceased, on 10 June 1610 encroached one-sixth of an acre, worth 6*d*. a year, of the king's soil within the perambulation of the Forest at Abenhall, adjoining the pond of his mill called Gunn's mill; John Wyntour of Lydney, kt., takes the issues and profits of it.[1] (fine £3, rent 12*d*.)

372 Richard Vaughan, late of Abenhall, the same day built a barn at Abenhall within the Forest, and took, etc. (fine 40*s*.)

373 Thomas Nelmes, late of Abenhall, the same day built a barn at Abenhall within the Forest, and took, etc. (fine 40*s*.)

374 John Nelmes, late of Flaxley, yeoman, on 1 July 1631 built a grist mill (*molendinum aquaticum anglice one grist mill or corne mill*)[2] at Flaxley within the regard and perambulation of the Forest, and took, etc. (fine £20)

[*f. 32*]

Mines in the Upper Part of the Forest[3]

It was presented by the foresters, regarders, and the twelve jurymen, and convicted by the verderers, that:

375 There are various mines in a place called Clearwell Meend (*Clowerwalls Myne*), within the regard and in the upper part of the Forest, commonly called by these names, viz. *Bush pitt*, *Rad pitt*, *Nowes of the green*, *Stayre pitt*, *Hall pitt*, *Pluckpenny*, and [there are] other mines adjoining them; and there are other mines in the park of Sir John Wintour, kt., within his free tenement within the Forest perambulation, one called *Hickells Wildern*, but they do not know the names of the others; and there are other mines in the free tenement of Baynham Throckmorton, kt. and bt., within the Forest perambulation, as appears in a particular, viz. one in a little close called *le Shraves*, another called *Cowlers Wylder*, another called *Browne Wilder*, another called *Beech pitt*, another called *Brownes Wilder pitt*, and others of which they do not know the names.

376 And that there are other mines in the land of the same Baynham Throckmorton, kt., in the Forest, [viz.] a mine called *Scar pitt* which lies in a little close or pasture called Noxon park, another called *Ash pitt* or *Wyth Wylder*, another called *Lady pitt*, another *Brownes pytt*, another *Little pytt*, and various others of which they do not know the names; and there are mines in other lands of Baynham Throckmorton within the perambulation of the Forest called Lambsquay (*Lambsquy*), one of which is called *Bridge pitt*, another *Etlow* or *Scarre pitt*, another *Wrok Wylder*, another *Horse pitt*, with other mines there of which they do not know the names; and there are various other mines in the lands of John Gonning, late of Bristol, merchant, in Newland parish called *le Nowes*, one of which is called *Great Nowes*, another *Great Nowes* (sic) or *Little Nowes*, and another *Cillies pitt*.

377 And that there are other mines in the free tenement of Thomas Sternhold of Staunton, gent., called Tufthorn in Newland parish, within the Forest perambulation, one of which is called *Old Orchard*, with various others the names of which [they] do not know; and there are other mines, of which [they] do know the names, in the free tenement of William Skyn of Clearwell called *Clay Oake*.

---

[1] Gunn operated the mill as a fulling-mill; it later became an iron furnace, owned by Winter in 1634: *VCH Glos.* v. p. 97.

[2] The literal translation would, of course, be 'water-mill'.

[3] The mines presented here, for the most part probably iron-ore mines, were in the western part of the Forest, both within the royal demesne and on private land (mainly the Throckmortons' Clearwell manor). The mines in the eastern part of the Forest, known as 'below the wood', were for some reason not presented at the swanimote. For mining and mining customs in the Forest, see Hart, *Free Miners*.

378   And that there are other mines in the free tenement of William Wyrrall called *le Clapps* within the Forest perambulation, one of which is called *Brownes Clap*, with various others of which they do not know the names; and there are other mines in the free tenement of Henry Worgan of Clearwell in a land or farm (*sive fundo*) within the Forest perambulation called *Packhaynes*, one of which is called *Hopwell*, another *Hamppitt*, another *Little Hame pitt*, another *Sally pitt*, with various others which cannot be distinguished by their names; and there are other mines in the land or farm of William Bond in Newland parish within the Forest perambulation called *Satwell field*, one of which is called *Great Dam pitt*, another *Little Dam pitt*, and two others called *Catwell* and *Little Catwell*.

[*f. 32v.*]

379   And that each miner (*unusque mineriorum anglice miners*), according to a custom from [a time beyond] the memory of man, ought to pay Stirleie Kedgwin and Christopher Worgan and others, the king's collectors or deputies commonly called galers (*gawlers*) 1*d.* for each week, provided that in that time of working he earns 9*d.*; and that each miner ought to pay to the same deputies or collectors one load of 'mine' at the four terms in the year, for the sole purpose that the mine court may be held and kept according to their custom.

380   And that the miners living in the lower part of the wood in the Forest are accustomed to pay the king's deputies or collectors commonly called galers at the four terms of the year 120 loads of mine and one load of charcoal for the king's use.

(*marginal note*: the mines to be seized because no claim)[1]

The Vert (*de Viridis*)[2]

It is presented by the foresters, regarders, and 12 jurymen, and convicted by the verderers, that:

381   John Nelme, late of the Merrin (*le Merringe*),[3] in Mitcheldean parish, labourer, on 28 August 1630 within the lord king's demesne of his Forest cut holly trees (*hollyes*) of the king's woodland to the quantity of 10 horse-loads of wood, worth 20*d.*, and converted them to his own use. (fine 5*s.*, and the value, etc.)

382   John Hopkins, late of Mitcheldean, labourer, the same day and year within the lord king's demesne of his Forest cut holly trees of the king's woodland to the quantity of six horse-loads of wood worth 12*d.*, and converted them to his own use. (fine 10*s.*, and the value, etc.)

383   William Lugge and Thomas Lugge, of the city of Gloucester, tanners, the same day and year within the lord king's demesne of his Forest at a place called Ruardean's Eaves, by grant of Robert Treswell, then a king's officer, stripped the bark from 16 oaks of the king's woodland, containing by estimation 200 tons of timber, each ton worth 3*s.* 4*d.* (fine £10 each)

---

[1] This note, which from its position in the MS might seem to refer only to the mines in no. 380, evidently refers to all those in the Forest: see above p. 18.

[2] After no. 390, the presentments in this long section are given here in much abbreviated form. Among standard phrases omitted are: 'within the king's demesne of his Forest; 'and converted it to his own use'; 'by estimation' (used in most cases before tonnages of timber); 'on the same day and year' (used in most presentments which follow one where a date is given and before another appears); 'late of' (used in most addresses and evidently meaning that the offender was resident there at the time of the offence, rather than that he had since died or moved away); 'and the value, etc.' (which usually follows the marginal note of the fine imposed by the eyre).

[3] The name of the road junction at the south end of Mitcheldean town: *VCH Glos.* v. p. 174.

384 John Dobbes, late of Soudley, labourer, the same day and year within the lord king's demesne of his Forest cut down the crown (*culmen*) of a beech of the lord king's woodland, containing by estimation four horse-loads of wood worth 4*d.*, with loss to the king 2*s.*, and converted it to his own use. (fine 2*s.* and the value, etc.)

385 Edward Wore, late of [English] Bicknor, labourer, the same day and year within the lord king's demesne of his Forest cut down the topmost branches of a beech of the lord king's woodland, containing by estimation one horse-load of wood worth 2*d.*, with loss to the king 6*d.* (fine 5*s.*, and the value, etc.)

386 Hugh Jones of Coleford, labourer, and Ambrose Vick of the same, labourer, the same day and year within the lord king's demesne of his Forest cut down a beech of the lord king's woodland, containing by estimation two wagon-loads of wood worth 5*s.*, and converted it to their own use. (fine 10*s.* each, and the value, etc.)

[*f. 33*]

387 James Morgan, late of Whitecliff, labourer, the same day and year within the lord king's demesne of his Forest cut down nine beeches of the lord king's woodland, containing by estimation 30 horse-loads of wood worth 7*s.* 6*d.*, and to his use, etc. (fine 40*s.*, and the value, etc.)

388 Thomas Trigge, late of [English] Bicknor, labourer, the same day and year within the lord king's demesne of his Forest cut down two beeches of the lord king's woodland, containing by estimation four wagon-loads of wood worth 10*d.*, and to his use, etc. (fine 40*s.*, and the value, etc.)

389 James Godwyn the younger, late of the same, labourer, the same day and year within the lord king's demesne of his Forest cut down the branches of a beech of the lord king, containing by estimation six horse-loads of wood worth 12*d.*, and to his use, etc. (fine 5*s.*, and the value, etc.)

390 Hugh Jones, late of Coleford, labourer, on 20 November 1632 within the lord king's demesne of his Forest cut down two beeches of the lord king's woodland of his Forest, containing by estimation 10 horse-loads of wood worth 20*d.*, and to his use, etc. (fine 5*s.*, and the value, etc.)

391 Christopher Phellps of the same, glover, 'girded' (*circumscidit anglice girded*)[1] a beech, containing one horse-load of wood worth 2*d.* (fine 5*s.*)

392 Thomas Awre of Awre, husbandman, cut down an oak, containing one horse-load of wood worth 2*d.* (fine 6*s.* 8*d.*)

393 John Foxe of Coleford, labourer, took two horse-loads of timber of the king's vert, and carried it out of the Forest with a horse worth 13*d.* (fine 5*s.*)

394 William Mason of [English] Bicknor, yeoman, entered the king's demesne with four oxen worth 40s. and dragged a beech, containing four loads of wood worth 8*d.*, out of the Forest into his own lands. (fine 10*s.*, and the value of the oxen)

395 Anthony Turner, George Turner, and Thomas Ashman of [Mitcheldean],[2] labourers, cut down a beech, containing four cords of wood worth 13*s.* 4*d.* (fine 10*s.* each)

[*f. 33v.*]

---

[1] See above, p. 46*n.*

[2] MS. reads *de Magna*, evidently intending *de Magna Dene*.

396   John Baker of the same, labourer cut down the topmost branches of a beech, containing three horse-loads of wood worth 6*d*. (fine 5*s*.)

397   John Norton of Lea (*le Lea*) (Glos.), labourer, cut down an oak, containing two wagon-loads of wood worth 6*s*. 8*d*. (fine 40*s*.)

398   The same John Norton cut down another oak, containing nine horse-loads of timber worth 4*s*. (fine 20*s*.)

399   Thomas Hopkins of Littledean, labourer, on 12 February 1631 cut down the topmost branches (*summos ramos anglice the tower bowghes*) of a beech, containing six horse-loads of wood worth 12*d*. (fine 10*s*.)

400   John Nelme of Mitcheldean, labourer, cut down the topmost branches of a beech, containing four horse-loads of wood worth 12*s*. (fine 6*s*. 8*d*.)

401   James Baddam of the same, labourer, cut down four horse-loads of holly trees of the king's vert, worth 3s. (fine 6*s*. 8*d*.)

402   John Browne of Awre, husbandman, 'girded' a beech, containing two horse-loads of wood worth 4*d*. (fine 20*s*.) [*item crossed through and note* added: fine paid to Thomas Leake, esq., the receiver]

403   John Bayly of Blakeney, butcher, 'girded' a beech, containing two horse-loads of wood worth 4*d*. (fine 20*s*.)

404   John Harris of Aylburton, labourer, cut down two of the topmost branches of a beech, containing two horse-loads of wood worth 4*d*. (fine 20*s*.)

405   Meredith Prosser of Coleford, labourer, cut down a beech, containing one wagon-load of wood, worth 4*s*. 4*d*. (fine 40*s*.)

[*f. 34*]

406   Christopher Sowdley of Clearwell, labourer, 'girded' a beech, containing one horse-load of wood, worth 2*d*. (fine 20*s*.)

407   William Morse, the younger, of the same 'girded' a beech, containing one horse-load of wood, worth 2*d*. (fine 20*s*.)

408   John Prosser of Clearwell, labourer, on 12 February 1632 cut down a beech, containing one wagon-load of wood worth 3*s*. 4*d*. (fine 40*s*.)

409   Thomas Keere of the same, husbandman cut down the topmost branches of a beech, containing two horse-loads of wood worth 4*d*. (fine 10*s*.)

410   Richard Keare of the same, butcher cut down a beech, containing four horse-loads of wood worth 6*d*. (fine 20*s*.)

411   Thomas Sibbraunce of St. Briavels, husbandman, cut down the topmost branches of a beech, containing two horse-loads of wood worth 4*d*. (fine 20*s*.)

412   John Leighton of Bream, labourer, and Hugh Harris of the same, labourer, cut down two beeches, containing two wagon-loads of wood worth 6*s*. (fine 15*s*. each)

413   John Clerke of [English] Bicknor, clerk, cut down a beech, containing four horse-loads of wood worth 8*d*. (fine 20*s*.)

414   Roger Rosser of Coleford, servant of Master Williams, gent., cut down three beeches, containing 12 horse-loads of wood worth 2*s*., and [converted] them to the use of the same Master Williams. (fine 20*s*.)

415   John Palmore of Whitecliff (*Whittcleve*), labourer, cut down the topmost branches of an oak, containing two horse-loads of wood worth 4*d*. (fine 20*s*.)

[*f. 34v.*]

416   John Hopkins of Mitcheldean, labourer, 'girded' a beech, containing three horse-loads of wood worth 12*d*. (fine 20*s*.)

417   Thomas Wilde of the same, labourer, cut down two oaks, containing two tons of timber, worth 10*s*. (fine £3)

418   George Saunders of Mitcheldean, labourer, cut down the topmost branches of a beech, containing one horse-load of wood worth 4*d*. (fine 5*s*.)

419   The same Thomas Wilde cut down the topmost branches of an oak, containing six horse-loads of wood worth 12*d*. (fine 20*s*.)

420   Richard Wirrall of the same cut down the topmost branches of two beeches, containing four horse-loads of wood worth 8*d*. (fine 20*s*.)

421   Thomas Wallwyn of Mitcheldean cut down an oak, containing four horse-loads of wood worth 8*d*. (fine 20*s*.)

422   John Hopkins of Whitecliff, within the king's demesne, 'girded' a beech, containing 12 horse-loads of wood, worth 2*s*. 8*d*. (fine 30*s*.)

423   Hugh Jones of Coleford, labourer, cut down a beech and the topmost branches of another beech, containing six horse-loads of wood worth 40*d*. (fine 20*s*.)

424   Richard Corsley of the same, labourer, cut down a beech, containing six horse-loads of wood worth 43*d*. (fine 20*s*.)

425   James Gunter of Highmeadow (*Hymeade*), labourer, cut down two little beeches, containing three horse-loads of wood worth 10*d*. (fine 20*s*.)

[*f. 35*

426   John Clarke of English Bicknor cut down two beeches, containing four horse-loads of wood, worth 12*d*. (fine 20*s*.)

427   Thomas Pirke of Mitcheldean cut down a beech, containing 10 horse-loads of wood worth 12*d*. (fine 20*s*.)

428   John Mayo of the same, husbandman, cut down the topmost branches of two beeches, containing six horse-loads of timber worth 12*d*. (fine 20*s*.)

429   John Hopkins of Mitcheldean cut down several holly trees, containing 10 horse-loads of wood worth 20*d*. (fine 40*s*.)

430   William Hyett of the same, labourer cut down the topmost branches of a beech, containing two horse-loads of wood worth 4*d*. (fine 20*s*.)

431   William Wirrall of the same cut down the topmost branches (*summos ramos anglice the tower bowes*) of two beeches, containing four horse-loads of wood worth 8*d*. (fine 20*s*.)

432   John Davis of English Bicknor, labourer, cut down a beech, containing six horse-loads of wood, worth 18*d*. (fine 20*s*.)

433   James Uncle of Ruardean, labourer, cut down an oak, containing four horse-loads worth 20*s*. (fine 20 nobles)

434   Alexander Lambe of the same, labourer cut down a beech, containing three tons worth 13*s.* 4*d.* (fine 20 nobles)

435   Leonard Beare of Littledean, labourer, cut down four horse-loads of holly worth 1*s.* 4*d.* (fine 20*s.*)

[*f. 35v.*]

436   It is presented by the foresters, regarders, and jury of 12, and convicted by the verderers, that the following persons on various days between 30 July and 22 October 1630 made waste by cutting down and 'girding' beeches, oaks, hollies, and crab trees of the king's woodland and vert, and carried away the wood from the same and converted it to their own use, to the king's loss, viz.

437   Paul Thomas of Lea Bailey, labourer, cut down topmost branches of an oak, containing six horse-loads of wood (*vi seam' ligni anglice sixe seames of wood*) worth 12*d.* (fine 20*s.*)

438   Anne Garway of Mitcheldean, widow, and William Worrall and William Griffith, of the same, labourers, cut down the topmost branches of four beeches, containing 15 horse-loads of wood worth 2*s.* 6*d.*, and carried them away with three horses worth 15*s.* (fine 13*s.* 4*d.* each, and the value of the horses)

439   John Hopkins of the same, labourer, cut down the topmost branches of a beech, containing three horse-loads of wood worth 6*d.*, and carried them away with one horse. (fine 20*s.*, and the value of the horse)

440   Richard Tompson of Ruardean, clerk, cut down the tops (*capita*) of two beeches in Ruardean's Eaves, containing four horse-loads of wood worth 2*d.*, and carried them away with one horse worth 6*s.* 8*d.*, with loss to the king 6*d.* (fine 10*s.*)

441   John Webb of Ruardean, turner, cut down two beeches in Ruardean's Eaves, containing six tons of timber worth 30*s.*, with loss to the king 7*s.* (fine £10)

442   Thomas Raynolde, a stranger (*peregrinus*), living in the Forest in a place called Howbrook near Lydbrook, cut down two oaks, containing three tons of timber worth 20*s.*, to build himself a cottage, with loss to the king 6*s.* 8*d.* (fine £3)

443   John Webb of Ruardean, turner, cut down a beech at Brierley, containing four wagon-loads of timber worth 12*s.*, with loss to the king 5*s.* (fine 20 nobles)

444   John Baker of Ruardean, yeoman, cut down a beech, containing four wagon-loads worth 12*s.*, with loss to the king 5*s.* (fine £5)

445   Richard Hodges of Etloe, yeoman, cut down a beech at Blakeney's Eaves, containing 10 horse-loads of wood worth 20*d.*, with loss to the king 10*d.* (fine 20*s.*)

446   William Hyet of Mitcheldean, yeoman, cut down the top (*caput*) of a beech, containing four horse-loads of wood worth 8*d.*; with loss to the king 6*d.* (fine 20*s.*)

[*f. 36*]

447   John Hopkins of Mitcheldean, labourer, cut down the the top of a beech, containing three horse-loads of wood worth 6*d.*, with loss to the king 8*d.* (fine 20*s.*)

448   William Wirrall of Mitcheldean, labourer, cut down the top of a beech containing two horse-loads of wood worth 4*d.*, with loss to the king 6*d.* (fine 20*s.*)

449   William Griffith of the same, labourer, cut down the top of a beech, containing one horse-load of wood worth 2*d.*, with loss to the king 4*d.* (fine 20*s.*)

450   William Hyet of Mitcheldean, labourer, cut down two horse-loads of wood, worth 4*d*, from the top of a beech, with loss to the king 6*d*. (fine 20*s*.)

451   John Heyward of Hillersland (*Hellarsland*) in [English] Bicknor, cardboard maker, on 3 December 1630 cut down a beech, containing five wagon-loads of wood and timber worth 5s. (fine £10)

452   Benedict Jorden of [English] Bicknor, yeoman, on 17 November 1629 cut down an oak in Coverham, containing two wagon-loads of wood and timber worth 6*s*. 8*d*., with loss to the king 12*d*. (fine 40*s*.)

453   Henry Godwyn, and William Smarte of Eastbach (*Eastpage*), labourers, on 18 November 1629 cut down a beech near le *Whitethornes peake,* containing three wagon-loads of wood and timber worth 6*s*., with loss to the king 12*d*. (fine £3 each)

454   William Nashe of Milkwall, labourer, on 30 November 1629 cut down the head of a beech in Birch hill, containing five horse-loads of wood worth 5*d*., with loss to the king 6*d*. (fine 20*s*.)

455   William Tresteed of Clearwell, mason, on 26 November 1629 cut down a beech in Birch hill, containing one horse-load of wood worth 6*d*., with loss to the king 6*d*. (fine 20*s*.)

456   James Sibbrance of Bream, labourer, on 2 December 1629 cut down a beech at Bream's Eaves, containing three wagon-loads of wood worth 3*d*. (fine £5)

457   William Yem, late of Coleford, yeoman, on 26 November 1629 cut down an oak near Milkwall, containing three wagon-loads of wood and timber worth 2*s*. 6*d*. (fine £5)

458   John Smith of Coleford, miner, on 1 December 1629 cut down a beech at Coverham, containing three horse-loads of wood worth 3*d*., with loss to the king 4*d*. (fine 20*s*.)

[*f. 36v.*]

459   James Passmore of Clearwell, labourer, on 18 and 20 November 1629 cut down a beech and holly trees, worth 2d., with loss to the king 6d. (fine 20s.)

460   John Pritchard of Mitcheldean, cooper, cut down the head of a beech, containing 20 horse-loads of wood worth 20*d*., with loss to the king 8*d*. (fine 40*s*.)

461   And [they present] that the several people underwritten on various days and various times between 30 December 1629 and 25 February 1630 made waste in the king's demesne of the Forest by cutting, felling, and 'girding' (*succidendo, prosternando, et circumscidendo*) beeches, oaks, hollies, and crab trees of the king's wood and vert, and carried away the wood and converted it to their own use, to the king's loss, as follows:

462   Thomas Dawe of Ruardean, labourer, grazed (*depascuit anglice browsed*) 10 animals (*averia*) in the Forest, and cut holly trees and hawthorns. (fine 5s.)

463   John Pritchett of Mitcheldean, labourer, 'girded' seven oaks in the middle of the Forest, containing 12 horse-loads of wood worth 2*s*., with loss to the king 12*d*. (fine 40*s*.)

464   John Williams of Mitcheldean, labourer, cut down the head of a beech, containing six horse-loads of wood worth 12*d*., with loss to the king 12*d*. (fine 20*s*.)

465   Richard Garway of Mitcheldean, labourer, cut down the head of a beech, containing four horse-loads of wood worth 8*d*., with loss to the king 2*d*. (fine 20*s*.)

466   John Cornewall of Mitcheldean, labourer, cut down a beech, containing two wagon-loads of wood worth 3*s*. 4*d*., with an axe worth 6*d*. (fine £3 6*s*. 8*d*.)

467   Samuel Parsons of *Iverdeane* in Abenhall, labourer, cut down the crown of a crab tree, containing two horse-loads worth 4*d.* (fine 20*s.*)

468   Peter Marshall and Richard Frewen of Ruardean, carpenters, on 25 February and 12 August 1630 cut down an oak near a place called *High Beeche*, containing seven wagon-loads of wood and timber worth 7*s.*, with loss to the king 12*d.* (fine 50*s.* each)

[*f. 37*]

469   John Birt of Coleford, miner, 'girded' a beech, worth 1*d.*, in Coverham; damage to the king 4*d.* (fine 10*s.*)

470   John Rudge of Weston under Penyard,[1] yeoman, in 12 August 1630 and 8 January 1633 cut down an oak in Lea Bailey, containing one ton worth 5*s*, and carried it away with four oxen worth £4, with loss to the king 12*d.* (fine 40*s.*)

471   William Baddam and William Wirrall of Mitcheldean, labourers, cut down two beeches, containing two tons of timber worth 10*s.*, and carried them away with two horses worth £2, with loss to the king 2*s.* (fine 40*s.* each and the value of the horses)

472   The same William Baddam and William Wirrall cut down a beech in Lea Bailey, containing six horse-loads of wood, and carried it away with three horses, worth 30*s.*, with loss to the king 2*s.* (fine 20*s.* each and the value of the horses)

473   Francis Acton of Littledean, carpenter, cut down an oak in Badcocks Bailey, containing two wagon-loads of wood worth 2*s.* (fine 5 marks)

474   Martha Bonde, widow, and Fortune Holliday, miner, late of Littledean, cut down the head of an oak, containing two wagon-loads of timber worth 2*s.*, with loss to the king 12*d.* (fine 40*s.* each)

475   Thomas Hopkins of Littledean, labourer, cut down a beech, containing one wagon-load of wood and timber worth 2*s.*, with loss to the king 12*d.* (fine 40*s.*)

476   Anthony Wisham of Staunton, husbandman, on 17 January and 28 February 1631 cut down an oak and a beech in Coverham, containing two wagon-loads of wood worth 2*s.*, with loss to the king 10*d.* (fine 40*s.*)

477   John Godwyn of Coleford, miner, cut down two beeches in Coverham, containing two wagon-loads of wood worth 2*s.*, with loss to the king 6*d.* (fine 40*s.*)

478   John Birt of Coleford, miner, cropped (*cirpsit*) an oak and cut holly trees at the base of the trunk (*pro le butt*), worth 2*s.*, with loss to the king 6*d.* (fine 40*s.*)

479   Giles Webb of Coleford, miner, cut down the head of a beech, worth 4*d.*, with loss to the king 6*d.* (fine 20*s.*)

480   William Parlor of Joyford (*Jayfford*) in [English] Bicknor, yeoman, cut down an oak in Winnells (*le Wynolls*),[2] containing one ton of timber worth 3*s.* 4*d.* (fine 20*s.*)

---

[1] Weston is given as in Gloucestershire: see below, p. 85*n.*

[2] Identifed ('*the Winnal*') *c.* 1680 at the edge of the demesne east of Coalway: TNA, F17/7; cf. Atkinson, *Plan of Forest of Dean*, where the name was used for Winnells Hill house in the adjoining parochial lands of Coleford.

[*f. 37v.*]
481   Richard Morgan, son of James Morgan, late of Ruardean, labourer, cut down a timber oak in Moorwood, containing four tons worth 20*s.* (fine £5)

482   Richard Jones of Ruardean, labourer, [is presented] for his son cutting down 10 little beeches in Moorwood, containing one horse-load of wood worth 2*d*, with loss to the king 2*s.* (fine 40*s.*)

483   Stephen Still of Littledean, saddle-tree maker, cut down three horse-loads of beech timber, worth 4*d.*, and carried it away with his horses worth 9*s.* (fine 20*s.*, and for the horses)

484   William ap Thomas of Etloe, in Awre, yeoman, [is presented] for carrying away two wagon-loads of timber, containing 1½ tons of timber worth 7*s.* 6*d.*, with four oxen worth £4. (fine 5 marks, and for the oxen)

485   John Smith, Thomas Smith, and Richard Jones of Aylburton, husbandmen, decapitated a beech in Lea Bailey, containing seven horse-loads of wood worth 13*d.*, with loss to the king 12*d.* (fine 10*s.* each)

486   Francis Bridgeman of Blakeney, gent., cut down two horse-loads of beech timber worth 12*d.*, with loss to the king 4*d.* (fine 20*s.*) [*item crossed through and note added*: fine paid to Thomas Leake, esq., the receiver]

487   William Baddam of Mitcheldean, labourer, cut down the crown of a beech, containing six horse-loads of wood worth 12*d.*, with loss the king 12*d.* (fine 20*s.*)

488   Thomas Heyward of Ayleford (*Arleford*) in Awre, cardboard maker, [is presented] for carrying eight horse-loads of timber, worth 10*s.*, with two horses worth 20*s.* (fine 5 marks, and for the horses)

489   James Hamon of [English] Bicknor, labourer, [is presented] for a third part of a cord of timber worth 2*s.* (fine 20*s.*)

490   William Wirrall of Mitcheldean, labourer, cut down green [*blank*], containing two wagon-loads of wood and timber worth 2*s.* (fine 40*s.*)

491   Thomas Trigge of [English] Bicknor, cut down a beech in Worral [hill] (*le Wyroll*), containing three horse-loads of wood worth 6*d.* (fine 20*s.*)

492   Hugh Hopkins of Coleford, labourer, cropped (*carpsit*) oaks and beeches in Coverham and *Buckinsole*, containing 10 horse-loads of brushwood (*tinnetti*) worth 2*s.* 6*d.*, and carried it with two horses, worth 20*s.*, with loss to the king 12*d.* (fine 30*s.*, and for the horses)

493   Giles Webb of Coleford, miner, 'girded' (*circumscidit*) an oak in Winnalls (*Winnoll*), containing two loads of wood worth 6*d.* (fine 20*s.*)

[*f. 38*]
494   Christiana Pello of Mitcheldean, widow, cut a load of holly in *Ashwod*, worth 12*d.*, and carried it away with a horse worth 10*s.*, with loss to the king 6*d.* (fine 20*s.*, and for the horse)

495   William Parlor of *le Goysen* in [English] Bicknor, millward, cut down an oak in Winnells (*le Wynolls*), worth 3*s.* 4*d.* (fine ?as before (*antea*))

496   Matthew Ricketts of Mitcheldean, mason, cut down an oak in Lea Bailey (*le Bayly*), containing one ton worth 3*s.* 4*d.*, with loss to the king 5*s.* (fine 10*s.*)

497   Richard Pacie of Mitcheldean, labourer, cut down the topmost branches of a beech, containing three loads of wood worth 6*d.*, and carried them away with a horse, worth 10*s.*, with loss to the king 12*d.* (fine 10*s.*, and for the horse)

498   Anthony Gonning and William Baddam of Mitcheldean, labourers, cut down a 'sealed' oak (*quercum sigillatum*), containing one ton of timber worth 3*s*. 4*d*., and carried it away with a horse, worth 12*s*., with loss to the king 3*s*. (fine 40*s*. [?each], and for the horse)

499   Robert Rudge of Lea (*le Lea*) (Glos.), labourer, cut down an oak in Lea Bailey, containing one ton of timber worth 4*s*., with loss to the king 2*s*. (fine 40*s*.)

500   William Baddam of Mitcheldean, labourer, cut down the topmost branches of a beech in Lea Bailey, containing four horse-loads of wood worth 12*d*., and carried them away with two horses worth £2, with loss to the king 12*d*. (fine 20*s*., and for the horses)

501   Thomas Flower of the said Lea, labourer, cut down the topmost branches of an oak, containing two loads of wood worth 4*d*., with loss to the king 2*d*. (fine 10*s*.)

502   John Prichard of Mitcheldean, cooper, cut down an oak in Lea Bailey, containing one ton worth 5*s*., and carried it away with a horse worth 15*s*., with loss to the king 2*s*. (fine 40*s*., and for the horse)

503   John Trigge of Mitcheldean, labourer, cut down divers oaks and beeches in Lea Bailey and other places in the Forest, containing 20 loads of wood worth 3*s*. 4*d*., and carried them away with two horses worth £2, with loss to the king 10*s*. (fine 40*s*., and for the horses)

504   Thomas Jones of Newnham, labourer, between 10 Feb. and 12 April 1631 took timber, worth 12*d*., and carried it away on his back. (fine 10*s*.)

[*f. 38v.*]

505   James Weekes of Ruddle, labourer, took timber, worth 5s., and carried it away on his back, with loss to the king 16*d*. (fine 10*s*.)

506   William Blast of Hope Mansell (Herefs.), husbandman, cut down an oak, containing four loads worth 8*d*., in Lea Bailey and carried it away on his back, with loss to the king 12*d*. (fine 10*s*.)

507   William Linche of Mitcheldean, labourer, cut down an oak, worth 3*s*. 4*d*., in Lea Bailey and carried it away on his back, with loss to the king 2*s*. 6*d*. (fine 10*s*.)

508   John Lewes of Lydbrook, gent., took and carried away 1¼ ton of timber, worth 8*s*. (fine 40*s*.)

509   James and William Hamon of English Bicknor, labourers, took three 'gross' (*grossas*) of beech timber of the king's woodland, worth 6*s*. (fine 40*s*.)

510   John Pritchett of Mitcheldean, cooper, cut down an oak in the skirts (*le Skirt*) of Lea Bailey, worth 3*s*. 4*d*., and carried it away with two horses worth 20*s*., with loss to the king 12*d*. (fine 40*s*., and for the horses)

511   Richard Beare of Littledean, smith, cut down six loads of brushwood worth 5*s*., and carried them away with six horses worth £4, with loss to the king £5. (fine 20*s*., and for the horses)

512   William Whettson of Littledean, nailer, 'girded' the crown of an oak near *le More head*, [containing] one cartload of wood worth 12*d*., with loss to the king 2*d*. (fine 40*s*.)

513   William Linch of Mitcheldean, labourer, cut down a little oak in Lea Bailey, containing half a ton of timber worth 2*s*. 6*d*., with loss to the king 6*d*. (fine 10*s*.)

514   William Baddam of Aston Ingham (Herefs.), yeoman, cut down an oak in Lea Bailey, containing one ton of timber worth 5*s*., with loss to the king 12*d*. (fine 40*s*.)

515   William Wirrall of Mitcheldean, labourer, cut down an oak in Lea Bailey, containing one ton of timber and wood worth 4*s*. (fine 40*s*.)

[*f. 39*]

516   Thomas Merrok of Lea Bailey cut down a beech in Lea Bailey, containing one ton of timber worth 5*s.* (fine 40*s.*)

517   Robert Meeke of Weston [under Penyard] (Herefs.), yeoman, cut down an oak in Lea Bailey, containing two tons of wood and timber worth 4*s.*, which was taken away from him by the king's officer William Rowles. (fine 40*s.*)

518   Thomas Rudge of Lea cut down an oak in Lea, containing one ton worth 5*s.* (fine 40s.)

519   John Rudge of Weston [under Penyard] (Herefs.), yeoman, cut down an oak in Lea Bailey, containing three tons of wood and timber worth 15*s.* (fine £3)

520   John Trigge of Mitcheldean, labourer, cut down divers oaks and beeches in Lea Bailey, containing 10 tons of wood and timber worth 40s. (fine 20 nobles)

521   Robert Kirke of Mitcheldean, mercer, cut down an oak in Lea Bailey, containing one ton of timber worth 4*s.* (fine 40*s.*)

522   James Baddam of Mitcheldean, 'girded' an oak in Haywood, containing three loads of wood worth 6*d.* (fine 10*s.*)

523   James Michell of Mitcheldean, cooper, cut down an oak in Lea Bailey, containing four loads of wood worth 12*d.* (fine 20*s.*)

524   John Tucker of Lea Bailey, carpenter, 'girded' an oak, containing three loads of wood worth 6*d.* (fine 10*s.*)

525   Matthew Ricketts of Mitcheldean, mason, cut down two oaks in Lea Bailey, containing two cartloads of wood and timber worth 5*s.* (fine £4)

526   William Linche of Mitcheldean, labourer, cut down an oak in Lea Bailey, containing three tons worth 4*s.* (fine £6)

527   John Homes of Mitcheldean, labourer, cut down an oak in Lea Bailey, containing ½ ton worth 2*s.* (fine 30*s.*)

[*f. 39v.*]

528   John Pritchett of Mitcheldean, cooper, cut down an oak in Lea Bailey, containing one ton worth 4*s.* (fine £5)

529   Edward Phelpes of Coleford, carpenter, cut down an oak in Winnells (*le Wynolls*), containing one cartload of wood and timber worth 3s. (fine £3)

530   Hugh Hopkins of Coleford, labourer, cut down an oak in *Rusledge*[1], containing three cartloads of wood and timber worth 10*s.* (fine £5)

531   Roger Norton and Brian Garwey of Mitcheldean, labourers, cut down three oaks, containing 10 loads of wood worth 20*s.* (fine 20*s* each)

532   John Workman of Mitcheldean, butcher, cut down two great oaks, containing eight tons of timber worth 16*s.* (fine £10)

533   William Wywooll[2] of Mitcheldean, labourer, cut down an oak on 28 May 1633, containing three cartloads of wood and timber worth 5*s.* (fine £4)

---

[1] See below, p. 152*n.*
[2] *sic* but probably a scribal error for 'Wyrall'.

534　William Baddam of Mitcheldean, labourer, cut down an oak in Lea Bailey, containing one cartload of wood and timber worth 3*s*. (fine 40*s*.)

535　Stephen Watkins of Bream, labourer, cut down a 'sealed' beech (*fagum sigillatum*), containing 1½ cords of wood (fine £3)

536　Francis Mason of the same, cooper, cut down a 'sealed' beech, containing two cords of wood worth [*blank*]. (fine £4)

537　William Davis of the same cut down a 'sealed' beech, containing 1½ cords worth 3*s*. (fine £3)

538　John Springe of the same cut down a 'sealed' beech, containing 1½ cords of wood worth [*blank*]. (fine £3)

[*f. 40*]

539　John Rudge of Rudge of Weston under Penyard,[1] cut down a beech, containing one ton of timber and wood worth 5*s*., and carried it away with four oxen worth £5 6*s*. 8*d*. (fine 40*s*., and for the oxen).

540　John Richards of Ruardean, labourer, between 4 July and 5 August 1633 cut down the crown of a green oak in Ruardean's Eaves, containing three loads of wood worth 3*d*. (fine 10*s*.)

541　James Taylor of Ruardean, labourer, cut down a green oak in *Newnhams Slade*, containing three cartloads of timber worth 6*s*. (fine £4)

542　Thomas Wylde of Mitcheldean, labourer, cut down two beeches and the crowns of six other beeches in a place called Birch hill, containing four cartloads of wood worth 6*s*. 8*d*., which he carried away with a horse worth 10*s*.; often he has been hired by other men to cut down woodland in the Forest and take the spoils of the timber. (fine £5, and for the horse)

543　Brian Garway of Mitcheldean, labourer, for the same (*sic*).

544　William Linche of the same, labourer, cut down two oaks, containing three cartloads of wood worth 5*s*. (fine £5)

545　Edward Reynolds of Whitecliff in Newland, labourer, cut down four oaks in Winnalls (*le Wynoll*), containing three cartloads of wood and timber worth 10*s*. (fine £5)

546　Hugh Hopkins of Coleford, labourer, cut down three beeches in Coverham, containing five cartloads of wood [worth] 5*s*. (fine £5)

547　Edward Dickes of Mitcheldean, smith, cut down an oak in *Horwood*,[2] containing two cartloads of wood worth 5*s*. 4*d*. (fine £4)

548　Thomas Capull of Newnham, innkeeper, cut down a beech in Blaize Bailey, containing two cartloads of wood worth 10*s*. (fine £4)

549　William Rawlings of Newnham, maltman, cut down two beeches in Blaize Bailey, containing two cartloads of wood worth 10*s*. (fine £4)

550　John Owen of Ruddle in Newnham, husbandman, took an oak from Blaize Bailey, containing one ton of timber worth 6*s*. 8*d*., and carried it away with four oxen worth £4. (fine 40*s*., and for the oxen)

---

[1] MS. here identifies the Herefordshire parish of Weston under Penyard as in Gloucestershire; complex boundaries – detached parts of Newland, comprising its tithing of Lea Bailey, lay close to Rudge farm – may have contributed to the confusion.

[2] See below, p. 136*n*.

[*f. 40v.*]

551   William Wirrall of Mitcheldean, labourer, cut down a beech upon Serridge (*Sheredge*), containing one cartload of wood worth 5*s.* (fine 40*s.*)

552   Hugh Jones and Richard Tomlins of Coleford, labourers, cut down five beeches in a place called Coverham, containing six cartloads of wood worth 6*s.* (fine £4 each)

553   William Davis of *Rawlings meade*[1] in Mitcheldean, husbandman, cut down an oak, containing two cartloads of timber worth 5*s.* (fine £4)

554   William Wirrall of Mitcheldean, labourer, cut down the crowns of oaks and beeches, containing two cartloads of wood worth 5*s.* (fine 20 nobles)

555   William Wirrall of Mitcheldean, labourer, between 17 February and 26 September 1633 cut down the crown of a green oak in Ruardean's Eaves, containing three loads of wood worth 3*d.* (fine 20*s.*)

556   Richard Morgan of Ruardean, son of James Morgan of the same, cut down an oak in Ruardean's Eaves, containing three cartloads of wood worth 3*s.* (fine £5)

557   Tanner Morse of Blackmore's Hale, yeoman, cut down an oak in Edge (*Nedge*) hills, containing one ton worth [*illeg.*], and carried out of the Forest ¾ ton of oak timber with four oxen worth £4. (fine £4, and for the oxen)

558   George Dalloway of Flaxley, cardboard maker, cut down a beech in Blaize Bailey, containing one cartload of wood worth 5s. (fine 40*s.*)

559   William Sayer of Flaxley, cardboard maker, carried eight loads of timber out of the Forest to outer parts, and converted it into 'scales' (*scalas anglice scales*)[2] worth 8s. (fine £3)

560   John Trigge of Mitcheldean, labourer, cut down the crown of a beech in Haywood (*Aywood*) worth 12*d.* (fine 20*s.*)

561   Bryan Dowle and James Hannys of [English] Bicknor, labourers, on 5 July 1633, on the orders of George Wirrall the elder, cut down six oaks in Hangerberry, containing two tons of timber and eight cartloads of wood worth 11*s.* 6*d.* (fine for Wirrall, 20 marks)

562   William Wode of Coleford, labourer, cut down six oaks near *le Perche walle*, containing four cartloads of timber and 12 cartloads of wood worth 44s. (fine £20)

563   Hugh Jones and Richard Tomlins of Coleford, labourers, cut down three little beeches in Coverham, containing 1½ cartloads of wood worth 18*d.* (fine 20*s.* each)

[*f.41*]

564   John Smith of Ruardean, carpenter, cut down an oak in Lea Bailey, containing ¾ ton of timber worth 6*s.* 8*d.* (fine 20*s.*)

565   John Reynolds of Whitecliff and Christopher Prosser of Coleford, miners, cut down an oak in Winnells (*le Wynolls*), containing three cartloads of wood and timber worth 10*s.* (fine 50*s.* each)

566   Christopher and Thomas Palmer of Whitecliff, smiths, cut down a beech near Bixslade, containing five cartloads of wood and timber worth 10*s.* (fine 50*s.* each)

567   Thomas Wysam, late of Staunton, yeoman, cut down a beech in Coverham, containing three loads of wood worth 6*d.* (fine 10*s.*)

---

[1] Also called *Rawlins Lease*: see below, p. 87*n.*
[2] Thin pieces of board: *OED.*

568 John Heyward of Hillersland in [English] Bicknor, cardboard maker, cut down a beech in Coverham, containing one cartload of wood and timber worth 5*s.* (fine 40*s.*)

569 William Smoute of [English] Bicknor cut down, for the use of and by order of Thomas Tilman of Mailscot, 14 beeches in Coverham, containing three cartloads of wood and timber worth 15*s.*, with loss to the king 14*s.* (fine on Thomas Tilman, £4)

570 And [they present] that the persons underwritten on various days and at various times between 26 September and 19 December 1633 made waste in the king's demesne land of the Forest by cutting down, felling, and 'girding' beeches, oaks, hollies, and crab trees of the king's wood and vert, and carried away the wood and converted it to their own use, to the king's damage, as follows:

571 John Bachelor of Mitcheldean, pinner, cut down the top branches of an oak, containing three loads of wood worth 6*d.* (fine 20s.) [*item crossed through and note added* : fine paid to Thomas Leake, esq., the receiver)

572 Edward Baddam of Blakeney, labourer, cut down the crown of a beech, containing two loads of wood worth 4*d.* (fine 20s.)

573 John Evans of Lea (Glos.), labourer, cut down three oaks, containing two cartloads of wood. (fine 40*s.*)

574 William Davys of Newland, husbandman, cut down an oak, containing three cartloads of wood worth 5*s.* (fine £3)

575 Edward Reynolds of Clearwell, labourer, cut down four oaks, containing 12 loads of wood worth 2*s.* (fine 20s.)

[*f. 41v.*]

576 the said Edward Reynolds cut down four oaks, containing 12 loads of wood worth 2*s.* (fine 20s.)

577 Thomas Gething of Clearwell, labourer, cut down an oak, containing two tons of timber and one cartload of wood worth 10*s.* (fine £3)

578 Anthony Norgate of the same, labourer, cut down the crown of an oak, containing six loads of wood worth 12*d.* (fine 20s.)

579 Francis Hawkins of the same, labourer, cut down the top branches of two oaks, containing four loads of wood worth 8*d.* (fine 20s.)

580 Edward Reynolds of Whitecliff, yeoman, cut down the top branches of two oaks, containing seven loads of wood worth 16*d.* (fine 20s.)

581 James Prichard of Clearwell, miner, cut down one load of wood called hollies worth 12*d.* (fine 20s.)

582 William Davis of *Rawlins lease*,[1] labourer, cut down two oaks, worth 15*s.* (fine £4)

583 John Tomkins of *Walton'* (Herefs.), labourer, cut down the top branches of a beech and an oak, containing two cartloads of wood worth 5*s.* (fine £4)

And [they present] that the several persons underwritten on various days and at various times between 19 December 1633 and 13 March 1634 made waste in the king's demesne land of the Forest by cutting down, felling, and 'girding' beeches, oaks, hollies, and crab

---

[1] Identified on a plan of *c.* 1680 as south-west of Mitcheldean, apparently the place later called Loquiers farm, a detached part of Newland parish: TNA, F 17/7; *VCH Glos.* v. p. 196 (see also no. 585).

trees of the king's wood and vert, and carried away the wood and converted it to their own use, to the king's loss, as follows:

584   James Yearworth of Eastbach (*Eastpadge*), yeoman, cut down an oak, containing two cartloads of wood and timber worth 6*s*. (fine £12)

585   William Davies of *Rawlins lease* near Mitcheldean (*Deane*), husbandman, cut down an oak, containing four cartloads of wood worth 10*s*., and carried it away with a cart and four oxen worth £4. (fine £12, and for the oxen)

586   Edward Reynolds of Coleford, labourer, cut down three oaks, containing two cartloads of wood and timber worth 10*s*. (fine 40*s*.)

[*f. 42*]

587   John Rudge of Rudge (Glos.),[1] yeoman, cut down an oak, containing six tons of timber worth 30*s*. (fine £5)

588   John Prichard of Mitcheldean, labourer, cut down two oaks, containing three tons of timber worth 15*s*. (fine £3)

589   William Baddam of the same, labourer, 'girded' the crown of a beech, (containing) one cartload of wood worth 3*s*. 4*d*., and carried it away with a horse worth 10*s*. (fine £3, and for the horse)

590   William Dunning of Purton, yeoman, (acting) through his servants (*pro familia sua*), cut down an oak, containing two tons of timber worth 10*s*. (fine 40*s*.)

591   Edmund Morgan of Littledean and Thomas Morgan his son, shovel makers, cut down a beech, [containing] three cartloads of wood and timber worth 6*s*. (fine 30*s*. each)

592   Thomas Hopkins of Littledean, labourer, cut down a beech, [containing] two cartloads of wood worth 5*s*. (fine £3)

593   Leonard Tompson alias Beare of the same, nailer, grazed (*frondit anglice browsed*) his cattle on the woodland and on holly wood, with loss to the king 10*s*. (fine 40*s*.)

594   Thomas Hopkins of the same, labourer, cut down a beech in a place called Staple Edge, (containing) two cartloads of wood and timber worth 8*s*. (fine 40*s*.)

595   John Chinne of Newnham, pinner, cut down the top branches of three beeches, containing four loads of wood worth 8*d*. (fine 20*s*.)

596   Daniel Morse of Mitcheldean, clothier, cut down two beeches, containing two cartloads of timber worth 3*s*. 4*d*. (fine 40*s*.)

597   John Sayer of St. White's in Flaxley, timberman, took and carried out of the Forest one load of 'scales' (*de scalis anglice scales*),[2] worth 10*s*. (fine £3)

598   John Prichard of Mitcheldean, cooper, cut down an oak, containing one ton of timber worth 4*s*. (fine 20*s*.)

[*f. 42v.*]

599   And [they present that] the several persons underwritten on various days and at various times between 13 May 1633 and 24 April 1634 made waste in the king's demesne land of the Forest by cutting down, felling, and 'girding' beeches, oaks, hollies,

---

[1] See above, p. 85*n*.
[2] See above, p. 86*n*.

and crab trees of the king's wood and vert, and carried away the wood and converted it to their own use, to the king's damage, as follows:

600   William Martin of Ruardean, labourer, cut down the top branches of an oak, (containing) four loads of wood worth 4*d.* (fine 20*s.*)

601   Robert Lewellyn of the same, timberman, cut down one load of beech wood worth 12*d.* (fine 20*s.*)

602   John Jefferyes of Parkend, labourer, 'girded' an oak, containing five loads of wood worth 12*d.* (fine 20*s.*)

603   John, the servant of John Peckover of Clearwell, collier, 'girded' the top branches of two oaks, containing 12 loads of wood worth 2*s.* (fine 30*s.*)

604   John Prichard of Mitcheldean, cooper, cut down an oak, containing ¾ ton of timber worth 3*s.* (fine 20*s.*)

605   George Barnewoode of Mitcheldean, shoemaker, cut down an oak, containing one ton of timber worth 5*s.*, and carried it away with a horse worth 20*s.* (fine 40*s.*, and for the horse)

606   John Gwillim of Flaxley, cardboard maker, cut down a beech, containing ½ ton of timber worth 2*s.* 6*d.* (fine 20*s.*)

607   Anthony Grove of Littledean. labourer, cut down a marked oak, containing ½ ton of timber worth 3*s.* 4*d.* (fine £3)

[*f. 43*]

608   Philip Edwards of Awre, cardboard maker, Henry Humfrey of the same, cardboard maker, and Christopher Browne of the same, husbandman, cut down a marked beech, containing one ton of timber worth 5*s.* (fine 20*s.* each)

609   William Davis of *Rawlins lease*,[1] husbandman, cut down hawthorns and hollies from the king's underwood, containing one cartload of wood worth 2*s.*, which they carried away with a cart and four oxen worth 40*s.* (fine £5, and for the oxen)

610   John Rudge of Rudge in Weston [under Penyard],[2] husbandman, cut down a beech containing ½ ton of timber worth 2*s.*, hauling it away with four oxen worth £5. (fine 40*s.*, and for the oxen)

611   Thomas Floyde of Ruardean, sawyer, hauled a cartload of planks, worth 6*s.* 8*d.*, out of the Forest into Herefordshire with John Bennett's cart and six oxen, worth £4. (fine 5 marks, and for the oxen)

612   Thomas Jones of Newland, labourer, on 24 April 1634 cut down two oaks, containing six cartloads of wood worth 15*s.* (fine £10)

613   The said Thomas Jones cut down the trunk of an oak, containing two cartloads of wood worth 5*s.* (fine £3)

614   Eleanor Pullen of Cannop cut down hawthorns, containing two loads of wood worth 12*d.* (fine 10*s.*)

615   Edward Reynolds of Whitecliff, labourer, cut down an oak, [containing] one cartload of wood worth 2*s.* 6*d.* (fine £3)

---

[1] See above, p. 87*n.*

[2] Identified as in Gloucestershire in MS.: see above, p. 85*n.*

616   Stephen Watkins of Ruardean, collier, on 4 July 1633 cut down a marked beech, containing 1½ cords of wood worth 5*s*. (fine £5)

617   Francis Mason of Blakeney, cabiner, cut down a marked beech, containing two cords of wood worth 6*s*. 8*d*. (fine £3)

[*f. 43v.*]

618   William Davys of the Forest, cabiner, cut down 1½ cords of wood worth 5*s*. (fine £3)

619   John Springe of *Thornehille*,[1] collier, cut down a marked beech, containing 1½ cords of wood worth 5*s*. (fine £3)

620   Thomas Pinnock of Aylburton, labourer, and Edward Cole of the same on 10 June 1634 cut down the top branches of a beech, containing 1½ cords of wood worth 5*s*. (fine 20*s*. each)

621   The said Edward Cole on the same day cut down the top branches of a beech, containing one cord of wood worth 3*s*. 4*d*. (fine 40*s*.)

622   Richard Jones of the same, husbandman, cut down the top branches of a beech, containing three loads of wood worth 3*d*. (fine 20*s*.)

623   The said Thomas Cole(*sic*) on 10 Dec. 1633 cut down the top branches of a beech, [containing] three loads of wood worth 3*d*. (fine 20*s*.)

624   Edward Baddam of Blakeney, labourer, on the same day cut down the top branches of a beech, containing two loads of wood worth 2*d*. (fine 20*s*.)

625   George Linch of Ruardean, labourer, cut down a beech, containing one cord of wood worth 3*s*. 4*d*. (fine 40*s*.)

626   Edward Reynoldes of Coleford on 10 June 1634 cut down the trunk of an oak, containing one cartload of wood worth 12*d*. (fine 40*s*.)

626 (*number repeated*) Thomas Hope of Aylburton, labourer, [is presented] for that a certain John Pynnocke, his servant, cut down several branches from a beech, containing two loads of wood worth 4*d*. (fine 20*s*.)

[*f. 44*]

626 (*number repeated*) Thomas Jones of the Forest, labourer, cut down two oak trunks, containing three cartloads of wood worth 3*s*. (fine £5)

627   Philip James and John Williams, [both] of Parkend, woodcutters, cut down 20 holly trees (*arbores anglice hollies*), containing 20 loads of wood worth 10*s*. (fine £3 each)

628   Richard Williams of the same, woodcutter, similarly cut down 10 hollies worth 5*s*. (fine £3)

629   Morgan James and Peter Beach, [both] of the same, labourers, with a certain stranger (*peregrino*) employed by them (*per ipsos mercinato anglice hered*), cut down 16 hollies worth 6*s*. (fine 40*s*. each)

630   Henry Gammon of Newnham, shoemaker, on 20 June – [*date not completed*] cut three loads of holly from the underwood, worth 18*d*. (fine 40*s*.)

631   William Browne of Ruddle, labourer, cut down an oak, containing four loads of wood worth 12*d*. (fine 40*s*.) [*item crossed through and note added:* fine paid to Thomas Leake, esq., the receiver]

---

[1] See above, p. 68*n*.

632   James Witts of Ruddle, labourer, took and carried away one load of timber worth 6d. (fine 40s.)

633   John Somner of Mitcheldean, labourer, cut down the top branches of a beech, containing one load of wood worth 3d. (fine 20s.)

634   John Gosling and John Bretherton, [both] of Parkend, labourers, cut down a marked beech, containing three cords of wood worth 6s. 8d. (fine 40s. each)

635   Richard Bleeke of Parkend, labourer, cut down two marked beeches, [containing] three tons of timber worth 20s. (fine 20 nobles)

636   John Evans of Ruardean, labourer, cut down an oak and a beech, containing four cords of wood[1] worth 26s. 8d. (fine £5)

[*f. 44v.*]

637   James Watkins of Ruardean, labourer, cut down four marked beeches, containing four tons of timber, worth 26s. 8d. (fine £5)

638   William Phellps of Cleeve in Ross-on-Wye (Herefs.), yeoman, cut down a yew (*yudre*), containing 12 tons of wood and timber worth 16s., and carried it away with six oxen worth £6. (fine £10, and for the oxen)

639   Richard Vaughan of Abenhall, husbandman, and William Vaughan of Mitcheldean cut down an oak, containing one ton of timber worth 5s. (fine 30s. each)

640   The said William Vaughan cut down an oak, containing one ton of timber worth 5s. (fine 40s.)

641   William Dowse of Ruardean, husbandman, on the same day cut down an oak, [containing] one ton worth 5s. (fine 2s., on account of his poverty)

642   William Whetson of Littledean, labourer, cut down an oak, containing ½ ton of timber worth 12d. (fine 30s.)

643   William Parlor of English Bicknor, yeoman, cut down a beech, containing one ton worth 4s. (fine 40s.)

644   Thomas Swayne of Littledean, carpenter, on the same day cut down four oaks, containing 14 tons of timber, each ton worth 5s. (fine £20)

645   The same Thomas Swayne cut down seven oaks, containing 30 tons, each ton worth 5s. (fine £40)

646   Richard Vaughton of Purton's Purlieu (*Purley*), labourer, cut down an oak, containing five tons, each ton worth 5s. (fine £5)

[*f. 45*]

647   Edmund Harris of Clearwell, labourer, with others unknown, cut down and cleft (*scinderunt*) 10 cords, each cord worth 2s. 6d. (fine £5)

648   Edward Worgan of Coleford, labourer, cut down a beech, containing one cartload of wood worth 3s. 4d. (fine £3)

649   Henry Bushe, servant of John Duncombe of London, gent., sold to Thomas Halle of Littledean the bark of 12 oaks, which oaks contained 18 tons of timber, each ton worth 5s.; and Thomas stripped (*expallivit anglice stripped*) the oaks and bark and converted them to his own use. (fine £5)

---

[1] In MS. replaces 'four tons of timber'.

650   The said John Duncombe and [*blank*] Dirham, his servant, stripped the bark of 20 marked oaks, containing 50 tons [worth] 5s. [each], and took the bark and converted it to Duncombe's use; and afterwards, on 25 June 1634, the said oaks were cut down and converted into charcoal. (fine £100)

651   Thomas Phillipps of the same(*sic*), timberman, cut down two tons of timber, each ton worth 5s. (fine £13 6s. 8d.)

652   Thomas Phillipps of *Quickslade* in the Forest, wood corder, cut down an oak, containing two tons of timber, each ton worth 5s. (fine £13 6s. 8d.)

653   James Tims, servant of William Morse of Clearwell, yeoman, cut down the top branches of a marked oak, containing four loads of wood worth 7d. (fine 40s.)

654   Henry Hulinge of Stowe, yeoman, cut down a beech, containing two cartloads of wood worth 5s. (fine £5)

[*f. 45v.*]

655   John Tayler of Clearwell, carpenter, cut down a marked oak, containing four tons of timber, each ton worth 6s. 8d. (fine £20)

656   Edward Reynolds and Richard Hawkins, [both] of Whitecliff, labourers, cut down two oaks, containing eight tons of timber, each ton worth 5s. *(*fine £8 6s. 8d. each)

657   The said Edward Reynolds cut down the top branches of an oak, [containing] two loads of wood worth 4d. (fine 20s.)

658   Richard Pullin of Purton's Purlieu (*Purley*), labourer, cut down one ton of timber worth 5s., and converted the wood and timber into treenails (*ad clavos ligneos anglice tre nayle pins*). (fine £5)

659   Philip James and John Williams, [both] of Parkend, labourers, on the same day cut down two oaks, containing six tons of timber, each ton worth 5s. (fine £13 6s. 8d. each)

660   John Prosser of the same, labourer, on th same day cut down an oak, containing two tons of timber, each ton worth 5s. (fine £5)

661   John Dobbes of the same, labourer, and his servants (*eius famulie*) cut down an oak, containing 12 loads of wood worth 2s., and converted it to the use of Dobbes. (fine 40s.)

662   John Homes and George Turner, [both] of Blackwell Meadows in Mitcheldean, labourers, at various times between 1 April 1632 and 30 April 1634 in places called (?*Harolds*) *Eves*, *Ravensford*, and *Goyrooke*[1] cut down 40 stub oaks (*truncos quercos anglice stubb oakes*), each worth 2s. 6d., and converted the timber and wood to their own uses. (fine £50 each)

[*f. 46*]

663   John Veare of Littledean, woodcutter, within the same period at Little Staple Edge cut down five oaks and 'girded' two others, worth £3 2s. 6d. (fine £5)

664   Rowland Millard of Blakeney, collier, within the same period cut down two oaks and eight beeches at Blakeney's Eaves, each worth 13s. 4d. (fine £80)

---

[1] On a plan of *c.* 1680 Ravensford is marked by the Dry brook north of Nailbridge and the other two places mentioned are perhaps represented by 'Harwood Eves' and 'Gorbrook' shown in the same area: TNA, F 17/7.

665   the said Rowland Millard, Luke Pullen of Ruardean, corder, and Francis Reade of Littledean, corder, within the same period cut down divers oaks and beeches, with loss to the king £60. (Millard's fine £400, and the other two £200 each)

666   Michael Robins of Ruardean, labourer, and Richard Allam of the same within the same period cut down an oak and a beech near Staple Edge, each worth 5*s*. (fine £10 each)

667   Charles Driver of Westbury [on Severn], gent., took and carried out of the Forest three tons of crooked ship's timber, each ton worth 6*s*. 8*d*. (fine 6*s*. 8*d*.)

668   Francis Bridgeman of Blakeney between 1 April 1631 and 30 April 1634 cut down divers oaks and beeches, with loss to the king £200. (fine £2,400) [*item crossed through and note added:* fine, reduced by petition to £50, paid to Thomas Leake, esquire, the receiver]

669   William Jones of Nass, gent., within the same period took and carried out of the Forest two tons of beech timber, each [ton] worth 3*s*. 4*d*. (fine £20)

670   the said Rowland Millard between (*sic*) 1 April 1634 cut down two oaks and 28 beeches, each worth 6*s*. 8*d*., at Blakeney's Eaves. (fine £130)

Woods Felled within the Perambulation of the Forest

It is presented by the foresters, regarders, jury of twelve, and the verderers that:[1]

671   Henry Mayle, late of Bledisloe, yeoman, deceased, within the last 30 years cut down a grove called *Wilseys More*, containing 4 a. worth £4, in the fee of Joan Vaughan, widow, and now or late in the occupation of John Hille. (fine £6 13*s*. 4*d*.)

672   John Hill, late of Newnham, gent., deceased, within the last six years cut down a grove, containing 2 a., in the fee of Richard Hill, gent., and now or late in the tenure of William Latham. (fine £6 13*s*. 4*d*.)

673   The said John within the last 12 years cut down another grove, containing 2 a. worth 40*s*., now in the possession of the said Richard, his son and heir. (fine £6 13*s*. 4*d*.)

674   The said Richard Hill within the last year cut down a grove, containing 1 a. worth 20*s*., in his fee; all the three groves lie within the perambulation. (fine 40*s*.)

675   Richard Hooper of Awre, mariner, within the last 12 years cut down a little grove called *Jordens grove*, containing ½ a., which he now holds in the fee of Richard Jorden. (fine £10)

676   William Kingston of Flaxley, esq., at divers times, viz. each 14th year, has cut down the woods called Abbots wood and Flaxley grove, containing 60 a. of woodland worth [*blank*], now in his fee, which he formerly cut as he pleased. (fine £200)[2]

677   Henry Custans, late of Newnham, yeoman, within the last half year cut down a grove lying next to Littledean, containing 20 acres. (fine £40) [*item crossed through and note added*: fine, reduced by petition to £10, paid to Thomas Leake, esq., the receiver]

678   Benedict Hall, late of Highmeadow, esq., [*blank*] last past converted [*eversit*] a parcel of barren and thorny ground, containing 6 a., in Staunton; it is now converted to

---

[1] In this section standard phrases of the original MS, omitted are: 'lying within the perambulation (or the metes and bounds) of the Forest'; and 'by estimation' (used for the acreages given).

[2] For this case, see also above, p. 13.

arable land but is not any grove; each new acre is worth 12*d*. (fine £40) [*item crossed through and note added*: fine £10, paid to Thomas Leake, esq., the receiver]

[*f. 47*]

679   The said Benedict Hall within [*blank*] converted one parcel and cut down divers groves in the king's demesne, containing 2 a. of woodland, and within the last 20 years cut down four other little groves. (fine £40) [*item crossed through and note added:* fine paid to Thomas Leake, esq., the receiver]

680   Richard Parsons and John Pullen, late of Mitcheldean, tanners, within the last half year cut down a parcel of oak timber, containing 1½ a., growing in a grove near Mitcheldean in the demesne of Nicholas Roberts, esq. (fine £20 each)

681   John Kirle, kt. and bt., late of [Much] Marcle (Herefs.), within the last 10 years cut down a grove called Howley (*Owley*) grove,[1] containing 12 a., in the demesne of the said Nicholas Roberts. (fine 20 marks)

682   William Blast of Hope Mansell (Herefs.), yeoman, within [*blank*] cut down a grove, containing 9 a. worth [*blank*], lying under Lea Bailey. (fine £50)

683   Thomas Gorway of Weston [under Penyard] (Herefs.), yeoman, within the last five years cut down a grove, containing [*blank*] worth [*blank*], lying under Lea Bailey in the demesne of John Joulding. (fine £10)

684   Christopher Bellamy, late of Westbury [-on- Severn], tanner, lately cut down a grove, containing 11 a., each acre worth [*blank*], lying next Chestnuts; he holds it of the said Nicholas Roberts. (fine 5 marks) [*item crossed through and note added*: fine paid to Thomas Leake, esq., the receiver]

685   John Kirle within [*blank*] cut down a grove, containing 12 a. worth [*blank*], lying next Lea Bailey; the said Nicholas Roberts now holds it as his demesne. [*note added*: he is pardoned, as before]

686   John Wintour, late of Lydney, kt., within [*blank*] cut down a grove or wood in his park (*septum anglice parke*), containing 4 a. worth [*blank*]. (fine 20*s*.)

687   Richard Catchmay of Bigswear, kt., within [*blank*] cut down a grove called *Wyes Hills grove*, containing 12 a. worth [*blank*], which Baynham Throckmorton, kt. and bt., holds in his demesne. (fine 40*s*.) [*item crossed through and note added*: fine, reduced to 26*s*. 8*d*., paid to Thomas Leake, esq., the receiver]

[*f. 47v.*]

688   The same Richard Catchmay within the last four years cut down a grove called *Moone grove,* containing 3 a. worth [*blank*], in his demesne. (fine 10*s*.) [*item crossed through and note added*: fine, reduced to 6*s*. 8*d*., paid to Thomas Leake, esq., the receiver]

689   Eleanor James, widow, within [*blank*] cut down two two little groves, containing 3 a. worth [*blank*], lying in Newland parish next to Wood mill (*Wodmyll*)[2]. (fine 5*s*.)

690   The said Richard Catchmay, kt., within [*blank*] cut down a grove, containing 3 a., which he holds in demesne, lying near his dwelling house. (fine 5*s*.) [*item crossed through and note added*: fine paid to Thomas Leake, esq., the receiver]

---

[1] The grove, north of Mitcheldean, was a detached part of Newland parish: *VCH Glos.* v. p. 196.
[2] The mill was at Rodmore in St. Briavels (ibid. 266); 'Newland' as the location of the groves may be an error.

Furnaces and Forges

It is presented that:

691   Richard Tyler of Goodrich (Herefs.), gent., now or late [is or] was seized or possessed of an iron forge (*fabrica ferria anglice oon iron forge*) situated at Lydbrook[1] within the Forest perambulation, built within the last 13 years or more. (fine £100) [*item crossed through and note added*: fine, reduced by warrant to £30, paid to Thomas Leake, etc.]

692   George Vaughan, late of the city of London, gent., was lately seized or possessed of an iron forge situated at Lydbrook, built or established within the last 44 years. (fine £100)

693   Benedict Hall, late of Highmeadow, esq., now or late [is or] was seized or possessed of an iron forge situated at Lydbrook, now or late in the tenure of John Lewes, established within the last 44 years. (fine £100) [*item crossed through and note added*: fine paid to Thomas Leake, esq., etc.]

694   The lord king was seized of an iron forge situated in a place called Howbrook (*Holbrooke*)[2] within his demesne, established within the last 44 years at his own expense (*propriis pecuniis suis*). [*nos. 694 to 698 have the marginal note*: dominus rex]

695   The lord king was seized of another iron forge and an iron furnace situated at Soudley within his demesne, established within the last 21 years at his own expense.

696   The lord king was seized of a double iron forge situated at Bradley within his demesne, established by Basil Brook, kt., and George Myn, esq., within the last five years.

[*f. 48*]

697   The lord king is now seized in demesne of another furnace and a double iron forge, called [Whitecroft][3] forge, established within the last five years and situated at a place in the Forest called the Park.

698   The lord king is now seized in demesne of another double iron forge, established within the last five years at a place in the Forest called Whitecroft forge.

699   John Wintour, late of Lydney, kt., now or late is [or was] seized of an iron furnace, built within the last nine years at a place called Gunn's mill[4] within the demesne of the Forest. (fine £400)

699 (*number repeated*) The same John Wyntour holds or occupies another iron furnace and an iron forge, built within the last five years next to Lydney, within Newland parish[5] and within the Forest perambulation. (fine £200)

700   The same John Wyntour now or late holds or occupies an iron forge called a slitting mill, built within the last five years in the king's demesne near and adjoining the aforesaid furnace. (fine £100).

701   The same John Wyntour now or late is [or was] seized of a double iron forge, [established] within the last five years outside the king's demesne and also outside the Forest perambulation. (*marginal note*: respited)

---

[1] For the Lydbrook forges, *VCH Glos*. v. p. 341.
[2] For the king's ironworks, Hart, *Ind. Hist. of Dean*, pp. 8–13.
[3] *sic* but apparently in error for 'Whitemead'.
[4] See *VCH Glos*. v. p. 97.
[5] For Winter's Lydney iron works, Hart, *Ind. Hist. of Dean*, pp. 44–5.

702 The heir of Edward James, late of Lydney, is seized of an iron furnace, now or late in the tenure of the said John Wyntour, kt., built about five years ago in St. Briavels parish[1] within the Forest perambulation. (fine £100)

703 Benedict Hall now or late holds [or held] an iron furnace, built about 20 years ago in the lordship of Staunton[2] within the Forest perambulation. (fine £300) [*item crossed through and note added*: fine, afterwards by warrant £150, paid to Thomas Leake, etc.)

704 The same Benedict Hall now or late [is or] was seized of another iron furnace,[3] [established] within the last five years within the Forest perambulation. (fine £300) [*item crossed through and note added*: fine, afterwards by warrant £150, paid to Thomas Leake, etc.]

705 William Kingston, late of Flaxley, esq., now holds or occupies two separate iron forges; one, built within the last three years, he enjoys (*gaudet*) within his fee and the other, built within the last seven years,[4] lies upon the furthest metes and bounds of the Forest. (fine £200)

706 Richard Catchmay, kt., holds an iron furnace, established within the last four years in his demesne[5] and within the Forest perambulation. (fine 100 marks) [*item crossed through and note added*: fine, reduced by petition to 20 marks, paid to Thomas Leake, esq., the receiver]

[*f. 48v.*]

[*no heading given*]

It is presented that:

707 William Donning, late of Purton, yeoman, within the last 17 years purchased and took 80 tons of timber, each ton worth 6*s*. 8*d*., in the king's demesne and the Forest perambulation. (fine £200, and the value, etc.)

708 George Donning of the Wellhouse[6] within the last 17 years purchased and took 70 tons of timber, each ton worth 6*s*. 8*d*., in the king's demesne of his Forest. (fine £150)

709 John White of Blakeney, ship carpenter, within the last 16 years purchased and took 25 tons of timber, each ton worth 6*s*. 8*d*., in the king's demesne of his Forest. (fine £100) [*item crossed through and note added*: fine, afterwards by petition £10, paid to Thomas Leake, esq., the receiver]

710 Thomas A Deane of Etloe, yeoman, within the last four years purchased and took from the king's officers 20 tons of timber in the king's demesne in the Forest, each ton worth 6*s*. 8*d*. (fine £40, and the value, etc.)

711 William Norton of [English] Bicknor, labourer, within the last three years burnt 10 a. of the cover (*cooperti anglice covert*) in a place called Hangerberry in the king's demesne in the Forest and within the perambulation. (fine £200)

---

[1] This was on the James family's estate at Rodmore in St. Briavels parish: *VCH Glos.* v. pp. 261, 266.

[2] At Knockalls hill above Upper Redbrook: *VCH Glos.* v. p. 217.

[3] Apparently at Upper Redbrook: ibid. p. 218.

[4] Both apparently on Kingston's Flaxley estate: ibid. p. 146.

[5] On his estate at Bigswear in St. Briavels: see below, p. 150 (no. 3).

[6] At Purton in Lydney parish: *VCH Glos.* v. p. 67. In a report of 1633 Donning was described as 'an old experienced ship-timber man': *Cal.S.P.Dom.*1633–4, p. 191.

712   John Dobbes of the Park within the last seven years dug a great ditch, one mile in length, in a certain 'land' (*laundam*) called Phelps mead[1] and in other 'lands' of the Forest, to the harm of the deer (*ferarum*) and to the danger of the king's subjects walking or riding there. (fine 40*s.*)

Dogs

713   It is presented that there are many mastiffs (*igolossi anglice mastives*) with other dogs within the Forest perambulation, but none are 'hambled' (*expeditati*) as they were accustomed to be from time immemorial. (fine £5 from each verderer for an insufficient presentment)[2]

Deer-Leaps (*de saltariis*)

714   It is presented that there are two deer-leaps in the inclosure (*clausulo*) or park of John Wintour, kt.; one of the leaps is within the Forest perambulation and the other outside.[3] (fine £10; the park is forfeited, etc.)

[no heading given]

715   It is presented that rents belonging to the king's castle of his manor of St. Briavels and his rents of agistment, herbage, and pannage within the Forest are collected and received annually by Richard Catchmay of Bigsweir, kt. (*marginal note*: by grant of William, late earl of Pembroke)[4]

[f. 49]

Fisheries

It is presented that:

716   Anthony Williams, late of Westbury [-on-Severn], yeoman, on 4 June 1634 fished in the king's water of his Forest in a place called Walmore[5] and took several fish, worth 2*s.* and did there as he wished. (fine £5)

717   John Coslet, William Morrell, and James Olliver, late of Bradley forge in the Forest, forgemen, on 6 June 1634 fished in the king's water in a place near Ayleford (*Arleyfford*). (fine 40*s.* each)

718   Richard Games the younger, late of Allaston in Lydney parish, tiler, and George Brayne, late of Badhamsfield quarry in Newland parish,[6] labourer, on 23 May 1634 fished in the king's water called Blackpool, near Moseley green within the Forest. (fine 40*s.* each)

719   John Harris of Hall mill, in Awre parish, on various days and times between 20 December 1633 and 20 June 1634 fished in the king's water of his Forest at Hall mill and took several fish, worth 12*d.*, and did there as he wished. (fine £3)

---

[1] By Blackpool brook, south of Saintlow Inclosure: Atkinson, *Plan of Forest of Dean.*
[2] For this matter, see below, p. 105.
[3] At Lydney where Winter's park evidently included land in the adjoining Bream tithing of Newland, within the Forest bounds as then constituted: *VCH Glos.* v. p. 50.
[4] The earl granted these and other assets of the St. Briavels castle estate to Catchmay in 1612: TNA, C99/36; *VCH Glos.* v. p. 256.
[5] A detached part of the demesne, within Westbury parish.
[6] Badhamsfield was a detached part of Newland in the Yorkley area.

[no heading given]

720   John Vast, late of the Park forge in the Forest, labourer, during the last four years kept five horses and other beasts (*averia anglice beasts*) pasturing in the king's demesne of his Forest without any warrant. (fine £5)

721   William Nurton of English Bicknor, carpenter, during the last four years had four horses and mares pasturing in the king's demesne of his Forest without any warrant. (fine £5)

722   William Morgan, late of Cannop in the Forest, labourer, during the last four years kept five horses and mares pasturing in the king's demesne without any warrant. (fine £6 13s. 4d.)

723   James Haller, late of *Ashe* (Herefs.), husbandman, during the last four years had four bullocks, six sheep, one cow, and three other beasts pasturing in the king's demesne of his Forest without any warrant. (fine £10)

724   Leonard Tompson alias Beare of Littledean, nailer, during the last seven years kept 12 horses and mares pasturing in the king's demesne of his Forest without any warrant. (fine £20)

[f. 49v.]

725   William Hale of the same, nailer, during the last seven years kept 12 horses and mares pasturing in the king's demesne of his Forest without any warrant. (fine £20)

726   The said Leonard Tompson alias Beare during the last seven years kept 20 pigs pasturing in the king's demesne of his Forest without any warrant. (fine £10)

Hunting (*de venatione*)

It is presented that:[1]

727   Thomas Kingston, late of Flaxley, gent., on 20 November 1633 entered the Forest and hunted the king's does with greyhounds at a place near *le Damme*,[2] and he killed and butchered one doe and carried away the meat at will (*ad voluntatem suam*). (fine £100)

728   The said Thomas Kingston and Charles Kingston, late of Flaxley, gent., on 23 November 1633 entered the Forest and hunted the king's does with two greyhounds. (fine £100 each)[3]

729   The said Charles and Thomas Kingston on 22 December 1633 entered the Forest and killed and butchered a doe and took the meat and carried it away at will. (fine £100 each)

730   Thomas Trehearne, late of Newland parish, millward, on 25 April 1633 entered the Forest and hunted a doe, called a 'soaken' doe,[4] with greyhounds. (fine £50)

---

[1] In this section the phrase 'to the king's loss', which appears in almost all the presentments, has been omitted; also, the marginal note *def' fac' cap'*, perhaps for 'he makes default and is to be arrested', which appears beside almost all. The phrase *trucidavit et occidit*, used in most cases of deer killing, has been rendered, in a more logical order, as 'killed and butchered'.

[2] Perhaps the place later called Dam pool, north-west of Cinderford: Atkinson, *Plan of Forest of Dean*.

[3] For this case, see also above, p. 7.

[4] A barren doe: *OED*, s.v. soaking.

731   Thomas Cole, late of Newland parish, miner, on 26 April 1633 entered the Forest and hunted a doe, called a 'soaken' doe, with greyhounds. (fine £50)

732   John Hamblin, late of Elton, gent., on 10 July 1633 entered the Forest and was found at a place called Blackpennywall with a gun (*cum tormento anglice a gunne*). (fine £10; the gun to be seized)

[*f. 50*]

733   The said Charles Kingston and Thomas Kingston, gents., in December 1633 entered the Forest and hunted the king's bucks and does, to the [king's] loss £10. (fine £100 each)

734   The said Charles Kingston on 18 January 1634 entered the Forest and killed a doe with a greyhound and butchered it, and took the meat and carried it away at will. (fine £200)

735   Charles Kingston on 24 October 1633 entered the Forest and killed and butchered a doe at a place called Cannop meadow, and took the meat and carried it away at will. (fine £200)

736   Charles Woodhouse, late of Westbury [-on-Severn], labourer, and John Cadell, late of Blaisdon, labourer, on 15 February 1634 entered the Forest and were found at a place called Haywood (*Aywood*) hunting bucks and does with two guns. (fine £40 each).

737   The said Charles Kingston on 16 November 1633 entered the Forest and hunted the king's bucks and does with greyhounds at a place called *Lanards hill*,[1] and he killed and butchered a doe and took the meat and carried it away at will. (fine £100)

738   John Sare, late of Flaxley, 'scalemaker',[2] on 13 April 1633 was found in the Forest with a gun. (fine £20; the gun to be seized)

739   The said Charles Kingston on 29 December 1633 entered the Forest and was found with a gun, which he fired (*exoneravit anglice did dischardge*). (fine £100)

740   Thomas Gowghe, late of English Bicknor, and Geoffrey (*Jefferidus*) Mayo, late of the same, clerk, with a certain servant of Geoffrey, on 22 December 1633 entered the Forest and were found at a place called Great Kensley (*Kenslow*) hunting the king's bucks and does with greyhounds. (fine £100 each)

741   William Worgan, late of Coleford, miner, on 2 April 1633 entered the Forest and killed a 'pricket'[3] with a gun at a place called Winnalls (*le Winnolls*), and butchered it and took the meat and carried it away at will. (fine £50; the gun to be seized)

742   William Worgan on 6 April 1633 was found in the Forest with a gun. (fine £20)

[*f. 50v.*]

743   The said William Worgan, on 24 May 1633 was found in the Forest with a gun. (fine £20)

744   The said William Worgan, Giles Webbe, late of Coleford, miner, John Goodwyn, late of the same, miner, and Henry Smith, late of the same, nailer, on 10 January 1633 entered the Forest and were found at Wet wood with a gun near (*erga*) the king's bucks and does. (fine £10 each; the gun to be seized)

---

[1] Perhaps Lennetshill, west of Bilson Green.

[2] See above, p. 86*n*.

[3] A buck in its second year: *Manwood's Forest Laws*, ed. Nelson, p. 48.

745   Drew Turcke, late of Parkend, forgeman , and with him two others unknown, on 20 April 1632 entered the Forest and were found at Stone Edge with a gun and a hunting dog (*cane investigario anglice a hounde*). (fine £50; the gun to be seized)

746   George Williams, late of Soudley, labourer, on the same day entered the Forest and was found at a place called Beechenhurst meadow hunting the king's bucks and does with a crossbow (*arcubalista anglice a crossebowe*). (fine £40; the crossbow to be seized)

747   William Worgan, late of Coleford, miner, on 28 January 1633 was found in the Forest with a gun. (fine £40)

748   Hugh Jones, Richard Tomkins, John Walkins, and Walter Jones, late of the same, woodcutters, on 16 October 1632, being at a place called Howlers (*Howley*) Slade in the Forest, killed and butchered a 'sorell' deer and took the meat and carried it away at will. (fine £20 each)

749   John Gardiner, late of [English] Bicknor, yeoman, and a certain stranger (*peregrinus*), on 23 May 1634 entered the Forest and killed and butchered a doe, and took the meat and carried it away at will. (fine £100)

750   Thomas Wirrall, late of Eastbach (*Eastpadge*) in [English] Bicknor parish, gent., on 4 April 1634 entered the Forest and at a place called Serridge after sunset fired a gun, which he then possessed, close to the king's bucks and does. (fine £20; the gun to be seized; he is committed)

751   James Roberts, late of Welsh Newton (Mon.), carpenter, and Philip Mason, late of Whitchurch (Herefs.), husbandman, on 22 April 1632 entered the Forest and killed a doe with a gun, and butchered it and took the meat and carried it away at will. (fine £40 each; the gun to be seized)

[*f. 51*]

752   Richard Howell, late of Clearwell, timberman, on 1 May 1634 had a gun and a greyhound in his house at Clearwell in the Forest. (fine £20; the gun and dog to be seized)

753   Widow Bande, late of the same, on the same day had a gun in her house at Clearwell within the perambulation of the Forest. (fine £5; the gun to be seized)

754   William Gough, late of [English] Bicknor, gent., on the same day kept greyhounds and hunting dogs (*canes leporarios et venaticos*) in the Forest. (fine; £40; [the dogs] to be seized)

755   John Davis, late of Parkend, timberman, on 31 March 1634 had a gun in his cottage at Parkend in the Forest. (fine £10; [the gun] to be seized)

756   Charles Kingston, late of Flaxley, gent., on 1 March 1628 was found in the Forest with a gun. (fine £50; the gun to be seized)

757   James Davis, late of Lea (Glos.), on 16 December 1628 was found in the Forest with a gun. (fine £20; [the gun] to be seized)

758   Edward Hodges, late of Elton in Westbury [-on-Severn] parish, Richard Hodges, late of Broadoak in the same parish, and Thomas Dawe, late of Longhope, labourers, on 2 January 1629 were found in the Forest with a gun. (fine £40 each; the gun to be seized)

759   John Cowsham, late of Aston [Ingham] (Herefs.), yeoman, on the same day entered the Forest with a gun, killed and butchered a doe, and took the meat and carried it away at will. (fine £100; the gun to be seized)

760   Richard Hannis, late of Mitcheldean, labourer, and Clement Dabbs, late of Longhope, yeoman, on the same day were found in the Forest with a crossbow, primed (*prompta*) and with an arrow in it. (fine £40 each; the crossbow to be seized)

761   Thomas Hobby, late of Longhope, tanner, on 15 September 1632 was found in the Forest with a gun. (fine £200; the gun to be seized)

762   Edward Hodges, late of Elton, tailor, on 1 January 1633 was found to have venison, two deer-skins, and a gun in his house at Elton. (fine £50; the gun to be seized)

[f. *51v.*]

763   William Conehill, late of *Harseberry*, labourer, on 1 September 1632 was found in the Forest carrying away a doe. (fine £60; memo. the value of the horse)

764   Nicholas Whittson, late of Littledean, nailer, on the same day was found in the Forest with a bow and arrows. (fine £30)

765   Walter Howell, late of Bream, collier, on the same day and on various other days during the last two years sold venison in the Forest. (fine £40)

766   Philip Ellis, late of Parkend, carpenter, on the same day was found in the Forest with a gun. (fine £100; the gun to be seized)

767   Thomas Thomas, late of Littledean, gent., on 10 July 1632 was found in the Forest with a crossbow, primed and with an arrow in it. (fine £40; the bow to be seized)

768   William Birch, late of the Forest, labourer, on the same day was found in the Forest carrying a doe on his back. (fine £40)

769   William Worgan, late of Coleford, miner, on 30 June 1633 was found in the Forest with a gun. (fine £20; the gun to be seized)

770   Robert Willmotts, late of Ruddle, carpenter, on 31 May 1634 was found in the Forest with a gun. (fine £20; the gun to be seized)

771   George Wintour, and Edward A Deane, late of Allaston, in Lydney parish, labourers, on 31 August 1631 entered the Forest with a gun. (fine £10 each)

772   Richard Chynne, late of Newnham, yeoman, on the same day entered the Forest with a gun. (fine £20)

773   John Gaynsford, late of Blakeney, gent., and another unknown person, on 1 August 1632 entered the Forest with a gun. (fine £20)

[*f. 52*]

774   Philip Lewys, late of Ruardean, glover, on 10 November 1630 entered the Forest with a gun. (fine £20)

775   Names of those who hunted in the lord king's Forest during the last four years but by what warrant is not known (*all bracketed as fined £10*):

Baynham Throckmorton, bt. (respited)

John Winter, kt. (fine by agreement £10)

William Howard, kt.

Edward Bainton, kt.

Benedict Hall, esq. (fine, by consent £10, paid to Thomas Leake, esq.)[1]

William Winter, late of Coleford, esq. (dead)

William Huntley, late of Frocester, esq. (dead)

Alexander Baineham, esq. (dead)

775 (*number repeated*) William Worgan and Henry Smith, late of Coleford, miners, on 9 December 1630 were found in the Forest with a gun. (fine £10 each; [the gun] to be seized)

776   Christopher Dowle, late of Coxbury[2], labourer, on 31 October 1627 was found in the Forest with a gun. (fine £10; [the gun] to be seized)

777   William Mason, late of [English] Bicknor, husbandman, and John Mason, late of Whitchurch (Herefs.), yeoman, on 3 November 1632 entered the Forest and killed and butchered a doe, and took the meat and carried it away at will. (fine £40 each)

[*f. 52v.*]

778   Henry Morgan and Richard Yearsley, late of Coleford, labourers, on the same day entered the Forest and killed and butchered a doe, and took the meat and carried it away at will. (fine £40 each)

779   William Cornehill and Henry Bishop, late of Huntley, labourers, on various days between 1 July 1628 and 30 April 1634 entered the Forest and killed several does with a gun, and butchered them and took the meat and carried it away at will. (fine £100 each)

780   Edward Hodges, late of Flaxley, tailor, on 14 March 1632 entered the Forest and killed and butchered a doe, and took the meat and carried it away at will. (fine £50)

781   William Jennings the younger, Anthony Sampson, Richard Hannys, and Christopher Hodges, all late of Mitcheldean, labourers, on 4 March 1629 entered the Forest and hunted does with guns and bows. (fine £20 each)

782   Richard Collyns, late of Lea (Glos.), one of the deputy foresters-in-fee of the Forest, on 10 August 1632 entered the Forest and, without any warrant, killed a doe with a gun, and butchered it and took the meat and carried it away at will. (fine £100)

783   John Meeke, late of Weston under Penyard (Herefs.), labourer, on 7 August 1631 entered the Forest at a place called Lea Bailey, killed a buck with a gun, and butchered it and took the meat and carried it away at will. (fine £60)

784   Charles Kingston, Edmund Kingston, and Thomas Kingston, late of Flaxley, gents., on 6 December 1633 entered the Forest and hunted the king's does with guns and greyhounds, and killed and butchered one and took the meat and carried it away at will. (fine £50 each)

785   John Hodges, late of Clifton,[3] gent., and John Hopkins, late of Ross [-on-Wye] (Herefs.), tailor, on 6 July 1631 entered the Forest and were found at a place called Hangerberry (?)stalking (*crepent' post*) bucks and does with a gun, loaded with two lead bullets (*duobus plumbatis anglice with a brace of loggetts*). (fine £30 each)

---

[1] For hunting foxes: see above, p. 8.

[2] A farmhouse in Newland parish, south of Redbrook.

[3] MS. *Clifton, Glos.*, so presumably this is the parish adjoining Bristol and then part of the county.

[*f. 53*]

786   Israel Atwell, late of the town of Monmouth, blacksmith, John Rawlings, late of the same, blacksmith, and Philip Mason, late of [Welsh] Newton (Mon.), husbandman, on 3 June 1631 entered the Forest, and at place called *Danyellmore* discharged a gun at bucks and does. (fine £30 each; [the gun] to be seized)

787   William Worgan, late of Coleford, miner, on 3 November 1627 entered the Forest and was found there with a gun. (fine £20)

788   John Williams, late of Lydbrook, forgeman, on the same day was found in the Forest with a hound (*venatorio anglice a hounde*) hunting a doe. (fine £30)

789   Servicens Boyse,[1] late of Littledean, labourer, on 1 December 1629 was found in possession of the venison and skins of four does in his house at Littledean. ((fine £100)

790   The said Servicens Boyse on various days and times in 1633–4[2] placed sharpened stakes and withy poles (*palulos stipites anglice sharpe stakes et salices anglice wythes*) near the Forest in order to catch and kill the king's bucks and does coming out of the Forest. (fine £100)

791   Thomas Gwillim, late of (?)*Tanhok* (Mon.), labourer, on 1 December 1629 entered the Forest and was found there with a loaded gun. (fine £20)

792   Richard Miller, late of Parkend, labourer, on 6 October 1628 was found in possession of venison from a doe at his house at Parkend. (fine £50)

[*f. 53v.*]

793   Benedict Jorden, late of [English] Bicknor, yeoman, John Jorden, late of the same, and James Sherston, late of Highmeadow, labourer, on 1 March 1634, hunted a hare in the Forest with hounds. (fine £5 each)

794   Thomas Morgan, late of Ruardean, labourer, and John Morse of the same, labourer, on the same day were found in the Forest with a gun. (fine £20 each)

795   Thomas Crooke, late of Coleford, mercer, on 1 April 1634 was found to have a gun in his possession in his house within the king's demesne of his Forest. (fine £10; [the gun] to be seized)

796   John Gardiner, late of Lydbrook, on the same day was found in possession of a gun and a hound in his house within the king's demesne of his Forest. (fine £20)

797   William Monmoth the younger, late of English Bicknor, gent., and Thomas Baker, late of *le Damme*,[3] labourer, on 10 July 1632 entered the Forest and killed a 'soarrell' buck[4] with a bow and arrows, and butchered it and took the meat and carried it away at will. (fine £20 each)

798   John Vaughan, late of Courtfield (Mon.],[5] gent., on 20 August 1630 was found in the Forest with a crossbow and arrows, and the crossbow was primed (*existentem promptam anglice bent*). (fine £10)

799   Brian Goughe, late of Mitcheldean, smith, William Read, late of the same, smith, William Stirley, late of the same, gent., George Worrall, late of the same, labourer,

---

[1] The unusual forename is given as 'Servis' above, p. 8.

[2] Dated only by regnal year (9 Chas. I).

[3] See above, p. 98*n*.

[4] A buck in its third year: *Manwood's Forest Laws*, ed. Nelson, p. 48.

[5] In Welsh Bicknor (Mon., later Herefs.).

Thomas Bainwoode, late of the same, labourer, Christopher Hodges, late of the same, labourer, and Richard Hannis, late of the same, labourer, are all poachers (*malefactores de venatione*) and together take hares and other animals in the Forest with 'hare pipes' (*leporaris*)[1] and other devices (*aliis ingeniis*). (fine £40 each)

[*f. 54*]

Names of the Regarders

Warren Gough	George Wyrall	Anthony Arnold	John A Deane
George Bond	John Jane	William Wargent	Anthony Bower
Richard Birkin	Thomas Aram	Nicholas Morse	Edmund Browne

Names of the Jurors

Thomas Morgan	William Carpender	Richard Derling	William Philpott
Arthur Ricketts	Roger Taylor	Henry Morris	William Aram
Charles Tripp	Richard Aylway	John Madocke	William Hopkins
Caleb Hulinge	John Calowe	Thomas Sellins	

[1] The word might be taken for a scribal error for *leporariis* ('greyhounds'), but see *OED*, sv. 'hare-pipe', and the mention of this offence above, at p. 8.

PRESENTMENTS OF THOSE KEEPING DOGS IN THE FOREST
(British Library, Harleian MS. 4850, ff. 60–2)

Gloucestershire, the Forest of Dean: Presentments of the Regarders made 16 July 1634 of those persons who keep dogs within the perambulation of the Forest, as follows[1]

LITTLEDEAN

1.   They present that Thomas Hall of Littledean, tanner, within the year last past kept a mastiff, not 'hambled' (*mastivum inexpeditatum*), within the Forest contrary to the forest laws and assizes. [2]

2.   Thomas Morse the elder

3.   Thomas Morse the younger

4.   Richard Brayne, gent.

5.   Richard Constable, gent.: 'a small mastiff (*parvum mastivum anglice a whelpe*)'

6.   John Swifte

7.   Leonard [Beare][3] alias Tompson

LEA

8.   Thomas Rudge of *Noke* in Lea parish

9.   Humphrey Kitton

10. Richard a Rudge

11. William Bennett

12. William Drewe

13. William Phillippes

MITCHELDEAN

14. Thomas Wade, gent.

15. John Workeman

16. Thomas Walling

17. Jasper Lugg, tanner

18. Humphrey Browne, tanner

---

[1] Under the forest law all dogs kept in the bounds of a forest were required to be 'hambled' (also known as 'lawing'), the balls of their feet being mutilated to prevent them pursuing game. This presentment was submitted during the eyre, after the judges censured the officers for an inadequate presentment at the swanimote of June 1634: see above, p. 9; p. 97 (no. 713).

[2] Subsequent entries follow (with the minor differences noted) the form given here.

[3] MS reads *Ware*, evidently a scribal error for *Beare*: see above, p. 88 (no. 593), and p. 98 (no. 724).

CLEARWELL

19. John Symonds

20. John Skyn

21. Kedgwyn Hoskyns

22. Thomas Kedgwin

23. William Bond

24. Alice Partridge, widow

25. Elizabeth Hooper, widow

FLAXLEY

26. John Nelme: 'a small mastiff'

27. Thomas Milles: 'a small mastiff'

28. John Hall

ST. BRIAVELS

29. John Hookeham, butcher: 'a small mastiff'

30. William Wargent, gent., one of the regarders of the Forest

COLEFORD BEAME[1]

31. Henry Mooreton: 'a small mastiff'

32. Thomas Yerroth, yeoman

33. John Yerroth, yeoman

34. Christopher Worgan, yeoman

35. Thomas Crucke, labourer

36. Sturly Kedgwin, miner

RUARDEAN

37. William Tutye, butcher

38. John Mutle, smith

39. Joan Vaughan, widow

40. John Rudge, labourer

41. Henry Rudge, yeoman

42. John Gwilliam, yeoman

43. Robert Cooke, victualler

ABENHALL

44. Thomas Morgan, husbandman: 'a small mastiff'

45. Richard Vaughan

---

[1] See above, p. 32*n*.

BLAKENEY

46. John Wintle, tanner

47. James Burle, tanner

48. Robert Yonge, joiner

49. Richard Vertue, joiner

50. Gough Chynn, yeoman

51. Edward Butler, yeoman

AWRE

52. Charles Trippett, gent.

53. John Bayse, yeoman

54. John Browne, yeoman

55. Thomas Browne, yeoman

56. Elizabeth Higgins, widow

57. Richard Walbrooke, husbandman

58. Joan Trippett, spinster

59. John Awre, yeoman

60. John Robbins, yeoman

61. Richard Hooper, tailor

62. Richard Driver, yeoman

63. John Hycman, yeoman

64. Morgan Griffin, yeoman

65. John Birkin, yeoman

66. Richard Browne, yeoman

(C 99/11)

no. 1 PHILIP, EARL OF PEMBROKE AND MONTGOMERY, CHAMBERLAIN OF THE KING'S HOUSEHOLD[2]

Holds the offices of constable of St. Briavels castle, keeper and warden of the Forest of Dean, and chief justice of the king's court in the Forest called the mine law court, held from time immemorial for the government of the mines of iron and coal and the workers of the same.

claims: The right to nominate and appoint seven officers under him, one of whom is called the bowbearer and should carry a bow and arrows, the other six called keepers; after swearing an oath to be good and faithful officers, they are to perambulate through the whole Forest and make attachments of vert and venison. The right to take 20*d.* from each charcoal pit (*puteo carbonis anglice colepitt*) in the Forest for every six weeks during which charcoal is made there. The right to take all ruined trees called 'moriers' in the royal demesne of the Forest.

title: By Letters Patent of 15 June 1631, granting the said offices during the king's pleasure to hold, together with the lordship and manor of Newland, in as full a manner as Edward Wintour, kt., Henry, earl of Pembroke, William, earl of Pembroke, George Baynham, kt., or William, the last earl of Pembroke, held them.[3]

no. 2 EDMUND BERROW, esquire

The manor of Blakeney; and the bailiwick of Blakeney belonging to said manor, with the office of bailiff and woodward and with two woodwards under him for keeping the said bailiwick.

claims: By right of the said manor he claims: court of view of frankpledge held for residents of the manor twice a year, viz. within a month after Easter and within a month after Michaelmas, before the steward of the manor, with all amercements and profits of the same court; goods and chattels called waifs and strays in the manor; common of pasture, for himself and the customary tenants of the manor, in all open and waste places outside the Forest cover, excepting only in the 'forbidden month' (*mense vetito*),[4] for all commonable beasts (*averiis communialibus*) 'levant and couchant' on the lands of the manor. By right of the bailiwick of Blakeney, he claims within the king's woods of the same bailiwick: housebote and heybote, by view and allocation of the foresters and verderers of the Forest, for repairs of his houses on the manor, and firebote of dry wood for burning as firewood; pannage of pigs and the whole after-pannage; windfallen trees;

---

[1] The claims are paraphrased here, omitting much verbiage and repetition; for one in its original form, see Nicholls, *Forest of Dean*, pp. 261–3.

[2] Each claim was delivered through an attorney, named in most cases as Edward Offley.

[3] For these, his recent predecessors in the office, see *VCH Glos.* v. p. 415.

[4] Also known as the 'fence month', a period of 30 days around Midsummer (24 June) when commoning and all other potential disturbances to the deer, then fawning, were prohibited: *Manwood's Forest Laws*, ed. Nelson, pp. 134–6.

the trunk of a tree at Christmas; eyries of goshawks and falcons; mines of sea-coal and iron.

title: Held by his ancestors and predecessors from time immemorial from the castle and manor of St. Briavels, paying the king or his farmer 19*s*. 6*d*. a year.

no. 3 JOAN VAUGHAN, widow

The manor of Littledean; and the bailiwick of Littledean with the office of bailiff and woodward in same.

claims: View of frankpledge (as above). Within the woods of the bailiwick she claims: wood and timber, by view and allocation of the foresters and verderers, for rebuilding and repairing the manor house and other buildings of the said manor and the hedges around her lands; one oak trunk at Christmas for her hearth; eyries of goshawks and falcons; all dead, dry, and windfallen trees; pannage of pigs at time of pannage, without rendering anything to the king, and after-pannage following the feast of St. Martin (when the king takes his profit of pannage); common of pasture (as above).

title: Held by her ancestors and predecessors from time immemorial from the king by military service, viz, the service of finding a suitable man to keep the said bailiwick.

no. 4 The same

The manor of Abenhall; the bailiwick of Abenhall with the office of bailiff and woodward in same.

claims (details as above): View of frankpledge; wood for repairs; an oak trunk at Christmas for her hearth; eyries of goshawks and falcons; pannage, and after-pannage; common of pasture.

title: Held by her ancestors and predecessors from time immemorial from the king by military service of finding two men to keep the bailiwick, paying a rent of 20*s*., and serving the king in war with a horse, a breastplate, two spears, and a bow and arrows when the king comes to war(*sic*) in the Forest.[1]

no. 5 The same

The manor of Ruardean; the bailiwick of Ruardean with the office of bailiff and woodward in same.

claims (details as above): View of frankpledge; wood for repairs; an oak trunk; eyries; dead, dry, and windfallen trees; pannage and after-pannage; common of pasture.

title: Held by her ancestors and predecessors from time immemorial from the king by military service of finding one man to keep the bailiwick, and paying a rent of 11*s*.

no. 6 NICHOLAS ROBERTS, esquire

The manor of Lea (*Lacu*); the bailiwick of Lea with the office of bailiff and woodward in same.

claims (details as above): By right of the manor: view of frankpledge; waifs and strays; common of pasture in all open and waste places outside the enclosed lands (*terras defensas*). By right of the bailiwick: housebote and heybote, by view and allocation of the foresters and verderers; firebote of dry wood for burning in the houses of the manor; the bark of all trees growing in the bailiwick given or delivered by gift of the king;[2] all windfallen trees in the bailiwick.

title: Held by his ancestors and predecessors from time immemorial from the king by military service, paying a rent of 15s. to the king or to his farmer of the castle and manor of St. Briavels.

---

[1] This is presumably a confused account of the ancient service: the service with bow and arrows was no doubt owed when the king came to *hunt* in the Forest.

[2] i.e. from any trees given away by the king to others.

no. 7 The same

The manor of Mitcheldean (*Deane Magna*); the bailiwick of Mitcheldean with the office of bailiff and woodward in the same.

claims (details as above): By right of the manor: view of frankpledge; waifs and strays; a market held on Monday each week and a fair on the feast of Michaelmas in the vill of Mitcheldean, with all tolls and profits of same; common of pasture. By right of the bailiwick: housebote, heybote, and firebote; bark of trees given by the king; windfallen trees.

title: Held by his ancestors and predecessors from time immemorial from the king by military service, paying a rent of 20s. to the king or his farmer of the castle and manor of St. Briavels.

no. 8 BENEDICT HALL, esquire

The manor of Staunton; the bailiwick of Staunton with the office of bailiff and woodward in the same.

claims (details as above): By right of the manor: view of frankpledge; the goods and chattels called waifs and strays in the manor; common of pasture. By right of the bailiwick: housebote, heybote, and firebote; bark of trees given by the king; windfallen trees.

title: Held by his ancestors and predecessors from time immemorial, paying a rent of 26s. 8d. to the king or his farmer of St. Briavels manor, and rendering the service of carrying the king's bow when he comes to hunt.

no. 9 The same

The manor of [English] Bicknor; the bailiwick of Bicknor with the office of bailiff and woodward in the same.

claims (details as above): By right of the manor: view of frankpledge; waifs and strays; common of pasture (claimed for himself and for his customary tenants). By right of the bailiwick: housebote, heybote, and firebote; bark of trees given by the king; windfallen trees.

title: Held by his ancestors from time immemorial, paying a rent of 15s. to the king or his farmer of St. Briavels manor.

no. 10 GEORGE SOUTH, gentleman

The office of one the rangers in the Forest of Dean with all the profits of same, receiving a fee of 6d. a day from the castle and manor of St. Briavels.

title: Letters Patent of 25 March 1626, to hold for his life (citing an earlier grant of the same by James I to John Norman, esq.).

(*C 99/12*)

no. 11   THOMAS, EARL OF ARUNDEL AND SURREY, MARSHAL OF ENGLAND, as guardian of HENRY, LORD STAFFORD, a minor (aged 14) in the king's wardship

The borough of Newnham in the Forest of Dean.

claims: View of frankpledge for all inhabitants of the borough twice a year, viz. a month after Easter and a month after Michaelmas, before his steward; waifs and strays; fairs within the borough on 11 June and the feast of St. Luke (18 October) and a market each Friday, with toll, stallage, and pickage (or stake pence) belonging to same; a several fishery in the part of the river Severn that runs within the borough.

no. 12 THE MEN AND TENANTS OF RODLEY MANOR (ancient royal demesne)[1] and lands and tenements within that manor but outside the Forest of Dean
claims: Estovers of the dead and dry wood from the king's woodlands in the Forest, to burn in their anciently-built houses; common of pasture in all commonable places of the Forest outside the enclosed lands, for all their commonable beasts 'levant et couchant' on their lands and tenements (excepting in the 'forbidden month'); pannage for their pigs in the time of pannage.
title: As enjoyed by their ancestors and predecessors from time immemorial.

no. 13 WARREN GOUGH, gentleman
The office of one of the verderers of the Forest of Dean.
claims: A doe in summer and a doe in winter each year; and he may fell and take each year, by allocation of the other verderers, one oak and one beech.
title: Elected to the office under the king's writ; enjoys the privileges as did his predecessors in the office.

no. 14. JOHN BERROW, gentleman
The office of one of the verderers of the Forest of Dean.
claims: As no. 13.
title: As no. 13.

no. 15. GEORGE WYRALL of Newland, gentleman
Six messuages, with barns, stables, and other necessary buildings, and lands in Newland parish, viz. a messuage and 4 a. in the tenure of Francis Humfries; messuage and 8 a. in tenure of John Griffiths; messuage and 12 a. in tenure of Thomas Lewes; messuage and 18 a. in tenure of Christopher Dubberley; messuage and 20 a. in tenure of Christopher Rive; messuage and 4 a. in tenure of Lewis (*Lodovicus*) Evans; also, 24 a. of land in Newland.
claims:[2] For each, housebote and heybote[3] from the waste and commonable places of the Forest for necessary repairs to the houses and buildings, to be allocated by the foresters and verderers on requisition made by the owner at the king's court held in the Forest called the speech court; estovers to use and burn in those houses taken from the dead and dry wood in the waste and commonable places of the Forest;[4] common of pasture in all open and commonable places in the Forest, except in the 'forbidden month', for all commonable beasts 'levant et couchant' on his lands and tenement*s*; pannage with his pigs in the Forest waste in the time of pannage, paying the king 1*d.* a year as swine silver. (For the 24 a. of land only common pasture and pannage is claimed).
title: The houses and lands were held by his ancestors and predecessors from time immemorial, paying to the king for each property 1*d.* a year as mark silver (and 1*d.* as swine silver).[5] The 24 a. is held of the king's manor of St. Briavels for a rent of 24*s.* 6*d.* and suit to the court of St. Briavels every three weeks.

---

[1] As used here the term refers to land recorded in the possession of the Crown at the time of Domesday Book.

[2] In some later entries these claims are made 'for [himself and] his heirs, farmers, and tenants', emphasising that all occupiers under the freeholder should enjoy the rights.

[3] For this right the terms 'housebote and heybote' are only used in some of the claims, others mentioning merely 'wood for necessary repairs' or some such phrase; for simplicity the terms are consistently used here.

[4] In some later claims this right is termed 'firebote' rather than 'estovers'.

[5] Here and in later claims the obligation to swine silver, given in the claim to pannage, is repeated in the statement of tenure and rent.

no. 16 BRIDGET WYRALL of English Bicknor, widow, and GEORGE WYRALL of Newland, gentleman

Five messuages and lands, viz. a messuage and 200 a. with barns, stables, etc. in Bridget's tenure;[1] messuage and 9 a. in English Bicknor in tenure of Richard Powell, gent.; messuage and 16 a. in English Bicknor in tenure of Thomas Mowsell; messuage and 18 a. in English Bicknor in tenure of James Potter; messuage and 6 a. in English Bicknor in tenure of William Pearce.

claims: (detailed as in no. 15) Housebote and heybote; estovers; common of pasture; pannage.

title: Held freely by Bridget for life, with remainder to George and his heirs, paying 1*d.* for mark silver.

no. 17 WILLIAM PERKINS, gentleman

A messuage and 100 a. of land in Newland.

claims: As no. 15.

title: Held by his ancestors and predecessors from time immemorial by suit to the king's court of St. Briavels castle every three weeks, paying a rent of 19*s.* 6*d.* to the king's farmer of the Forest.

no. 18 WILLIAM SKYNNE

A messuage and 20 a. of land at Platwell in Newland parish.

claims: As no. 15.

title: Held by his ancestors and predecessors from time immemorial, by suit to the king's court of St. Briavels castle every three weeks, and rent of 8*s.* 8*d.* to the farmer of the Forest.

no. 19 ANTHONY CALOW

Twenty messuages, three orchards, and 100 a. of land in Mitcheldean and Abenhall.

claims: As no. 15.

title: Held by his ancestors and predecessors from time immemorial.

no. 20 THOMAS MATHEWES

A messuage, garden, orchard, and 12 a. of land in Newland.

claims: As no. 15.

title: Held by his ancestors and predecessors from time immemorial, paying 1*d.* as mark silver to king's farmer.

(*C 99/13*)

no. 21 THOMAS YERWORTH of Coleford in Newland, yeoman

An ancient messuage called *Morses house*, with barns, stables, and 60 a. of land in Coleford in his own tenure; an ancient messuage, garden, and parcel of meadow (5 a.) in tenure of James Parlor; an ancient messuage called *Yearslies house*, garden, and buildings in Coleford in tenure of James Wintle; an ancient messuage called 'le handsmith'[2] in Coleford in tenure of John Gilberd; an ancient messuage, barns, stables, and 5 a. of land called Blackalls field in Staunton in tenure of John Hoskins.

claims: As no. 15

title: Held by his ancestors and predecessors from time immemorial, paying for each tenement a rent of 5*s.* 6*d.* to the king's farmer of the Forest, and 1*d.* as mark silver.

---

[1] The Bicknor Court estate: *VCH Glos.* v. p. 108.

[2] The usual term for a forge in the early period of the Forest iron-making industry.

no. 22 EDMUND BERROW, esquire

An ancient messuage called North Hall, 200 a. of land, 100 a. of meadow, and 100 a. of pasture in the township of Awre.[1]

claims: As no. 15 (except that for pannage he owes his rate and portion of the sum of 8*s*. 6*d*. which the township of Awre owes to the king as swine silver).

title: Held by his ancestors and predecessors from time immemorial.

no. 23 LAWRENCE SLEDD, gentleman

An ancient messuage, barns, stable, and 100 a. of land called Inwood farm in Newland.

claims: As no. 15.

title: Ancestors and predecessors from time immemorial.

no. 24 JOHN COURTE

An ancient messuage, barns, stables, and 4 a. of land in Newland.

claims: As no. 15.

title: Ancestors and predecessors from time immemorial, paying fee-farmer of the Forest 1*d*. as mark silver.

no. 25 RICHARD KATCHMAY, knight

Lands and tenements called 'suit land' in St. Briavels parish.

claims: As no. 15.

title: Ancestors and predecessors from time immemorial.

no. 26 ATHANASIUS ELY of Redbrook, in Newland

An ancient messuage, in his tenure, with 100 a. of land in Newland.[2]

claims: As no. 15 (but no payment of swine silver mentioned).

title: Ancestors and predecessors from time immemorial, held from the king as of manor of St. Briavels, owing a rent of 22*s*. 6½*d*. to its farmer and suit of court there every three weeks.

no. 27 JOHN BUFFORD the elder

Three messuages, three gardens, and 6 a. of land in Ruardean.

claims: As no. 15.

title: Held by his ancestors and predecessors from time immemorial.

no. 28 RICHARD SMYTH, yeoman, a free tenant of Staunton manor

An ancient messuage and 20 a. of land in Staunton.

claims: As no. 15.

title: Ancestors and predecessors, etc.

no. 29 HENRY DOWLE, yeoman, a free tenant of Staunton manor

A messuage and 12 a. of land in Staunton.

claims: As no. 15.

title: Ancestors and predecessors, etc.

no. 30 JOHN HOSKINS, a free tenant of Staunton manor

A messuage and orchard in Staunton.

claims: As no. 15.

title: Ancestors and predecessors, etc.

---

[1] The Hall Farm estate, based on a house near Awre village: *VCH Glos*. v. p. 29. Here and in the reference to swine silver 'township' probably refers to the tithing of Awre, a division of Awre parish.

[2] Lower Redbrook (later Lodges) farm in the valley of the Red brook below Newland village: *VCH Glos*. v. p. 213.

no. 31 EDWARD SMYTH, yeoman, a free tenant of Staunton manor.
A messuage in Staunton.
claims: As no. 15.
title: Ancestors and predecessors, etc.

no. 32 THOMAS WYSAM, yeoman, a free tenant of Staunton manor
A messuage and 12 a. of land in Staunton.
claims: As no. 15.
title: Ancestors and predecessors, etc..

no. 33 WILLIAM MARSHAL, yeoman, a free tenant of English Bicknor manor
A messuage and 8 a. of land in English Bicknor.
claims: As no. 15.
title: Ancestors and predecessors, etc.

no. 34 WILLIAM GODWYN, yeoman, a free tenant of English Bicknor manor
A messuage and 3 a. of land in English Bicknor.
claims: As no. 15.
title: Ancestors and predecessors, etc.

no. 35 WILLAM GARDNER, yeoman, a free tenant of English Bicknor manor
A messuage and 100 a. of land in English Bicknor.
claims: As no. 15.
title: Ancestors and predecessors, etc.

no. 36 JOHN BATCHELLOR, pinmaker, a free tenant of English Bicknor manor
A messuage and 5 a. of land in English Bicknor.
claims: As no. 15.
title: Ancestors and predecessors, etc.

no. 37 JAMES KEARE, a free tenant of Staunton manor
A messuage and 16 a. in Staunton.
claims: As no. 15.
title: Ancestors and predecessors, etc.

no. 38 JOHN FISHER, yeoman, a free tenant of English Bicknor manor
A messuage and 125 a. of land in English Bicknor.
claims: As no. 15.
title: Ancestors and predecessors, etc.

no. 39 HENRY WORGAN
An ancient messuage, with barns, stables, etc. and 40 a. of land in Clearwell, Newland parish.
claims: As no. 15.
title: Held by his ancestors and predecessors from time immemorial, paying the king's farmer I*d.* as mark money.

no. 40 ROGER LEWIS, yeoman, a free tenant of English Bicknor manor
A messuage and 50 a. of land in English Bicknor.
claims: As no. 15.
title: Held by his ancestors and predecessors from time immemorial.

no. 41   FRANCES CARPENTER of St. Briavels, widow, and NATHANIEL HODGES of the city of Gloucester and MARGARET, his wife (which Frances and Margaret are daughter and heirs of WILLIAM WHITTINGTON, gentleman, deceased)
An ancient messuage with barns, stables, etc. and 120 a. of land in St. Briavels parish.

claims: As no. 15 (but no mention of swine silver)

title: From time immemorial, held from the king as of his manor of St. Briavels, paying 1*s*. rent and suit of court every three weeks to the court of St. Briavels.

no. 42 ANDREW HORNE

Two messuages with barns, stables, etc. and 30 a. of land in Awre parish.

claims: As no. 15 (but paying 2d. for swine silver).

title: Held by his ancestors and predecessors from time immemorial.

no. 43 GEORGE BIRKIN

An ancient messuage with barns, stables, etc. and 10 a. in Awre parish.

claims: As no. 15 (paying 2*d*. for swine silver)

title: Ancestors and predecessors, etc.

no. 44 CHARLES BRIDGMAN, esquire

The site of the manor of Poulton (*Poltons*) Court[1] within the Forest of Dean.

claims: As no. 15 (the housebote for the repair of the ancient manor house on the estate).

title: Ancestors and predecessors, etc.

no. 45 ROBERT YOUNGE

Two messuages and 17 a. in Awre parish.

claims: As no. 15 (paying 6*d*. for swine silver).

title: Ancestors and predecessors, etc.

no. 46 THOMAS SALENCE

A messuage with barns, stables, etc. and 30 a. of land in Awre parish.

claims: As no. 15 (paying 2*d*. for swine silver).

title: Ancestors and predecessors, etc.

no. 47 EDWARD MORSE

Two ancient messuages with barns, stables, etc. and 4 a. of land in Mitcheldean parish.

claims: As no. 15 (paying 2*d*. for swine silver).

title: Ancestors and predecessors, etc.

no. 48 RICHARD HOPKINS, yeoman

An ancient messuage with barns, stables, etc. and 20a. of land in Awre parish.

claims: As no. 15 (paying 3*d*. for swine silver).

title: Ancestors and predecessors, etc.

no. 49 JOHN WINTLE

Three ancient messuages with barns, stables, etc. and 40 a. of land in Awre parish.

claims: As no. 15 (paying 2*d*. for swine silver).

title: Ancestors and predecessors, etc.

no. 50 JOHN BROWNE

An ancient messuage with barns. stables, etc. and 11 a. of land in Awre parish.

claims: As no. 15 (paying 2*d*. for swine silver).

title: Ancestors and predecessors, etc.

(C 99/14)

no. 51 JOHN NELME

An ancient messuage with barns, stables, etc. and 4 a. of land in Ruardean parish.

claims: As no. 15.

title: Ancestors and predecessors,etc.

---

[1] In Awre parish: *VCH Glos*. v. pp. 26–7.

no. 52 MORGAN GRIFFITH
An ancient messuage with other buildings and 3 a. in Coleford, in Newland parish.
claims: As no. 15 (paying 2*d.* for swine silver).
title: Ancestors and predecessors, etc.

no. 53 CHARLES TRIPPETT
Three ancient messuages with barns, stables, etc. and 120 a. in Awre parish.[1]
claims: As no. 15 (paying 15*d.* for herbage and pannage by name of herbage and swine silver).
title: Ancestors and predecessors, etc.

no. 54 WILLIAM HODGES
An ancient messuage with barns, stables, etc. and 3a. in Awre parish.
claims: As no. 15 (paying 2*d.* for swine silver).
title: Ancestors and predecessors, etc.

no. 55 THOMAS A DEANE
An ancient messuage with other buildings and 3 a. of land in Awre parish.
claims: As no. 15 (paying 2*d.* for swine silver).
title: Ancestors and predecessors, etc.

no. 56 GOUGHE CHINNE
Nine messuages with barns, stables, etc. and 45a. of land in Awre and Newnham parishes.
claims: As no. 15.
title: Ancestors and predecessors, etc.

no. 57 ALEXANDER THORNE, a minor.
An ancient messuage with barns, stables, etc. and 80a. of land in Clearwell, in Newland parish.
claims: As no. 15.
title: Claimed by Christopher Thorne (*sic*)[2] to have been held by his ancestors and predecessors from time immemorial, paying the king's farmer of the Forest 1*d.* a year for marke silver.[3]

no. 58 JOHN HARRIS
An ancient messuage with a garden, orchard, and barns, stables, etc. and 12 a. of land in Blakeney, in Awre parish.
claims: As no. 15.
title: Held by his ancestors and predecessors from time immemorial.

no. 59 JOHN PREECE
An ancient messuage with a garden, orchard and barns, stables, etc. and 4 a. of land in Woodfield, in Awre parish.
claims: As no. 15 (paying ½*d.* for swine silver).
title: Ancestors and predecessors, etc.

no. 60 HENRY HULYN
An ancient messuage with an orchard and barns, stables, etc. and 40a. of land in Clearwell, in Newland parish.
claims: As no. 15.

[1] Evidently the Field House estate: *VCH Glos.* v. p. 30.
[2] Presumably Christopher was Alexander's late predecessor as owner.
[3] This payment appears in these claims variously as 'marke silver' and 'marke money.

title: Held by his ancestors and predecessors from time immemorial, paying the king's farmer of the Forest 1d. a year for marke silver.

(*C 99/15*)

no. 61 THOMAS WHOPER
An ancient messuage with garden and barns, stables, etc. and 4 a. in Clearwell, in Newland parish.
claims: As no. 15.
title: As no. 60.

no. 62 ALICE PARTRIDGE, widow, and THOMAS PARTRIDGE, son and heir apparent of EDWARD PARTRIDGE of Clearwell, deceased
An ancient messuage with garden, orchard and barns, stables, etc. and 20 a. in Clearwell.
claims: As no. 15.
title: As no. 60.

no. 63 THOMAS WHOPER the elder
An ancient messuage with garden, orchard and barns, stables, etc. and 4 a. in Clearwell, in Newland parish
claims: As no. 15.
title: As no. 60.

no. 64 THOMAS KEARE
An ancient messuage with garden and barns, stables, etc. in Clearwell, in Newland parish.
claims: As no. 15.
title: As no. 60.

no. 65 JOHN BUCKE
An ancient messuage with garden, orchard and barns, stables, etc. and 60 a. in Blakeney, in Awre parish.
claims: As no. 15 (paying ½d. for swine silver)
title: Held by his ancestors and predecessors from time immemorial.

no. 66 RICHARD HOOPER
An ancient messuage with barns, stables, etc. and 50 a. in Gatcombe, in Awre parish.[1]
claims: As above (paying 1d. for swine silver).
title: Ancestors and predecessors, etc.

no. 67 THOMAS BATCHCROFT, professor of sacred theology, master and warden of GONVILLE AND CAIUS COLLEGE, CAMBRIDGE, founded in honour of the Annunciation, and the fellows of the college
Five messuages with other buildings and 160 a. of land in Awre parish, held by tenants and farmers under the college.[2]
claims: As no. 15 (paying 2s. for swine silver).
title: Held by their predecessors from time immemorial.

no. 68 WILLIAM STEVINGTON, esquire
Two ancient messuages with barns, stables, etc. and 70 a. in Mitcheldean.
claims: As no. 15 (paying 2d. for swine silver).
title: Held by his ancestors and predecessors from time immemorial.

---

[1] Evidently Oatfield farm: *VCH Glos*. v. p. 22.
[2] This was apparently a part of what became the Hagloe estate, in which in 1853 the college held a right in reversion under an ancient lease: TNA, CRES 38/611; *VCH Glos*. v. pp. 30–1.

no. 69 KETFORD BRAYNE, gentleman
Twenty ancient messuages with barns, stables, etc. and 500a. of land in Littledean.[1]
claims: As no. 15 (paying 20*d.* for swine silver).
title: Ancestors and predecessors, etc.

no. 70 CHARLES BRIDGEMAN, esquire
An ancient messuage with barns, stables, etc. and 60 a. of land in Littledean.[2]
claims: As no. 15.
title: Ancestors and predecessors, etc.

no. 70 (*sic*) **JOHN BIRKIN**
Two messuages with barns, stables, etc. and 30 a. of land in Awre.
claims: As no. 15 (paying 2*d.* for swine silver).
title: Ancestors and predecessors, etc.

(*C 99/16*)

no. 71 WARREN GOUGH
A messuage and 200 a. of land in the manor of St. Briavels.[3]
claims: As no. 15 (paying 2*d.* for swine silver).
title: Ancestors and predecessors, etc.

no. 72 JOHN GUNNINGE, gentleman
A messuage and 200 a. in the manor of St. Briavels;[4] and a tenement in *Clayhall*.
claims: As no. 15 (paying 2*d.* for swine silver).
title: Ancestors and predecessors, etc.

no. 73 WILLIAM CATCHMAY, gentleman
Various messuages with barns, stables, etc. and 100 a. of land in Newland.
claims: As no. 15 (paying 2*d.* for swine silver).
title: Ancestors and predecessors, etc.

no. 74 HUGH DOWLE[5]
Two messuages with barns, stables, etc. and 20 a. in Clearwell, in Newland parish.
claims: As no. 15 (paying 2*d.* for swine silver).
title: Ancestors and predecessors, etc.

no. 75 JOHN KNIGHT
A tenement with barns, stables, etc. in Ruardean.
claims: As no. 15 (paying 2*d.* for swine silver).
title: Ancestors and predecessors, etc.

no. 76 EDMUND BROWNE, yeoman, a free tenant of English Bicknor manor.
An ancient messuage, buildings, and 60 a. of land in English Bicknor.
claims: As no. 15.
title: Ancestors and predeceesors, etc.

no. 77 MATTHEW DOWLE, a free tenant of English Bicknor manor
An ancient messuage, buildings and 6 a. of land in English Bicknor.
claims: As no. 15.

---

[1] For the Braynes' Littledean estate: *VCH Glos.* v. p. 163–4.
[2] Bridgeman (the same claimant as in no. 44) held the Dean Hall estate: *VCH Glos.* v. p. 164.
[3] The Willsbury estate*: VCH Glos.* v. p. 261.
[4] This was an estate based on a house known as the Great House (since demolished): *VCH Glos.* v. p. 262.
[5] Later in the entry, however, the owner is named as Christopher Dowle.

title: Ancestors and predecessors, etc.

no 78 RICHARD MORSE the younger, a free tenant of English Bicknor manor
An ancient messuage, buildings and 10 a. in English Bicknor.
claims: As no. 15.
title: Ancestors and predecessors, etc.

no. 79 CHRISTOPHER WORGAN
An ancient messuage with garden, orchard, barns, stables, etc. and 40 a. in Clearwell, in Newland parish.
claims: As no. 15.
title: Held by his ancestors and predecessors from time immemorial, paying the king's farmer of the Forest 1d. for marke silver.

no. 80 AVIS BAYLIE, widow, and THOMAS BAYLIE, a minor, son and heir apparent of JOHN BAYLIE of Blakeney, yeoman
A messuage with garden, orchard and barns, stables, etc, and 20 a. in Blakeney, in Awre parish.
claims: As no. 15.
title: As no. 79.

(*C99/17*)

no. 81 WILLIAM PHILLIPS of the Lea (*le Lea*) , in Newland parish,[1] husbandman
A close of pasture called *le Harp* containing *c*. 5 a. in the Forest of Dean.
claims: As no. 15 (but no claim made for estovers)
title: As no. 79.

no. 82 HENRY PHILLIPS of the Beach grove in Newland parish, husbandman
A messuage called the Beach grove and 12a. in Newland parish.
claims: As no. 15.
title: As no. 79.

no. 83 WILLIAM LOVELL of Newland, husbandman
An ancient messuage and 23 a. in Newland.
claims: As no. 15.
title: As no. 79.

no. 84 ROBERT PHILLIPS of Lea Line, in Newland parish,[2] husbandman
An ancient messuage and 12 a. at the Lea, in Newland parish.
claims: As no. 15.
title: As no. 79.

no. 85 JOHN BERROWE
A messuage and 7 a. in Bream, in Newland parish; and two messuages and 4 a. in Blakeney, in Awre parish.
claims: As no. 15 (but paying 2d. for swine silver).
title: Held by his ancestors and predecessors from time immemorial.

no. 86 THOMAS JAMES aged 8; claims made for him by GEORGE RAYMOND, admitted as his guardian by the Court of Wards
An ancient messuage and buildings in Newnham.

---

[1] Evidently an inhabitant of Lea Bailey tithing, which comprised detached parts of Newland parish near or adjoining Lea parish: *VCH Glos*. v. p. 195–6.
[2] A part of Lea Bailey tithing was at Lea Line, on the Ross–Gloucester road north of Mitcheldean.

claims: As no. 15.

title: Ancestors and predecessors, etc.

no. 87 THOMAS JAMES (as above)

Ancient messuage and buildings in Ruardean.

claims: As no. 15.

title: Ancestors and predecessors, etc.

no. 88 GEORGE BOND of Newland, gentleman

Six ancient messuages and lands in Newland parish, viz. A messuage in Clearwell with barns, stables, etc. and 6 a.; a messuage and garden in Newland called *Whitsons house* in the tenure of Christopher Gethinge; a messuage in Newland in the tenure of Robert Corbett; a messuage in Newland in the tenure of Edmund Symonds; a messuage in Redbrook with barns, stables, etc. and 50 a.; a messuage in Redbrook called *Ellis house* with barns, stables, etc. and 10 a.

claims: For each, as no. 15 (but no payment for swine silver mentioned).

title: All held by his ancestors and predecessors from time immemorial from the king's manor of St. Briavels, owing suit every three weeks to the court there, and paying for the first property a rent of 6*s*. 2*d*., for each of the next three 2*s*. 2*d*., for the fifth 14*s* 2*d*., and for the sixth 10*s*.

no. 89 BLANCHE BOND of Newland, widow, seized for her life, with remainder to GEORGE BOND of Newland, gentleman

Four ancient messuages with barns, stables, etc. and lands in Newland parish, viz. A messuage and 100 a.; a messuage and 5 a.; a messuage and 10 a. in the tenure of Edward Reeve; a messuage and 6a. in the tenure of Hugh Jones.[1]

claims: For each, as no, 15 (but no payment for swine silver).

title: All held as no. 88 from St Briavels manor, paying for the messuage and 100 a. a rent of 10*s*., and for each of the other three a rent of 3*s*. 4*d*.

no. 90 KEDGWIN HOSKINS of Clearwell, in Newland parish, yeoman.

An ancient messuage with barns, stables, etc, three gardens, an orchard, and 50a.[2] in Newland.

claims: As no. 15 (but no payment for swine silver).

title: As no. 88 from St. Briavels manor, paying a rent of 7*s*.

(C 99/18)

no. 91 CHRISTOPHER DUBBERLEY, of Newland, cordwainer (*cordiner*)

An ancient messuage and garden in Coleford, in Newland parish, in the tenure of George Dubberley.

claims: As no. 15.

title: Held by his ancestors and predecessors from time immemorial, paying the king's farmer of the Forest 1*d*. for marke silver.

no. 92 JOHN YERWORTH of Coleford in Newland parish, yeoman

An ancient messuage with barns, stables, etc. and 12 a. in Coleford.

claims: As no. 15.

title: As no. 91.

---

[1] Blanche's estate (or the main part of it) was apparently Upper Redbrook farm, in the Red brook valley below Newland village: *VCH Glos*. v. p. 213.

[2] Later in the entry, however, the acreage is given as 30.

no. 93 ANNE DOWLE of Clearwell, in Newland parish
An ancient messuage in Coleford with barns, stables, garden, orchard, and 16 a. in her tenure; an ancient messuage with garden and orchard in Clearwell, also in her tenure.
claims: For each, as no. 15.
title: For each, as no. 91.

no. 94 STURLEY KEDGWIN of Clearwell, in Newland parish, yeoman
An ancient messuage with garden and orchard, containing ¼ a., in Clearwell, in the tenure of Roger Williams.
claims: As no. 15.
title: As no. 91.

no. 95 RICHARD STROUDE alias FREEMAN of Cradley (Herefs.)
An ancient messuage with barns, stables, etc. and 53 a. of land in Coleford, in the tenure of John Williams; another ancient messuage, garden, and 2 a. of land in Coleford, in his own tenure.
claims: For each, as no. 15.
title: for each, as no. 91.

no. 96 JOHN KEDGWIN of Coleford, yeoman
An ancient messuage and garden in Coleford.
claims: As no. 15.
title: As no. 91.

no. 97 RICHARD MORETON of Coleford, in Newland parish,
An ancient messuage and 2 a. of meadow in Coleford; an ancient messuage and 4 a. of meadow in Whitecliff, in the tenure of Simon Griffith.
claims: For each, as no. 15.
title: For each, as no. 91.

no. 98 WILLIAM CARPENDER of Coleford, in Newland parish, gentleman
Ten ancient messuages and lands, viz. a messuage called *Gamells hill* with barns, stables, etc. and 100 a. of land in Coleford; messuage, garden, and orchard in Coleford, containing 2 a., in the tenure of Henry Nayler; messuage and garden in Coleford in the tenure of John Cowcombe; messuage and garden in Coleford in the tenure of John Phillipps; messuage and garden in Coleford in the tenure of Richard Cliftow; messuage and garden in Coleford in the tenure of Richard Hibbes; messuage and garden in Coleford in the tenure of James Fox; messuage in Coleford in the tenure of William Cromsell; messuage in Coleford in the tenure of Stephen Weathen; messuage and 40 a. of land in Stowfield, in English Bicknor, in the tenure of Julia Stevens.
claims: For each , as no. 15.
title: For each, as no. 91.

no. 99 ROBERT JORDAN of Coleford, in Newland parish
Six ancient messuages and lands, viz. messuage with barns, stables, garden, orchard, and 30 a. of land in Coleford in his own tenure; another messuage and garden in Coleford in his tenure; messuage and garden in Coleford in the tenure of Sibyl Jones, widow; messuage and garden in Coleford in his (Robert's) tenure; messuage, garden, and 5a, of land in Newland parish in the tenure of Thomas Clarke; messuage in Staunton in the tenure of Roger Davis.
claims: For each, as no. 15.
title: For each as no. 91 (except that for the messuage in tenure of Sibyl Jones no liability to marke silver is mentioned).

no. 100 HENRY MARSHE of Whitecliff, in Newland parish

Five ancient messuages and lands viz. messuage, three gardens, and an orchard in Whitecliff, containing 2 a., in his own tenure; messuage, garden, orchard, and a parcel of land, containing ½ a., in the tenure of Nathaniel Cowles (no location given); messuage and garden in the tenure of John Dew (no location given); messuage and garden in the tenure of James Powell (no location given); messuage called *Huntlands house* with barns, stables, etc. and 8 a. of land in Whitecliff in his (Henry's) tenure.

claims: For each, as no. 15

title: For each, as no. 91.

no. 101 HENRY MORTON of Coleford, in Newland parish, yeoman

An ancient messuage, garden, and parcel of meadow containing ½ a. in Coleford, in the tenure of Alice Hartford.

claims: As no. 15.

title: As no. 91.

no. 102 EDWARD WORGAN of Millend, in Newland parish, yeoman

Six ancient messuages and lands in Newland parish, viz. messuage, garden, orchard, and 10 a. of land in his own tenure; messuage, garden, orchard, and 8 a. in Clearwell, in the tenure of Thomas Jenkins; messuage in Clearwell called *Clehay*, with garden, orchard, and 8 a. of land called *le Hedhill* in the tenure of James Tresteed; messuage, garden, orchard, and 8 a. of land, in the tenure of Thomas Worgan; messuage in Millend called *Sternholds house* with barns, stables, garden, orchard, and 12 a. of land, in the tenure of Christian Worgan; messuage in Millend with garden, barns, stables, etc. and 12 a. of land, in the tenure of John Worgan.

claims: For each, as no. 15.

title: For each, as no. 91.

no. 103 JOHN SYMONDS of Clearwell, in Newland parish, yeoman

An ancient messuage with barns, stables, etc., garden, orchard, and 16 a. of land in Clearwell.

claims: As no. 15.

title: As no. 91.

no. 104 WILLIAM DOWLE of Coleford, in Newland parish, yeoman

An ancient messuage and garden in Coleford.

claims: As no. 15.

title: As no. 91.

no. 105 WILLIAM YMME of Coleford, in Newland parish, yeoman

An ancient messuage and parcel of meadow containing 1 a., in Coleford.

claims: As no. 15.

title: As no. 91.

no. 106 JANE BIRTE of Clearwell, in Newland parish

An ancient messuage with barns, stables, etc., and 4 a. of land in Newland; an ancient messuage in Clearwell called *Keares house* with barns, stables, etc. and 6 a. of land, in the tenure of Edward Keare.

claims: For each, as no. 15.

title: For each, as no. 91.

no. 107 RICHARD HILL, gentleman

One ploughland (*carucatam*) of land called Blythes Court (*Bleyth Court*) in Newnham parish; the bailiwick of Blaize (*Bleyth*), belonging to the same ploughland, with the office of forester or woodward, and one woodward under him for keeping the same.

claims: In right of the bailiwick: housebote to build and repair the houses on the ploughland; heybote from the dead and dry wood of the woodland of the bailiwick to burn in the hearths of the houses; the trunk of a tree at Christmas by view of the constable of St Briavels and the verderers of the Forest. In right of the bailiwick and the ploughland: common pasture in all waste and commonable places outside the enclosed lands of the Forest, excepting only in the 'forbidden month', for all commonable beasts 'levant and couchant' on the said ploughland, and pannage for his pigs and piglets in all the woodland of the bailiwick.

title: Held by his ancestors and predecessors, as holders of the ploughland and bailiwick, from the king as of his castle and manor of St. Briavels, paying an annual rent of 5s. to the king or his farmer of the castle and manor.

no. 108 ARTHUR RICKETTS of Newland, gentleman

Three ancient messuages and lands, viz. a messuage with barns, stables, etc. and 100 a. of land[1] in Newland in his own occupation; a messuage and garden in Newland in the tenure of Christopher Yeroth; a messuage, with barns, stables, etc. and 20 a. of land in the Forest of Dean (no other location given).

claims: For each, as no. 15 (but no payment for swine silver mentioned for the first property).

title: Held by himself, his ancestors and predecessors from time immemorial, the messuage and land in his own occupation from the king as of the manor and castle of St Briavels for the annual rent of 13s. 7½d. and suit every three weeks at the court of that manor, but the other two properties owing only a payment of 1d. as marke silver.

no. 109 JOHN BULLOCKE and JOAN TRIPPETT

Three ancient messuages with barns, stables, etc. and 20 a. of land in Awre parish

claims: As no. 15 (but paying 3d. for swine silver).

title: Held by their ancestors and predecessors from time immemorial.

no. 110 THOMAS DE AWRE

An ancient messuage and 30 a. of land in Awre parish.

claims: As no. 15 (paying 4d. for swine silver).

title: Ancestors and predecessors, etc.

(C99/20)

no. 111 CHARLES BRIDGMAN, esquire

The office of one of the verderers of the Forest of Dean.

claims: A doe in summer and a doe in winter each year; and he may fell and take each year, by allocation of the other verderers, one oak and one beech.

title: Elected to the office under the king's writ; enjoys the privileges as did his predecessors in the office.

no. 112 JOHN WINTOUR, knight

The office of one of the king's foresters of the Forest of Dean.

claims: All the fees and profits belonging to the office (no details are given).

title: Held by his ancestors from time immemorial.

no. 113 JOHN JANE of Brockweir, gentleman

An ancient messuage with barns, stables, etc. and 24 a. of land in St. Briavels in the tenure of Thomas Grundhill.

claims: As no. 15 (but no payment for swine silver mentioned).

---

[1] But later in the entry stated to be 60 a.

title: Held by his ancestors and predecessors from time immemorial from the king as of his manor of St. Briavels, owing an annual rent of 4s. and suit to the court of that manor every three weeks.

no. 114 JOHN JANE of Brockweir, gentleman, and his wife ELEANOR, and ARTHUR RICKETTS of Newland, gentleman, and his wife PHILLIPPA

Three ancient messuages in St. Briavels parish, viz. messuage and garden in the tenure of Matilda Marshe, widow; messuage, garden, and 1a. of land in the tenure of John Braband; messuage and curtilage called *Beldams* in the tenure of the claimants.

claims: As no. 15 (but no payment for swine silver mentioned).

title: Held, in right of Eleanor and Phillipa in copartnership, of the king as of his manor of St. Briavels, owing for each property an annual rent of 2*d.* and suit of court every three weeks.

no. 115 The same claimants as no. 114

An ancient messuage with garden, barns, stables, etc. and 60 a. of land in St. Briavels parish in the tenure of Eleanor Lewis, widow; another ancient messuage, garden and 1a. of land in St. Briavels parish in the tenure of Blanch James.

claims: As no. 15 (but no payment for swine silver mentioned).

title: As no. 114 (owing for the first an annual rent 4*d.* and for the second 2*d.*).

no. 116 RICHARD WORGAN, a minor, son and heir apparent of THOMAS WORGAN, late of Clearwell, deceased

Eight ancient messuages and lands in Clearwell (in Newland), viz. messuage, with garden, orchard, barns, stables, etc. and 6 a. of land in the tenure of Fortune Keare, widow; messuage with garden, orchard, barns, stables, etc. and 7a. in the tenure of Henry Lynam; messuage with garden and 5 a. in the tenure of John Peckover; messuage with garden, orchard, barns, stables, etc, and 6 a. in the tenure of Thomas Browne; messuage with garden, barns, stables, etc. and 6 a. in the tenure of Joan Morgan, widow; messuage with garden, barns, stables, etc. and 5 a. in the tenure of Thomas Bannister; messuage with garden, barns, stables, etc. and 4 a. in the tenure of Thomas Morse; messuage with garden, barns, stables, etc. and 8 a. in the tenure of Richard Keare. Also, an ancient messuage in Coleford, in Newland parish, with garden, orchard, barns, stables, etc. and 5 a. of land in the tenure of Christopher Griffith.

claims: For each, as no. 15.

title: Held by his ancestors and predecessors from time immemorial, owing for each property 1*d.* for marke silver to the king's farmer of the Forest of Dean.

no. 117 WILLIAM,[1] BISHOP OF LLANDAFF

The tithe of the profits of the king's iron mines in Newland parish.

title: Granted to John,[2] bishop of Llandaff, as appropriator of the church of All Saints, Newland, and his successors by Edward II by letters patent of 15 November 1320 directed to the warden of the Forest of Dean (and stating that the king received great profit from the iron mines in the parish).

no. 118 The same

All the tithes of assarts in the Forest of Dean which are outside the limits of any parish.

title: As granted to John, bishop of Llandaff, as appropriator of the church of All Saints, Newland, by Edward I by letters patent of [1305], granting that the tithes of all new

---

[1] William Murray, bishop of Llandaff 1627–40.
[2] John of Monmouth, bishop of Llandaff 1297–1323.

assarts in the Forest that are outside the bounds of any existing parish shall belong to the church of Newland in perpetuity.[1]

no. 119 WILLIAM MONMOUTH

An ancient messuage and 70 a. of land in the manor of English Bicknor.

claims: As no. 15.

title: Held by his ancestors and predecessors from time immemorial.

no. 120 BAYNHAM THROCKMORTON, baronet

The office of chief riding forester (or master forester) of the Forest of Dean, having under him a walking forester, called a bowbearer, to make attachments of vert and venison in the Forest; the walking forester is appointed by Sir Baynham and makes oath to the king faithfully to perform his office.

claims: In right of his office, the right shoulder of all bucks and does killed in the forest; 10 bucks in summer (excepting in the 'forbidden month') and 10 does in winter each year, which he may kill and dispose of without licence of the king, the constable, or any other officer of the Forest; 16*d*. from the profits of each charcoal pit (*putei carbonis anglice colepitt*) for every six weeks in which charcoal is made there.

title: Holds the chief forestership and the said liberties as appurtenant to a messuage and yardland in St Briavels called Hathaways manor (or Hathaways Place), which his ancestors and predecessors have held from time immemorial from the king from the castle and manor of St. Briavels by the service of performing the said office and an annual rent of 28*s*. 4*d*.

---

[1] MS. has the date as '15 July 18 Edward I' (i.e.1290), presumably a clerical error, for the grant was made in 1305: *Calendar of Patent Rolls*, 1301–7, p. 319. It was as a result of this grant that Newland parish came to include detached portions scattered around the fringes of the Forest: *VCH Glos*. v. pp. 195–6.

(British Library, Harleian MS. 4850)

[f. 62v.]

Forest of Dean in Gloucestershire: Court of Swanimote held at Mitcheldean 15 Sept 1634 before Charles Bridgeman, Warren Gough the elder, and John Berrowe, esquires, Verderers of the Forest

In this roll the perambulation of the Forest made 3 September 1634 was enrolled.[1]

[f. 63]

Forest of Dean in the Counties of Gloucestershire, Herefordshire, Monmouthshire, and the County of the City of Gloucester[2]: Court of Swanimote of Charles, King of England, Scotland, France, and Ireland, Defender of the Faith, held at Mitcheldean in the said Forest 15 September 1634 before Charles Bridgeman, Warren Gough the elder, and John Berrowe, esqs., Verderers of the Forest

At this court it is presented by the foresters, regarders, and the 12 jurymen, and convicted by the verderers, that:[3]

1   John Homes, late of Blackwell Meadows in Mitcheldean parish, labourer, on 31 December 1634 cut down a beech, worth 5*s*., in the king's demesne of his Forest, and converted to his own use the timber and wood from it.

2   Thomas Collins, late of Blakeney, yeoman, on 1 August 1634, at *Thorney hills* in the Forest demesne cut down a dry beech, containing two loads of wood, that had been 'sealed' for use as timber (*existentem pro maeremio anglice being sealed for timber*), and [converted] the wood from it, etc.

3   Thomas Jones, late of *le Woodside*, and John Nichols, late of Coleford, labourer, within the last six weeks cut down two oaks, worth 18*s*. 4*d*., and [converted] the timber and wood from them, etc.

---

[1] A new perambulation had evidently been ordered by the justices, setting out the ancient bounds of the Forest as restored by the decision made at the eyre: see above, pp. xxi–xxiv.

[2] The heading of these courts reflects the restoration of the ancient bounds, which included several parishes and tithings in Herefordshire, the hamlets of Hadnock and Wyesham (part of the Monmouthshire parish of Dixton Newton) lying beside the river Wye opposite Monmouth, and the hamlets of Highnam, Linton, and Over which as part of Dudstone and King's Barton hundred were then in Gloucester city's 'inshire'.

[3] After the first few entries the presentments in these swanimotes are here paraphrased, omitting standard phrases such as: 'and converted to his own use the wood and timber'; and 'with [or to] the great destruction of the Forest'. A phrase 'in, etc.', used in many entries as shorthand for 'in the king's demesne of his Forest', is, however, expanded here to read 'in the Forest demesne'.

4   Henry Godwyn, late of English Bicknor, labourer, on 4 August 1634 in the Forest demesne cut up beech logs for making into trenchers (*pro quadr*[*atio*] *anglice sawing ... for trenchers*), and converted to his own use the timber and wood from them, with loss to the king 2*s.*

5   Isaac a Frenche of Parkend, collier, within the last six weeks set fire to an oak, containing one cord of 'sealed' wood worth 6*s.* 8*d.*

6   John Sayre, late of Ruardean, and William Sayre of the same, labourer, on 20 August 1634 set fire to a beech tree, containing two cords of wood and timber, at Staple Edge in the Forest demesne; and afterwards they cut down half a beech by night, and [converted] the wood and timber from it, etc.

7   Leonard Beare of Littledean, yeoman, on 20 August 1634 in the Forest demesne carried away with his horse, worth 20*s.*, one load of wood or timber from a cottage (*cottagii anglice of a cabbyn*), and [converted] to his own use the wood or timber, with loss to the king 6*d.*

8   David Jones, late of St. White's in Littledean parish, on 20 August 1634 in the Forest demesne cut down (*sic*) one horse-load of wood from the said cottage, and converted it to his own use.

[*f. 63v.*]

9   Henry Pumfrey, late of Blakeney, yeoman, on 20 August 1634, in the king's demesne, carried away by night on his horse, worth 30s., one load of timber, and converted it to his own use, with loss to the king 18*d.*

10   John Knyght, late of Ruardean, labourer, on 13 July 1634, in the king's demesne of his Forest, carried away wood and timber from a cottage with his four oxen and one mare, worth £4, and converted to his own use the wood and timber, with loss to the king 2s.

At this court the perambulation of the Forest and all the presentments and indictments recorded above were affirmed by unanimous agreement of the foresters, verderers, regarders, and other officers of the Forest.

[*the names of the three verderers – in the original rolls presumably signatures – appear at the end of this and succeeding courts*]

[*f. 64*]

Forest of Dean in Gloucestershire, Monmouthshire, Herefordshire, and the County of the City of Gloucester: Court of Swanimote of King Charles held at Mitcheldean on 9 December 1634 before Charles Bridgeman, Warren Gough, and John Berrow, Verderers of the Forest

The names of the various officers are written in two rolls,[1] and in one of them this following presentment.

Rolls by the Regarders

It is presented that:

---

[1] In the original swanimote rolls the record of each session would have begun with a full list of the forest officers, together with the reeves and 'four men' from each township: for examples, see GA, D 36/Q2; D 4431, incomplete roll for 9 June 1637.

1 James Hawkins, late of Flaxley, gent.,[1] by his agents and servants, within the last 20 years felled and entirely destroyed a parcel of great timber and woodland called Perlieu[2] wood, containing by estimation 100 a., in the fee of the bishop of Gloucester, lying near Lea Bailey (*le Baylie*), in the county of Herefordshire and within the perambulation of the king's Forest; he converted it to his own use, with loss to the king £100 and great destruction, damage, and harm to the Forest, contrary to the forest laws and assizes.

2 The said James Hawkins, late of Flaxley, gent., by his agents and servants, on 31 October 1634 felled a grove or wood called *Henypole*, containing by estimation 10 a., in the fee of the said James Hawkins, lying in the parish of Hope Mansell (*Mouncelle Hope*) (Herefs.) within the Forest perambulation, with loss to the king £5.

[*f. 64v.*]

Rolls by the Regarders

It is presented that:

1 Robert, earl of Essex, lately deceased, and his countess,[3] by their agents and under-servants, within the last 40 years felled and entirely destroyed a parcel of great woodland and timber called Bishop's wood (*boscum episcopale*), containing by estimation 1,000a., at Bishopswood (Herefs.) within the Forest perambulation, and converted it to their own use, with loss to the king £1,000 and great destruction and harm to the Forest, contrary to the forest laws and assizes.

2 Gilbert, earl of Shrewsbury, lately deceased,[4] by his agents and servants, felled and entirely destroyed a parcel of great timber and woodland called Huntley's wood, containing by estimation 1,000a., at Huntley in [the Forest perambulation] , and [converted] to his use etc., with loss to the king £1,000 and great, etc.

3 Henry, earl of Kent, and William Purefie[5] of Drayton (Leics.), esq., by their agents and servants, within the last 10 years felled another part of the great timber and woodland called Huntley's wood in [the Forest perambulation], and [converted] to their use, etc., with loss to the king £30 and great, etc.

4 Robert Parkhurst, alderman of London,[6] by his agents and under-servants, within the last 10 years felled and entirely destroyed a parcel of great timber and woodland called Taynton's wood, containing by estimation 100a., at Taynton within the perambulation, with loss to the king £100.

5 John Kyrle, bt., of [Much] Marcle (Herefs.), for the last 15 years had in his possession, and still has at present, a furnace for making iron at Burton's pool (Herefs.)[7] within the Forest perambulation, with loss to the king £5.

---

[1] Hawkins held the estate called the Grange at St. White's: *VCH Glos.* v. p. 143.

[2] MS. *Purleys*; evidently Perlieu wood in Hope Mansell parish (Herefs.).

[3] Robert Devereux, executed in 1601, and his widow Frances (who married the earl of Clanricarde and died in 1632); the destruction was evidently to fuel the ironworks established by the earl and carried on under his successors at Bishopswood and Lydbrook: *VCH Glos.* v. pp. 107, 240, 340, 345.

[4] Gilbert Talbot, who was lord of Huntley and Longhope manors and died in 1616: ibid. xii. pp.181, 234.

[5] Henry Grey (d.1639), who succeeded his father-in-law Gilbert Talbot at Huntley and Longhope; Purefie (Purefoy) leased the former under him in the 1620s: ibid.

[6] Parkhurst (d.1636) was lord of the manor of Great Taynton: ibid.p. 327.

[7] This furnace was apparently at Bishopswood: Hart, *Ind. Hist. of Dean*, p. 45.

6   Henry, earl of Kent, for the last 20 years had, and still has at present, a park (*leporarium*), surrounded by palings, called Penyard's park at Penyard near Weston (Herefs.) within the Forest perambulation, with loss to the king £5, contrary to, etc.

7   John Wintour, kt., of Lydney, for the last eight years had, and still has at present, a small park (*leporarunculus anglice a smale park*), surrounded by stone walls (*meniis lapidariis*)[1] at Lydney within the Forest perambulation, with loss to the king £5, contrary to, etc.

8   Robert Cooke, kt., of Highnam in the county of the city of Gloucester, for the last 10 years has had a small park called Highnam park, surrounded by palings, with loss to the king £5, contrary to, etc.

[*f. 65*]

9   John Browne, esq.,[2] of the city of Gloucester, during the last 10 years felled a coppice (*boscum anglice a coppice grove*) called Bird wood, containing 51 a. and worth £3, at Birdwood within the Forest perambulation.

10   Benedict Hall, esq., late of Highmeadow in Newland parish, by his agents or under-servants, during the last five years felled a coppice (*subboscum anglice one parcell of coppice wood*) called Hadnock, containing 4a. and worth 40s., at Hadnock (Mon.) within the Forest perambulation.

11   The high road leading from Gloucester to Monmouth in the parish of Dixton (Mon.) within the Forest perambulation, is in an extreme state of disrepair and most dangerously broken up on account of the king's subjects who travel by that way, with loss to the king £40.

12   Henry, earl of Worcester, by his agents and under-servants, during the last four years, felled a coppice called *lords grove*, containing 10 a., at Dixton, with loss to the king £5.

13   Basil Brooke, kt., and George Mynne, esq., by their agents and under-servants, during the last five years felled 680 oaks, comprising timber worth £200, and 370 beeches, comprising timber worth £150, at various places in the king's demesne of his Forest called the Old Speech House, the edge of Great Kensley, Little Kensley, and *Dannell moore*, with loss to the king £1,000 and contrary to the laws, etc.

which presentments were not presented to the last justice seat [3]

14   Robert Banister, kt.,[4] from 1 August 1634 to the 8 December following kept, and still keeps at present, a parcel of pasture and underwood called Cannop Vallets *(Fellet)*, containing by estimation 900 a. surrounded by a 5-ft. wall, at Cannop in the king's demesne of his Forest, to the harm and hindrance of the king's ironworks in the Forest.

15   Thomas Okey, late of Longhope, yeoman, during the last three years cut down 100 oaks, containing 100 tons of timber worth 40 marks, at Huntley's wood in the Forest

---

[1] Though *meniis* looks like a scribal error for *muris*, it was apparently intended: see Latham, *Medieval Latin Word-list* (1965) p. 295.

[2] Lessee (under the dean of chapter of Gloucester) of Churcham manor which included part of Bird wood: *VCH Glos*. x. 11, 17.

[3] *sic*, presumably referring to nos. 1–13 (though only no. 13 would have qualified for presentment under the bounds as then accepted).

[4] For Banister's estate (formerly John Gibbons's), above pp. xi–xii, xix.

perambulation, and he laid them waste and converted and disposed of them to his own use, with great defrauding and loss to the king and great destruction and harm to the Forest.

[*f. 65v.*]

16 Peter Langley, late of Lydney, labourer, on 31 September 1634 in the king's demesne at *le Haye end* in Blakeney bailiwick cut up and charcoaled 20 cords of felled wood, worth 20*s.*, not yet released [? by the forest officers], and converted and disposed of it to his own use, with great defrauding and harm to the king.

17 William Beard, late of (?)Staple Edge (*Stapletch*) near *le Meerebrooke* in the king's Forest, woodcutter, on 16 November 1634 cut down seven great holly trees (*aquifoli[as] anglice hollyes*) and other trees called hawthorns (*hatherns*), amounting to one wagon load worth 5*s.*

18 Richard Tompson, late of Flaxley, labourer, during the last two years encroached ¼ a. of land, worth 6*d.* a year, in Abbots wood within the Forest perambulation, and built a cottage on it, and took, and continues to take at the present, the issues and profits to his own use.

19 Richard Wollridge, late of Soudley, labourer, on 31 March 1633 enlarged a cottage at Cinderford in the Forest, and cut down a holly grove, containing one horse-load of timber worth 2s., in the king's demesne.

20 Thomas Rosser, late of Newnham, labourer, on 18 October 1634 in the king's demesne felled and uprooted by the butts (*per metas anglice the butts*) holly trees, containing by estimation one horse-load of timber worth 3d., with loss to the king 6d.

21 John Arthur, late of Parkend, labourer, on 18 October 1634 in Staunton bailiwick within the king's demesne cut down part of a log of timber, containing by estimation ¼ ton worth 20d.

22 Trestram Tresteede, late of Ellwood, and Brian Smyth of the Bearse near St. Briavels, miners, on 4 October 1634 in Staunton bailiwick in the king's demesne cut up a timber log, containing by estimation one ton worth 6*s.* 8*d.*, for their mine (*pro sua minera caverna [anglice] for their myne pitt*).

23 Richard Jenkins, late of Oakwood in the Forest, labourer, and Robert Fowler of the same, labourer, in Staunton bailiwick in the king's demesne cut down two young beeches, one holly tree, and one tree called a birch for building a cottage, with loss to the king 2s.

[*f. 66*]

24 Thomas Reynalds, late of Stowe, labourer, on 20 October 1634 at [*place-name indecipherable*] in Staunton bailiwick in the king's demesne, took two tons of timber to make boards and rafters (*lignos lignaros anglice boards and rafters*) after it had been assigned for the king's use and delivered into the custody of Benedict Hall, woodward of Staunton bailiwick.

25 Thomas Jones, late of St. Briavels, labourer, on 22 October 1634 in Staunton bailiwick in the Forest demesne cut down part of timber log, containing by estimation one ton worth 6*s.* 8*d.*

26 Thomas Evans, late of Ruardean, labourer, [is presented for] on 10 November 1634 digging out the king's earth and clay for making earthenware pots (*vasa terrena*) in a place near Ruardean called *Cowldwale* in the Forest demesne, for making pits in the

Forest, and also, on 20 July 1634, taking two cartloads of wood, worth 4*s*., from the king's woodland for making clay pots (*vasa lutea*).

27   William Davys, late of Mitcheldean, labourer, on 5 December 1634 carried timber, amounting to ½ ton worth 5s., out of the king's woodland.

28   Simon Mathewes, late of Drybrook near the Forest, John Adames of the same, labourer, William Dowse of Blackwell (*Blackholl*) Meadows, in Mitcheldean parish, labourer, Thomas Davies of the same, Elizabeth Probert of Lea (*le Lea*), and John Morris of the same, labourer, during the last two years kept, and keep up to the present time, male and female goats pasturing in the king's demesne without any warrant

[*f. 66v.*]   **The Roll by the Four Men and Reeve**

It is presented that:

29   George Russell, late of Oakwood near Bream, labourer, within the last three years built a cottage at Oakwood in the king's demesne of his Forest with cordwood (*cum tumulo ligni anglice with cordwood*), with loss to the king 6*d*., and took the issues and profits to his own use and takes them up to the present.

30   Thomas Imbery, late of the same labourer, within the same time built a cottage at Oakwood with cordwood, with loss to the king 6*d*., and [took] the issues, etc.

31   William Jenkins, late of the same, labourer, within the same time built a cottage at Oakwood with cordwood, with loss to the king 6*d*., and [took] the issues, etc.

32   William Nashe alias Gilbert, of Gorsty Knoll in the Forest, labourer, on 30 September 1634 enlarged a cottage at Gorsty Knoll, which was presented at the last eyre held for the Forest at Gloucester, and for that enlargement took a horse-load of wood, worth 2*d*., and [took] the issues, etc.

33   Richard Hannys, late of Mitcheldean, labourer, keeps a gun and a net in his house contrary to the forest law.

34   Joan Phelps, late of Shortstanding near the Forest, on 1 November 1634 lived in, and still does, a newly-built cottage with a garden enclosed and annexed to it, worth 2s. a year, and [took] the issues, etc.

35   Michael Hurst, late of English Bicknor, gent., on the same day cut down, and caused to be cut down, two beech trees, worth 5*s*. 6*d*., in the demesne, and converted and disposed of them to his own use, with great defrauding and loss to the king and great destruction and harm to the Forest.

36   The same Michael Hurst on the same day cut down, and caused to be cut down, a timber oak, worth 20*s*., in the demesne.

[*f. 67*]

37   Thomas Catchmay, late of Bishopswood (Herefs.), gent., within the last eight years built a house at Bishopswood within the Forest perambulation, containing six bays of building (*vi loca distincta tectorum anglice six bays of romth*).

38   John Broughton, late of Ruardean, gent., within the last three years built a house at Bishopswood within the Forest perambulation, containing two little bays of building (*duo parvula loca tectorum* [*anglice*] *two little bays of romth*), and took the issues and profits to his own use, and still does.

39   Francis Mathewes, late of Bishopswood, labourer, within the last 12 years built a house at Bishopswood within the Forest perambulation, containing two little bays of building, and [took] the issues, etc.

40   Roger Baylie, late of Bishopswood, labourer, within the last 10 years built a cottage at Bishopswood, containing one bay of building, and [took] the issues, etc.

41   Richard Williams, late of Bishopswood, within the last 10 years built a cottage at Bishopswood within the perambulation, containing one bay of building, and [took] the issues, etc.

42   John Shoreman, late of Bishopswood, labourer, within the last 12 years built a sheephouse at Bishopswood within the perambulation, containing two bays of building, which sheephouse encroached ¼ a. of the king's soil.

43   William Lawrence, late of Bishopswood, within the last 12 years built a cottage at Bishopswood within the perambulation, containing one bay of building (*unum locum tectorum anglice one baye of building*), which cottage encroached one-eighth of an acre of the land of the king's soil.

44   William Davys, late of Bishopswood, labourer, within the last 12 years built a cottage at Bishopswood within the perambulation, containing one bay of building, with which he encroached one-eighth of an acre of the king's soil.

45   Richard Davys, late of Bishopswood, on 28 February 1634 built a little cottage at Bishopswood within the perambulation, containing one bay of building, and [took] the issues and profits from it to his use, etc.

[*f. 67v.*]

46   John Vincent, late of Bishopswood, within the last 10 years built a cottage at Bishopswood within the perambulation, and took, and still takes, the issues and profits to his own use.

47   The same John Vincent on 28 February 1634 built another cottage at Bishopswood, and [took] the issues, etc.

48   Thomas Lodge, late of Bishopswood, labourer, on 20 March 1634 built at house at Bishopswood, containing one bay of building, and by it encroached ¼ a. of land of the king's soil.

49   John Morys, late of Bishopswood, labourer, within the last year built a house at Bishopswood and by it encroached ¼ a. land of the king's soil.

50   James Kyrle of Walford (Herefs.), esq., within the last 12 years built a house at Bishopswood, containing two bays of building, and [took] the issues and profits, etc.

51   Philip Jenkins of Walford, labourer, within the last 16 years built a cottage at Walford within the perambulation, containing two bays of building, and [took] the issues, etc.

52   Richard Fisher, late of Walford, labourer, on 28 February 1633 encroached one-eighth of an acre of the king's soil at Bishopswood.

53   William Penn of the same on the same day encroached one-eighth of an acre of the king's soil at Bishopswood.

54   William Hancocke of the same, labourer, on the same day encroached one-eighth of an acre of the king's soil at Bishopswood, and [took] the issues, etc.

55   Hugh Townsend of the same, labourer, on the same day encroached one-eighth of an acre of the king's soil at Bishopswood, and [took] the issues, etc.

[*f. 68*]

56   Richard Penn, late of the same, labourer, on the same day encroached one-eighth of an acre of the king's soil at Bishopswood, and [took] the issues, etc.

57   Thomas Jollye, late of the same, labourer, within the last two years built a cottage at Bishopswood, containing one bay of building, and [took] the issues, etc.

58   John Bennett, late of *le Bushes* near Mailscot,[1] labourer, within the last two years newly built a house at *Bromholde* near the Forest and within its regard, for building which he took two tons of timber of the king's woodland, and [took] the issues, etc.

59   William Howell, late of the *le Bushes* aforesaid, labourer, within the last three years newly built a cottage at *Bromholde* within the Forest regard, for building which he took a ton of timber of the king's woodland, and [took] the issues, etc.

60   Richard James, late of Berry hill near Coleford, labourer, within the last four years newly built a cottage at Berry hill within the Forest regard, for building which he took two tons of timber of the king's woodland, and [took] the issues, etc.

61   Roger Higgins the elder and Roger Higgins the younger of Berry hill near Coleford, husbandmen, within the last 20 years built a cottage and a barn at Berry hill, for building which they took six tons of timber of the woodland, etc.

62   The said Roger Higgins the elder and Roger Higgins the younger within the last seven years encroached from the king's soil of the Forest one bay of building adjoining the said cottage at Berry hill, and for building it they took a ton of timber of the woodland, etc.

63   George Marshall, late of Berry hill, husbandman, within the last 10 years built a cottage at Berry hill adjoining the Forest and within its regard, for which he took three tons of timber of the woodland, etc.

64   John Jefferyes, late of Lea (*le Lea*), labourer, within the last five years carried away ½ ton of the king's timber from a place called Lining wood in the king's demesne of his Forest.

[*f. 68v.*]

65   James Hall, late of Lea, labourer, within the last five years carried away ½ ton of the king's timber from a place called Lining in the king's demesne.

66   Robert Griffith, late of Staunton, and James Parrie, of *Knaven Greene*[2] near the Forest, miners, between 30 April 1631 and 30 April 1632 dug a coal-pit (*unum puteum carbonarium anglice one colepitt*)[3] at Berry hill in a parcel of land within the Forest regard and adjoining the highway, by reason of which Christopher Phelps of Coleford, glover, lost his life in the said pit, with loss to the king 40s. Also, the same Robert and

---

[1] *The Bushes* is marked on a map of *c.* 1680 between Mailscot wood and Berry hill: TNA, F 17/7.

[2] Marked on a map of c. 1680 to the west of Berry hill: TNA, F 17/7.

[3] The term usually means a 'charcoal-pit' at this period, but the offenders' occupation suggests that in this case a small coal-mine is meant.

James dug two other coal-pits in the same parcel of land at Berry Hill and have left them open and unfilled with loss to the king, contrary to the forest laws, etc.

67   James Hawkins, late of Flaxley, gent., within the last six years, in a place called Perlieu (*le Purley*)[1] in the parish of Hope Mansell (Herefs.) near Lea Bailey within the Forest perambulation, caused to be cut down 4,629 trees of oak timber, worth £200, and 22 oak saplings (*albur' querc' anglice saplings of oake*), worth £5, with great loss and harm to the king and great harm to the Forest, contrary to the laws, etc.

68   The said James Hawkins within the last 15 years, at Perlieu in Hope Mansell near Lea Bailey within the Forest perambulation, caused to be cut down four [*word indecipherable*] trees of beech timber, worth £100, and converted and disposed of them to his own use, with the great defrauding, etc.

69   The said James within the same period at the Perlieu cut down and rooted up the stumps and roots (*truncos et radices ... anglice le stubbs and the stowles*) of the trees he had formerly cut down and caused them to be made into charcoal.

[*f. 69*]

70   The said James Hawkins on 31 October 1634 cut down a coppice called *Hengrove*, containing 12 a. of woodland worth £6, lying in the parish of Hope Mansell (Herefs.) within the Forest perambulation.

At this court all the presentments and indictments recorded above and separately proved were affirmed in the court by the agreement of all the foresters, verderers, regarders, and other officers of the Forest.

[*f. 69v. is blank*]

[*f. 70*]

Forest of Dean in Gloucestershire, Herefordshire, Monmouthshire, and the County of the City of Gloucester: Court of Swanimote held at Mitcheldean 9 June 1635 before Charles Bridgman, Warren Gough, and John Berrowe, esqs., Verderers of the Forest

The names of the officers of the Forest are entered in the two following rolls.

The Roll for the Officers of the Forest

At this court it is presented that:

1   William Reynolds, servant of Benedict Jordan of English Bicknor, yeoman, on 23 May 1635 at Blackpennywall in the king's demesne of his Forest stripped the leaves and grazed 11 cattle on small green oak branches, containing by estimation four loads of wood worth 2*s.*, with loss to the king 4*s.*

2   Joseph Merricke, late of Mitcheldean, labourer, on 9 February 1635 cut down an oak at Lining wood in Lea bailiwick in the Forest demesne, with loss to the king 6*d.*

---

[1] See above, p. 129*n.*

3 Edmund Morgan, Thomas Morgan, and Walter Morgan, late of Littledean, labourers, on 26 February 1635 at *Meyseyhurst* in the Forest demesne cut down timber of the king's woodland to make instruments called shovel (*showle*)[1] timber.

4 James Wick, late of Ruddle, labourer, on 11 March 1635 at *Meyseyhurst* in the Forest demesne cut down timber of the king's woodland to make instruments called shovel timber.

5 John Sayre, late of Flaxley parish, labourer, on 26 February 1635 at *Meyseyhurst* in the Forest demesne cut down timber of the king's woodland.

6 Thomas Rosse, late of Littledean, labourer, on 5 March 1635 in the Forest demesne stripped the leaves and grazed his cattle on green holly trees, and felled by the roots two holly trees, amounting to one horse-load of wood.

[*f. 70v.*]

7 John Hopkins of Mitcheldean, labourer, on 8 March 1635, which was a Sunday, cut an oak in the king's demesne, with loss to the king 6*d.*

8 Paul Dellahay, late of Coleford in Newland, parish, gent.. and his servants on 25 March 1635 in the Forest demesne cut down and stripped leaves so that they might graze Paul's cattle on green hawthorns (*spinis anglice hathornes*), with loss to the king 6*d.*

9 Alexander Morgan, late of Ruardean, labourer, on 10 February 1635 at Moorwood in the Forest demesne cut down a green oak, containing two cords (*tumulos*) of wood, with loss to the king 13*s.*

10 Sara Swift, late of Littledean, widow, on 5 February 1635 at Haywood (*Eywode*) in the Forest demesne felled by the roots hollies and thorns, containing one horse-load of wood, with loss [to the king] 3*d.*

11 John Sayre, late of Flaxley parish, 'scalemaker',[2] on 5 March 1635 at *Meyseyhurst* in the Forest demesne cut up beech timber, amounting to one horse-load of timber, with loss to the king 2*d.*

12 Thomas Morgan and Walter Morgan, late of Littledean, labourers, on 5 March 1635 stripped the leaves from beech timber, amounting to three hose-loads of timber, with loss [to the king] 6*d.*

13 Giles Pope, late of Chestnuts in the Forest of Dean, labourer, on 25 May 1635 in the Forest demesne 'girded' (*succidit per medium ... anglice girded*) an oak, amounting to two horse-loads of wood worth 6*d.*, with loss to the king 2*s.*

14 Thomas Wilde, late of Mitcheldean, labourer, on 25 January 1635 cut down an oak, containing one-third of a ton of timber worth 3*s.* 4*d.*, at Lining wood in the Forest demesne, with loss [to the king] 6*d.*

15 Brian Conwaye, late of Mitcheldean, labourer, on 24 February 1635 'girded' an oak, amounting to six horse-loads of wood, at *Horwoods Eves*,[3] with loss to the king 12*d.*

---

[1] See above, p. 88 (no. 591), which confirms this meaning.

[2] A maker of thin boards from the outer cuts of a tree: *OED*.

[3] *Harwood Eves* is marked on a map of c. 1680 in the Harrow Hill area, south of Drybrook: TNA, F 17/7.

[f. 71]

16   Richard Frewin, late of Ruardean, husbandman, on 24 February 1635 at Ruardean's Eaves in the king's demesne of his Forest cut down the top branches (*summos ramusculos anglice the tower boughes*) of an oak, containing by estimation two horse-loads of wood worth 6*d.*, with loss to the king 12*d.*

17   Thomas Hopkins, late of Littledean, husbandman, on 25 February 1635 at Haywood felled by the roots green holly trees, containing by estimation two horse-loads of wood worth 6*d.*, with loss to the king 12*d.*

18   The said Thomas Hopkins on 5 February 1635 felled by the roots holly trees, amounting to one horse-load of wood, at Haywood in the Forest demesne, with loss to the king 3*d.*

19   George Dallaway, late of Newnham parish, labourer, and Thomas Treherne, and John Treherne of the same, labourers, on 16 February 1635 cut down a beech, containing ½ cord of wood, at Blaize Bailey, with loss to the king 3*s.* 4*d.*

20   Roger Norton, late of Mitcheldean, labourer, on 2 March 1635 cut up an oak, containing a wagon-load of wood, at *Dawkins hill* in the Forest demesne, with loss to the king 3*s.* 4*d.*

21   The same Roger Norton on 10 March 1635 cut down a young oak, containing a wagon-load of wood, at *Dawkins hill* in the Forest demesne, with loss to the king 3*s.* 4*d.*

22   Anthony Grynninge, late of Mitcheldean, labourer, on 18 March 1635 cut down the trunk of an oak, containing one cord of wood, at Lining wood in the Forest demesne, with loss to the king 3*s.* 4*d.*

23   William Cutler, late of Mitcheldean, labourer, and John Trigge of the same, labourer, on 26 March 1635 cut down an oak, containing one cord of wood, at Lining wood in the Forest demesne, with loss to the king 6*s.* 8*d.*

[f. 71v.]

24   Thomas Trigge, late of English Bicknor, labourer, on 18 December 1634 cut down two beeches, containing by estimation 10 horse-loads of wood worth 2*s.* 6*d.*, at Coverham in the king's demesne, with loss to the king 5*s.*

25   The same Thomas Trigge on 31 May 1635 cut down three beeches, containing three wagon-loads of wood worth 6*s.* 8*d.*, in Bicknor bailiwick in the Forest demesne, with loss to the king 12*s.*.

26   Benedict Jorden, late of English Bicknor, yeoman on 20 March 1635 stripped the leaves and grazed 11 cattle on small green branches (*ramusculis viridibus*) in the Forest demesne, with loss to the king 3*s.* 4*d.*

27   Humphrey Browne, late of Mitcheldean, labourer, on 31 March 1635 cut down the top of a yew, containing by estimation two horse-loads of wood, at Haywood in the Forest demesne, and carried off the wood with a black horse worth 10*s.*

28   Thomas Trigge, late of English Bicknor, timberman, on 24 March 1635 cut down a green timber beech, worth 12*d.*, at Coverham in the Forest demesne, with loss to the king 4*d.*

29   Richard Dowle, late of Whitecliff in Newland parish, husbandman, on 10 March 1635 at Winnalls (*le Wynnolls*) in the Forest demesne cut down two horse-loads of green oak, which he hauled out of the Forest with two horses worth 20*s.*, with loss to the king 12*d.*

30   Richard Bleeke, late of Parkend in the Forest, collier, on 20 February 1635 cut down an oak, containing a ton of timber worth 6*s.* 8*d.*, near Parkend in Staunton bailiwick in the Forest demesne, with loss to the king 20*d.*

31   The same Richard Bleeke on the same day cut up a timber trunk, containing by estimation a ton of timber worth 6*s.* 8*d.*, near Parkend in Staunton bailiwick in the Forest demesne.

[*f. 72*]

32   Christopher Foxe, late of Parkend in the Forest, woodcutter, on 10 February 1635 cut up part of a tree called a 'morier',[1] containing by estimation a ton of timber worth 6*s.* 8*d.*, at Parkend in the king's demesne of his Forest.

33   The same Christopher Foxe on the same day cut up part of the timber of an oak, containing by estimation ½ ton of timber worth 3*s.* 4*d.*, at Parkend in the Forest demesne.

34   Richard Whittington the younger, late of Bream in Newland parish, gent., on 31 May 1635 at Oakwood in Staunton bailiwick in the Forest demesne took out of the Forest various parcels of oak timber, containing by estimation two tons of timber worth 13*s.* 4*d.*, [using] four oxen worth 53*s.* 4*d.*

35   Thomas Ellys, late of Brockhollands (*Brookhollyns*)[2] near the Forest, carpenter, on 31 May 1635 cut down an oak, containing by estimation three tons of timber worth 20*s.*, at Parkend in Staunton bailiwick in the Forest demesne, with loss to the king 40*s.*

36   Anthony Molton, late of St. Briavels, labourer, on 31 May 1635 at Oakwood in Staunton bailiwick in the Forest demesne took four parcels of (?)saw*n* (*serat'*) beech timber out of the Forest, containing by estimation three tons worth 20*s.*

37   Richard Jones, late of Parkend in the Forest, labourer, and Leonard Jones of the same, labourer, on 31 May 1635 cut up various trunks of timber, containing by estimation four tons worth 26*s.* 8*d.*, at Oakwood in Staunton bailiwick in the Forest demesne, with loss and defrauding of the king.

38   Nicholas Whittson of Littledean, nailer, on 16 January 1635 in the 'meend' (*le myne*)[3] at Littledean called Master Brayne's meend within the Forest perambulation hunted a hare (?)in the snow (*nive*) with a female dog contrary to the law and statute ordained in such cases.

39   Richard Thomas of Flaxley parish, gent., on 1 February 1635 killed a brace of 'rascal'[4] does (*duas damas anglice a brace of rascall deere*) with his female dog (*canem femellam anglice by his mungrell bitch*) in the Forest regard, and took the meat and disposed of it at his will, with harm and damage to the king's deer, contrary to the forest law, etc.

[*f. 72v.*]

40   Richard Chynn, late of Newnham, yeoman, is a daily malefactor of the king's (?*le vaidue*) and on 8 June 1635 had the skin of a doe in his house at Newnham within the Forest perambulation.

---

[1] A 'ruined' tree: see above, p. 110 (no. 1).

[2] In Bream tithing, Newland parish.

[3] The local term for a parcel of common or waste land.

[4] A young, thin, or otherwise inferior animal: *OED*.

41   Hercules Loveden, late of the Hayes, near the Forest cover in Awre parish within the Forest perambulation, keeps a female dog in his house, which dog is not 'hambled' (*expeditatam*) in accordance with the forest law.

42   Richard Pallmer, late of Poolway near Coleford in Newland parish, labourer, on 30 January 1635 entered the king's Forest, and killed a 'sorrel' deer[1] with a mongrel dog at *Voylehay* in the king's demesne of his Forest, and took and carried off the meat at will.

43   The same Richard Pallmer, with an unknown person, on the same day killed a female fawn (*damam iuvenilem anglice a fawne*) at Wet wood, and took the meat, etc.

44   Henry, earl of Worcester, by his agents or undertenants, during the last four years cut down small parcels of coppice and underwood, containing 4 a., parts of a vill called the Garth (*le Garff*) at Wyesham in Dixton parish (Mon.) within the Forest perambulation.

45   Thomas Mark, late of Coleford in Newland parish, on 31 May 1635 built a cottage, containing one bay of building (*unum locum tectorum anglice one baye of romth*), on the king's soil of the Forest, and took, and still takes, the profits to his own use.

46   Walter Jones, late of Coleford, labourer, on the same day enlarged a cottage near Coleford, which cottage was built on the king's soil beforehand, viz. of a bay of building containing 8ft.

47   Richard Lawrence, late of Soudley in the Forest, labourer, during the last year has kept four horses and mares pasturing on the king's demesne of his Forest without any warrant.

[*f. 73*]

48   William Allen, late of Soudley in the Forest, labourer, during the past year has kept four horses and mares pasturing on the king's demesne without any warrant.

49   Ralph Collier, late of Bishopswood (Herefs.), labourer, during the past year has a cottage, built on the king's soil of the Forest at Bishopswood within the Forest perambulation, and took, and still takes, the profits of it to his own use.

50   Charles Hughes, late of Bishopswood, labourer, during the last two years encroached one-eighth of an acre of the king's soil of his Forest at Bishopswood within the Forest perambulation, and took the profits, etc.

51   Walter Preist of Walford (Herefs.), labourer, during the last two years built a sheephouse, containing two bays of building, at Bishopswood within the Forest perambulation, and [took] the profits, etc.

At this court all the presentments and indictments recorded above were affirmed by the unanimous agreement of all the foresters, verderers, regarders, and other officers of the Forest.

[*f. 73v. is blank*]

---

[1] A buck in its third year: *Manwood's Forest Laws*, ed. Nelson, p. 48.

[*f. 74*]

Forest of Dean in Gloucestershire, Herefordshire, Monmouthshire, and the County of the City of Gloucester: Court of Swanimote held at Mitcheldean 14 September 1635 before Charles Bridgman, Warren Goughe, and John Berrowe, esqs., Verderers of the Forest.

The names of the officers of the Forest are entered in the two rolls following.

It is presented that:

1   Richard Morgan, son of James Morgan, late of Ruardean, labourer, on 5 August 1635 at Ruardean Eaves in the king's demesne of his Forest cut down a green oak, amounting to a wagon-load of wood, with loss to the king 6*s*. 8*d*.

2   Edward Elliot, late of Awre, labourer, on 30 June 1635 in Blakeney bailiwick in the Forest demesne cut down two horse-loads of beech timber, worth 2*s*., to make 'spitters'[1] and shovel-trees (*instrumenta anglice spitters and shovell trees*).

3   John Webb, late of Blakeney, turner, on 30 June 1635 in Blakeney bailiwick in the Forest demesne felled by the roots the trunk of a beech, containing by estimation five horse-loads of wood worth 10*d*.

4   George Thorne and Edward Addams, late of Clearwell in Newland parish, labourers, on 30 June 1635 at Oakwood in Staunton bailiwick in the Forest demesne cut up part of an oak, containing by estimation one-eighth of a ton of timber worth 20*d*., after it had been assigned to the king's use and delivered into the custody of Benedict Hall, esq., the woodward of Staunton bailiwick.

5   William Cassall, late of Parkend in the Forest, labourer, on 30 June 1635 at Wet wood in the Forest demesne felled by the roots willow trees, containing by estimation eight horse-loads of wood worth 2*s*.

6   William Morgan, late of Whitecliff in Newland parish, labourer, on 30 June 1635 in Staunton bailiwick in the Forest demesne 'girded' by the middle (*succidit pro dimidia anglice girded by the middle*) an oak, containing by estimation three horse-loads of wood worth 9*d*.

7   John Dowle, late of Whitecliff in Newland parish, labourer, on 30 June 1635 in Staunton bailiwick in the Forest demesne cut down from the king's woodland four horse-loads of bills (*billorum* [*anglice*] . . . *stackes*), worth 12*d*., and carried them away with two horses worth 30*s*.

[*f. 74v.*]

8   Giles Webb, late of Coleford in Newland parish, labourer, on 30 June 1635 in Staunton bailiwick in the king's demesne cut down a green beech, amounting to one horse-load worth 3*d*., and carried it away with a horse worth 12*s*. 3*d*.

9   Henry Morton of Coleford in Newland parish, husbandman, on 30 June 1635 at Wet wood in Staunton bailiwick in the Forest demesne took out of the Forest three parcels of timber, containing by estimation one ton worth 6*s*.

10   Arnold Davis, late of Mitcheldean, labourer, on 13 July 1635 at Birch wood in Mitcheldean bailiwick in the Forest demesne cut down a piece of beech timber, amounting to half a cord of wood, and carried it away with two horses worth 20*s*.

---

[1] spades: *OED*.

11   William Holliday and Thomas Hopkins, late of Littledean, miners, on 25 July 1635 at Haywood (*Aywood*) in Ruardean bailiwick in the Forest demesne cut in half a green beech, worth 6*s.* 8*d.* and amounting to a wagon-load of timber, for use in their mine pits (*pro sua minera caverna anglice for their myne pitts*).

12   John Stevens, late of *Fayre moore* in the Forest, labourer, within the last year built a cottage on the king's soil of his Forest at a place called *Little Fayre moore* in the Forest demesne, and [took] the profits, etc.

13   John Addams, late of *Fayre moore*, labourer, within the same time built a cottage on the king's soil at *Little Fayre moore*, and [took] the profits, etc.

14   Thomas Baker, late of *Fayre moore*, labourer, within the same time built a cottage on the king's soil at *Little Fayre moore*, and [took] the profits, etc.

15   Thomas Williams, late of Dixton parish (Mon.), labourer, within the last year built a cottage on the king's soil at Wyesham (*Wisam*), and [took] the profits, etc.

16   John Griffith, late of Dixton parish (Mon.), labourer, within the last three years built a cottage on the king's soil at Wyesham within the Forest perambulation, and [took] the profits, etc.

[*f. 75*]

17   William Heynes, late of Staunton, shepherd, maintains a cottage, built some time ago near Staunton, and within the last 20 years he has inclosed and encroached a parcel of land [adjoining] the said cottage, containing 1a. of the king's soil, and [takes] the issues and profits from the same, etc.

18   Thomas Williams, late of Staunton, labourer, within the last year built a cottage near Staunton on the king's soil, and [takes] the issues and profits from the same, etc.

19   John Hodges, late of Flaxley, tailor, with another unknown person on 10 September 1635 entered [the Forest] at Badcocks Bailey with a gun and a mongrel dog, to the harm and disturbance of the king's deer in the Forest.

20   James Berrowe, late of Quedgeley, gent., and John Gaynsford, late of Blakeney, gent., on 1 September 1635 entered [the Forest] near a place called *Cowlery Oake* with a gun and a hunting dog, and there Berrowe shot (*sagittavit*) at a doe and chased it from there with the dog.

At this court all the presentments and judgements recorded above were affirmed by unanimous agreement of the foresters, verderers, regarders, and other officers of the Forest.

[*f. 75v. is blank*]

[*f. 76*]

Forest of Dean in Gloucestershire, Herefordshire, Monmouthshire, and the County of the City of Gloucester: Court of Swanimote held at Mitcheldean 8 December 1635 before Charles Bridgman, Warren Gough, and John Berrowe, esqs., Verderers of the Forest

The names of the officers of the Forest follow in the next roll.

It is presented that:

1   Thomas Ellye, son of James Ellye, late of Coleford in Newland parish, miner, on 20 October 1635 at Coverham in the king's demesne of his Forest cut down the topmost branches (*summos ramos anglice the tower boughes*) of an oak, containing by estimation two horse-loads of wood worth 6*d.*, with loss to the king 12d.

2   The wife and daughter of Richard Howell, late of the Peak in Clearwell in Newland parish, on 22 November 1635 at Ellwood in the Forest demesne felled green holly trees by their roots (*funditus*), containing by estimation one horse-load of wood, and by that felling he took the last of the hollies, with loss to the king 2*s.*

3   Thomas Hopkins, late of Littledean, miner, on 7 December 1635 at Haywood (*Eywood*) in the Forest demesne cut in half a young beech, containing by estimation two horse-loads of wood worth 6*d.*, with loss to the king 6*d.*

4   Simon Mathewes of the Morse in the Forest, labourer, on 7 December 1635 at *Horwoods Eaves* in the Forest demesne cut down the top branches of two oaks, containing by estimation four horse-loads of wood worth 12*d.*, with loss [to the king] 12*d.*

5   Hugh Hopkins, late of Coleford, servant of Leonard Wilson of the same place, gent., on 27 May 1635 at Barnhill in Staunton bailiwick in the Forest demesne cut down two horse-loads from an oak, worth 6*d.*, which he hauled out of the Forest with two horses worth 10*s.*, with loss [to the king] 12*d.*

6   Richard Bleeke, late of Ivy Moor[1] near Parkend within the Forest, labourer, on 26 October 1635 at Barnhill in Staunton bailiwick in the Forest demesne cut up a piece of oak timber, containing by estimation a ton of timber worth 10*s.*, with loss [to the king] 10*s.*

[*f. 76v.*]

7   Edward Addams, late of Clearwell in Newland parish, miner, on 21 November 1635 at Oakwood in Staunton bailiwick in the Forest demesne cut down four horse-loads of wood, worth 2*s.*, from two oaks, with loss to the king 4*d.*

8   Thomas Banister, late of Clearwell in Newland parish, miner, on 25 November 1635 at Oakwood in Staunton bailiwick cut down one horse-load [of wood], worth 6*d.*, from an oak, with loss to the king 12*d.*

9   James Wyntell, late of Coleford in Newland parish, tailor, on 24 November 1635 at Winnalls (*le Wynnolls*) in Staunton bailiwick in the Forest demesne cut down from an oak and a beech two loads of green wood, worth 8*d.*, which he hauled out of the Forest with a horse worth 13*s.* 4*d.*

10   Thomas Jones of *le Woodside* in the Forest, labourer, on 3 November 1635 at *Deanes Waye* in Staunton bailiwick in the Forest demesne cut down a young oak (*iuvenem querculum anglice one stubb oake*), containing by estimation a ton of wood, worth 6*s.* 8*d.*, with loss [to the king] 10*d.*

11   Richard Yersley, late of Coleford in Newland parish, labourer, on 7 November 1635 at *Deanes Waye* in Staunton bailiwick in the Forest demesne cut up two horse-loads, worth 8*d.*, from a windfallen oak, with loss [to the king] 12*d.*

12   Richard Richfield alias Richbyll, late of Littledean, saddle-tree maker, on 18 September 1635 cut up two 'kibbles'[2] (*segmenta anglice two kibbles*), containing by estimation two horse-loads of timber worth 12*d.*, from a windfallen beech.

[1] See above, p. 51*n.*

[2] In Dean this term was used for pieces of stolen timber cut into suitable lengths for use by coopers or wheelrights: *Third Report of the Commissioners to Enquire into the Crown Woods, Forests and Land Revenues* (1788), p. 29.

13 William Morgan, late of Whitecliff in Newland parish, labourer, on 27 November 1635 in Abenhall bailiwick in the Forest demesne cut up 'sealed' timber[1] from a birch tree, containing ½ ton worth 5s.

[f. 77]

14 William Worgan, late of Whitecliff in Newland parish, labourer, on the same day at Winnalls in Staunton bailiwick in the Forest demesne felled by the roots a crab-apple tree (*unam arborem silvestrem*)[2] containing by estimation ½ horse-load of wood worth 6d., with loss [to the king] 12d.

At this court all the presentments and judgements recorded above were affirmed by unanimous agreement of all the foresters, verderers, regarders, and other officers of the Forest.

[f. 77v. is blank]

[f. 78]

Forest of Dean in Gloucestershire, Herefordshire, Monmouthshire, and the County of the City of Gloucester: Court of Swanimote held at Littledean 9 June 1636 before Charles Bridgman, John Berrowe, and Warren Goughe, esqs., Verderers of the Forest.

The names of the officers follow in the two rolls following and then the presentments.

It is presented that:

1 Thomas Godwyn of Huntsham (Herefs.),[3] doctor of sacred theology, during the last two years at Mailscot in the king's demesne of his Forest has (?)obstructed (*interludit*) the highway leading from Huntsham ferry to Coleford, with loss to the king 6d. and hindrance of the king's subjects travelling on that road, contrary to the form of the statute ordained in this matter and contrary to the king's peace.

2 George Wirrall, late of Monmouth, during the same time at *Sars grove* near the river Wye within the Forest perambulation dug up a designated road (*denotandam viam* [*anglice*] *a marke waye*), to the hindrance of the public.

3 William Welshman, late of Wye's Green[4] in the Forest, labourer, within the last year encroached a parcel of land of the king's soil of his Forest at Wye's Green, worth by estimation 4d., and built a cottage on it, and took, and still takes, the issues and profits from the same to his own use.

4 James Taylor, late of Ruardean, labourer, on 25 Jan 1636 at Serridge in Mitcheldean bailiwick in the king's demesne of his Forest cut up a 'kibble'[5] (*unum segmentum anglice one kibble*) of a windfallen beech, containing by estimation two horse-loads of wood, which he carried out of the Forest on his back, with loss [to the king] 12d.

---

[1] i.e. sealed or marked by the officers for official use.

[2] For this meaning, see below, p. 146 (no. 37).

[3] See above, p. 59n.

[4] On the bank of the Wye in Newland parish, at the place later called Lower Redbrook: *VCH Glos.* v. p. 206.

[5] See above, p. 142n.

5   Charles Jones, late of *Horwoods Eaves* in the Forest, labourer, on 12 March 1636 at *Horwoods Eaves* in Mitcheldean bailiwick in the Forest demesne cut up (?)a bundle of oak (*nexa querc'*), containing three horse-loads of wood, which he carried out of the Forest on his back.

[*f. 78v.*]

6   David Harbard, late of the Forest, labourer, on 20 May 1636 at *Cowldwale* in Ruardean bailiwick in the king's demesne encroached a parcel of land of the king's soil, worth 6*d.*, and built a cottage on it, and took, and still takes, the issues and profits from it to his own use.

7   George Skynner, late of Lydbrook in the Forest, labourer, and Francis Landen, John Preddye, and John Lawrence, all of the same, labourers, on 31 January 1635 at Hangerberry in English Bicknor bailiwick in the Forest demesne felled by the roots six beeches, and cut down four other beeches, containing three horse-loads of wood worth 3*s.*, with loss to the king 5*s.*

8   James Marshall, late of Lea Bailey, labourer, in 1635–6[1] at Lea Bailey in Lea bailiwick in the Forest demesne cut down a small oak sapling, containing ¼ ton of timber worth 2*s.* 6*d.*, which he carried out of the Forest on his back, with loss [to the king] 12*d.*

9   John Rudge, late of Rudge[2] in the Forest, labourer, on 15 February 1636 at Lea Bailey in Lea bailiwick in the Forest demesne cut down a small oak sapling, containing by estimation ½ ton of timber worth 5*s.*, which he carried out of the Forest on his back, with loss [to the king] 2*s.*

10   John Huntley, late of Awre in the Forest, and Richard Ellotts and Edward Ellotts of the same, all timbermen, on 16 May 1636 near Blakeney in Blakeney bailiwick in the Forest demesne cut up a piece of beech timber, containing by estimation ½ ton worth 5*s.*.

11   The same John Huntley, Richard Ellotts, and Edward Ellotts on 30 April 1636 in Blakeney bailiwick in the Forest demesne cut up ½ ton of beech timber, worth 5*s.*

12   John Webb, late of Blakeney in Awre parish, timberman, on 30 April 1636 near Blakeney in Blakeney bailiwick cut up two horse-loads of beech timber worth 2*s.*

[*f. 79*]

13   Thomas Trigge, late of English Bicknor, timberman, on 14 January 1636 in English Bicknor bailiwick in the Forest demesne felled by the roots two beeches, containing two cords of wood worth 13*s.* 4*d.*, with loss to the king 20*s.*

14   The said Thomas Trigge on 14 March 1636 in English Bicknor bailiwick in the Forest demesne felled by the roots a beech, containing by estimation ½ cord of wood worth 3*s.* 4*d.*, with loss to the king 6*s.* 8*d.*

15   Roger Higgins, late of Berry hill in the Forest, husbandman, on 13 January 1636 in the Forest demesne felled by the roots a beech, containing by estimation ½ cord of wood worth 3*s.* 4*d.*, with loss [to the king] 6*s.* 8*d.*

16   Robert Banister, late of [*blank*], kt., by his agents and servants between 1 March and 6 April 1636 at Cannop Vallets (*Fellet*) in Staunton bailiwick in the Forest demesne

---

[1] Only the regnal year (11 Chas. I) is given.
[2] In Weston under Penyard parish east of Lea Bailey woods.

felled 1,000 sapling oaks and beeches to make wooden fences (*sepes oblignas*) for the said 'fellet',[1] hauling them away with a horse worth 26*s.* 8*d.*, with loss [to the king] £5.

17   Thomas Phillips the younger, late of *Quisclade* in the Forest, labourer, on 14 March 1636 at *Quisclade*[2] in the Forest demesne cut down the stump of a green beech (*viridis fagi anglice a greene stubb beech*), containing by estimation three-quarters of a cord of wood worth 6*s.*, with loss [to the king] 3*s.* 4*d.*

18   Enoch Tomlinson, late of Coleford in Newland parish, innholder, on 8 March 1636 at Winnalls in the Forest demesne cut down a green oak, containing two horse-loads of wood worth 12*d.*, with loss [to the king] 2*s.*

19   George Skynner, late of Lydbrook in the Forest, 'finer',[3] on 5 March 1636 at Hangerberry in the Forest demesne 'girded' the head of a young oak, containing by estimation one horse-load of green wood worth 6*d.*, with loss [to the king] 12*d.*

20   William Sayre, late of Flaxley, and John Sayre of the same, 'scalemakers',[4] on 5 May 1636 in the Forest demesne cut up by night two 'kibbles'[5] (*segmenta anglice two kibbles*) of beech wood in the king's woodlands; and the same on 19 May 1636 in the Forest demesne cut up a half 'kibble' (*halfe a kibble*), amounting to three horse-loads of timber, which they hauled away to the house of John Watkins.

[*f. 79v.*]

21   William Parlor, late of Joyford near English Bicknor, husbandman, during the last three years, without any licence, cut down 13 trees standing on his land at Joyford in the Forest demesne, from which William caused to be made five (?)loads (*vehes*) of charcoal, which he sold for £5, without any warrant and contrary to the forest laws.

22   The same William Parlor within the same period cut down three beeches and other logs (*truncos anglice loggs*) in the king's woodland in the demesne of his Forest, and hauled them onto his land with six oxen, and from them caused [to be made] three (?)loads (*vehes*) of charcoal, which he sold for £3.

23   The same William Parlor within the same period cut down, and caused to be cut down, five oak trees, worth 53*s.* 4*d.*, and four other tons of oak timber of the king's woodland of his Forest, worth 26*s.* 8*d.*, which he hauled out of the Forest with six oxen.

24   Anthony Grynnynge of Mitcheldean, labourer, on 5 January 1636 at Lining wood in the Forest demesne cut down a green oak trunk, which he carried out of the Forest on his back.

25   David Madocke, late of Serridge, cabiner, on 11 January 1636 at Serridge in the Forest demesne cut away (*presecavit(?) did chippe*) a piece (*frustillum anglice a peece*) of oak timber, containing by estimation one ton.

26   John Pritchett, late of Mitcheldean, labourer, on 23 December 1635 at Lining wood in the Forest demesne cut down a green oak trunk, containing ½ cord of wood worth 5*s.* 6*d.*, which he carried out of the Forest on his back.

---

[1] The word was used for a coppice designated for felling.

[2] See above, p. 63*n.*

[3] One who carried out the refining process at an ironworks.

[4] See above, p. 136*n.*

[5] See above, p. 142*n.*

[*f. 80*]

27   Thomas Jones, late of (?)*Erowalls* near Newland parish, labourer, on 26 January 1636 in Staunton bailiwick in the Forest demesne cut one horse-load of wood, worth 2*d.*, from an oak.

28   The said Thomas Jones on 10 February 1636 in Staunton bailiwick in the Forest demesne felled by the roots an oak, worth 20*s.*, with loss to the king 40*s.*

29   The same Thomas Jones on the same day in Staunton bailiwick in the Forest demesne cut one horse-load of wood, worth 2*d.*, from a beech, and hauled it out of the Forest with a mare, worth 10*s.*, with loss [to the king] 4*d.*

30   Thomas Ellis, late of Coleford in the Forest, labourer, on the same day in Staunton bailiwick in the Forest demesne felled two green holly trees by the roots, with loss to the king 4*s.*

31   Richard Bleeke, late of Ivy Moor near Parkend in the Forest, labourer, on 14 December 1635 in Staunton bailiwick in the Forest demesne felled by the roots a beech, containing two cords of wood worth 13*s.* 4*d.*, with loss [to the king] 20*s.*

32   The said Richard Bleeke on 14 January and 27 February 1636 in Staunton bailiwick in the Forest demesne cut down two other beeches, containing three cords of wood worth 20*s.*, with loss [to the king] 20*s.*

33   Richard Howell, late of Clearwell in the Forest, labourer, on 26 February 1636 in Staunton bailiwick in the king's demesne cut down two tons of oak timber after they had been assigned to the king's use and delivered into the custody of Benedict Hall, esq., woodward of Staunton, with loss to the king 13*s.* 4*d.*

[*f. 80v.*]

34   John Taylor, late of Clearwell in the Forest, carpenter, on 26 February 1636 in Staunton bailiwick in the king's demesne cut down a piece (*unum frustillum anglice a peece*) of oak timber, containing one ton, after it had been assigned to the king's use and delivered into the custody of Benedict Hall, esq., woodward of Staunton, with loss [to the king] 6*s.* 8*d.*

35   Richard Yersley, late of Coleford in the Forest, labourer, on 25 November 1635 in Staunton bailiwick in the Forest demesne uprooted (*extirpavit per radices*) five oak saplings, containing by estimation one horse-load of wood worth 12*d.*, with loss [to the king] 5*s.*

36   Giles Webb, late of Coleford in the Forest, miner, on 8 and 9 December 1635 in Staunton bailiwick in the Forest demesne cut down two oaks, containing by estimation two cords of wood worth 13*s.* 4*d.*, which he hauled away with three horses, worth £3, with loss [to the king] 10*s.*

37   William Morgan, late of Whitecliff in Newland parish, labourer, on 2 December 1635 in Staunton bailiwick in the Forest demesne felled by the roots a green crab-apple tree (*unam viridem silvestrem* [*anglice*] *a greene crabtree*), containing by estimation one horse-load of wood worth 12*d.*, with loss [to the king] 18*d.*

38   Thomas Worgan, late of Blakeney in Awre parish, tanner, on 19 May 1636 in Staunton bailiwick in the Forest demesne felled by the roots green sallows (*salves anglice sallies*), containing by estimation one horse-load of wood worth 2*s.*, which he hauled away with a horse, worth 26*s.* 8*d.*, with loss [to the king] 12*d.*

At this court all the presentments and judgements recorded above were affirmed by unanimous agreement of all the foresters, verderers, regarders, and other officers of the Forest.

[f. 81]

Forest of Dean in Gloucestershire, Herefordshire, Monmouthshire, and the County of the City of Gloucester: Court of Swanimote held at Littledean 14 September 1636 before Charles Bridgman, Warren Goughe, and John Berrowe, esqs., Verderers of the Forest.

The names of the officers are written in one roll.

It is presented that:

1   John Webb of Awre parish, timberman, on 28 May 1635 in Blakeney [bailiwick][1] in the king's demesne cut up ¼ ton of a windfallen timber beech, worth 5s. 3d., and also another 12 horse-loads (*sarcinas anglice seames*) of wood, worth 3s.

2   John Fryer, late of Blakeney, yeoman, deputy of the woodward of Blakeney bailiwick, on 6 April 1636 in Blakeney bailiwick in the king's demesne sold without licence to Edward Bradshawe of Blakeney, timberman, three cords of beech timber (?)lacking 2ft in length (*caren' duobus pedibus*), worth 21s.

3   William Preece, late of English Bicknor, labourer, on 14 January 1636 took one horse-load of wood from the king's cordwood, and hauled it away with a horse, worth 13s. 4d., with loss [to the king] 5s.

4   Thomas Preece, late of Redbrook in Newland parish, labourer, on 11 February 1636 at the Glydden[2] in the Forest demesne cut down a crab tree (*unum arbutum anglice a crabtree*), containing by estimation four horse-loads of timber worth 10s., with loss [to the king] 3s. 4d.

5   Simon Mathewes, late of Drybrook in the Forest, labourer, on 6 June 1636 near *Ravens Ford* in Ruardean bailiwick in the Forest demesne cut down three horse-loads of green wood, with loss [to the king] 12d.

6   William Foxe, late of Coleford in [Newland] parish,[3] (*word indecipherable*) maker, on 17 September in Staunton bailiwick in the Forest demesne cut down a piece (*frustillum anglice a peece*) of a timber oak, containing two horse-loads of timber worth 2s., formerly assigned to the king's use.

[f. 81v.]

7   Evan Williams, late of Bream's Eaves in the Forest, labourer, on 6 July 1636 in Staunton bailiwick in the Forest demesne felled by the roots a beech, amounting to one wagon-load of wood worth 5s., with loss [to the king] 2s. 6d.

8   Simon Upsimond, late of Brockhollands (*Brockhollyns*)[4] in the Forest, labourer, on 10 September 1636 in the Forest demesne cut down, and caused to be cut down, 13 oak saplings, containing by estimation six horse-loads worth 6s., with loss [to the king] 20s.

9   Cecilia Whittington, widow of Richard Whittington late of Oakwood mill in Newland parish, gent., deceased, by her servants and agents, on 8 July 1636 at Oakwood in Staunton bailiwick in the Forest demesne cut four horse-loads of wood, worth 2s., from two oaks.

[1] MS. has scribal error: *in Blackney de Blackney.*
[2] A detached part of the extraparochial demesne near Redbrook, later absorbed in Newland parish: *VCH Glos.* v. p. 197.
[3] MS. has scribal error: *in parochia de Coleford.*
[4] In Bream tithing, Newland parish.

10   John Huntley, late of Awre parish, timberman, and Richard Ellets of the same place, timberman, on 6 January 1636 in Blakeney bailiwick in the Forest demesne cut up a log from a timber beech, containing four horse-loads of timber worth 4*s*., with loss [to the king] 5*s*.

11   John Edwards, late of Cannop in the Forest, woodcutter, on 28 February 1636 in the Forest demesne took wood, amounting to ¼ cord, from the king's cordwood.

12   James Morgan, late of *Langosse* in the Forest, labourer, on 28 February 1636 at *Dennalls moore* in the Forest demesne took wood, amounting to ¼ cord, from the king's cordwood in order to make a fire.

13   William Sayre and John Sayre, late of Flaxley, timbermen, on 31 July 1636 at Serridge (*Sheridge*) in the Forest demesne cut up five 'kibbles'[1] (*sigmenta anglice five kibbles*) from a beech, and carried them away on his back, with loss [to the king] 5*s*.

14   Emanuel Buckler, late of Chepstow (Mon.), yeoman, within the last two years at Tidenham within the Forest perambulation cut down an underwood called *le Warren*, containing 51 a. and worth £3.

[*f. 82*]

15   John Teage, late of Lea (Glos.), labourer, on 15 May 1635 in Lea bailiwick in the Forest demesne cut down an oak sapling, amounting to ¼ ton of timber , which he carried away on his back, with loss [to the king] 5*s*.

16   Paul Thomas, late of Lea Bailey Side in the Forest, labourer, on 15 March 1636 in Lea bailiwick in the Forest demesne cut down the top branches of a beech, containing three horse-loads of wood, which he carried away on his back.

17   Henry Pumfrey, late of Blakeney, yeoman, on 11 February 1636 at Blakeney's Eaves in Blakeney bailiwick in the Forest demesne cut up ¼ of a cord of timber, worth 5*s*. 3*d*.., from a windfallen beech.

18   Thomas Hayward, late of Blakeney, timberman, by his servants and agents, on 11 February 1636 at Blakeney's Eaves in Blakeney bailiwick in the Forest demesne cut up a cord of timber, worth 21*s*., from a windfallen timber beech.

19   Edward Bradshawe, late of Blakeney, timberman, on 11 February 1636 at Blakeney's Eaves in Blakeney bailiwick in the Forest demesne cut up ¼ of a cord, worth 5*s*. 6*d*., from a windfallen timber beech.

20   Thomas Berrowe, late of Blakeney, and Philip Edwards, late of the same place, timberman, on 11 February 1636 at Blakeney's Eaves in Blakeney bailiwick in the Forest demesne cut up two cords, worth 42*s*., from a windfallen timber beech.

21   Thomas Wood and Thomas Symonds, late of Blakeney, labourers, on 10 February 1636 at Blakeney's Eaves in Blakeney bailiwick in the Forest demesne cut 1½ cords, worth 32*s*. 6*d*., from a windfallen timber beech.

22   Alexander Worgan, late of Blakeney, labourer, on 10 February 1636 at Blakeney's Eaves in Blakeney bailiwick in the Forest demesne cut up a short cord (*brevem tumulum anglice a short corde*), worth 10*s*. 6*d*., from a windfallen timber beech.

23   Christopher Hawkins, late of Coleford in Newland parish, labourer, during the last year built a cottage, 10ft. square (*decem pedum quadratum*), on the king's soil at Coleford, and took, and still takes, the issues and profits from it to his own use.

[1] See above, p. 142*n*.

[f. 82v.]

24   William Rogers, late of *le Rock* in Newland parish, labourer, during the last year built a cottage, 8 ft. square, on the king's soil at Coleford, and took, and still takes, the issues and profits from it to his own use.

25   Joseph Okey, late of Longhope, yeoman, during the last two years cut down, and caused to be cut down, 10 timber oaks, worth 40*s.*, on the soil and land of the earl of Kent at Longhope within the Forest perambulation.

26   John Hannys, late of *Gotherdge* (Herefs.),[1] yeoman, on 31 May 1636 at Bishopswood (Herefs.) within the Forest perambulation cut down underwood, containing three-quarters of an acre worth 20*s.*

27   William Caldicott of Bishopswood (Herefs.), gent., on 31 May 1636 at Bishopswood in Walford parish within the Forest perambulation cut down underwood, containing 2 a. worth 40*s.*

28   Robert Banister, kt., and John Tomes of Cannop in the Forest, husbandman, Robert's servant, for the last year have stopped up the common highway (*vestigiam publicam anglice the comon highway*) at Cannop, leading from English Bicknor through a parcel of land and underwood called Cannop Vallets to Purton passage (*transmissum anglice ... the passage*), with loss to the king 2*s.*, to the great loss of the king's subjects, contrary to the form of the statute passed in connexion with this matter, contrary to the king's peace and dignity, and to the harm of the deer in the king's Forest.

29   The said Robert Banister and John Tomes, his servant, during the same time have stopped up the common highway at Cannop, leading from English Bicknor through Cannop Vallets to *Hoppershill* and so to Serridge (*Sheridge*) and from thence to Newnham, a market town (*villatam for[ensam] anglice a markett towne*), with loss [to the king] 2*s.*[2]

At this court all [the presentments and judgements recorded above were affirmed by unanimous agreement of all the foresters, verderers, regarders, and other officers of the Forest].

[f. 83]

Forest of Dean in Gloucestershire, Herefordshire, Monmouthshire, and the County of the City of Gloucester: Court of Swanimote held at Littledean 14 September 1636(*sic*) Charles Bridgman, John Berrowe, and Warren Goughe, esqs., Verderers of the Forest.

It is presented that:

1   John Wyntour of Lydney, kt., by his agents and servants, for the greater part of a year since the sessions of the Justices of the Forest has continued in possession, and still

---

[1] Possibly Goodrich.

[2] The two routes mentioned in nos. 28 and 29 have, in the sections of their course through Banister's Cannop Vallets estate, been since obscured and made redundant by the later plantations and road improvements in the area. The former presumably ran south, along or parallel to the Cannop valley, to Parkend, to reach Purton by way of the road down Viney hill, and the latter south-eastwards over Serridge to join the main Forest road at or before Cinderford bridge, to reach Newnham by way of Littledean. *Hoppershill* on the latter route is recorded *c.* 1680 (as *Hoopers Hill*) in the Mirystock area at the north end of the estate: TNA, F 17/7; and for the estate, see pp. xi–xii.

does, of two furnaces for making iron within the Forest perambulation, one called Rodmore furnace and the other called Gunn's mill, with loss to the king, etc.

2   The said John Wyntour, by his agents and servants, for the greater part of a year since the sessions of the Justices of the Forest has continued, and still does, a double forge (*duplicem ferramentum anglice a double forge*) for making [iron] at Lydney within the Forest perambulation.

3   Richard Catchmay of Bigswear (*Bixeweare*), kt., by his agents [and servants], for [the greater part of a year since the sessions of the Justices of the Forest] has continued, and still does, a furnace for making [iron] at Bigswear within the Forest perambulation. (*note in margin*: fine £100)

4   Thomas Godwyn of Huntsham (Herefs.), doctor of theology, by his agents [and servants], for [the greater part of a year since the sessions of the Justices of the Forest] has continued, and still does, a furnace for making [iron] at Bishopswood (Herefs.) within [the Forest perambulation]. (*note in margin*: fine £100)

5   John Broughton of Ruardean, gent., by his agents [and servants], for two months has continued, and still does, a bloomery forge (*ferramentum anglice a bloomery*) to make [iron].[1]

6   William Kingston of Flaxley, esq., by his agents [and servants], for the greater part of a year since the sessions of the Justices of the Forest has continued, and still does, a forge (*ferramentum anglice a forge*) to make [iron]. (*note in margin*: fine £100)

7   Giles Foster of Coleford in Newland parish, gent., on 22 August 1636 at Phelps Meadow in the king's demesne of his Forest entered with a handgun (*tormento anglice a handgunne*) to the great harm [of the Forest]. (*note in margin*: fine £100)

[*f. 83v.*]

8   James Berrowe and Richard Berrowe, sons of Edmund Berrowe of Quedgeley, esq.,[2] on 31 August 1636 at Phelps Meadow in the king's demesne entered with a gun and killed a buck, with loss [to the king]. (*note in margin*: fine £61 13s. 4d. each of them)

9   John Buckler of Chepstow (Mon.), tailor, on 31 August 1636 at Tidenham within the Forest perambulation entered [the Forest] with a handgun, with loss [to the king]. (*note in margin*: fine £5)

10   John Foxe of Coleford, miner, on 9 August 1636 at Blackpennywall in the Forest demesne entered [the Forest] with a handgun and shot (*saggitavit anglice did shote*) at the king's deer. (*note in margin*: fine £40)

[*f. 84*]

Forest of Dean in Gloucestershire, Herefordshire, Monmouthshire, and the county of the City of Gloucester: Court of Swanimote held at Littledean 14 December 1636 before Charles Bridgman and John Berrowe, esqs., Verderers of the Forest[3]

---

[1] For Broughton's forge, an experimental variation of the traditional bloomery process, see *Cal. S.P. Dom. 1636–7*, pp. 300, 449, 482.

[2] See above, p. 61n.

[3] The third verderer, Warren Gough of Willsbury, who died a few days later, was evidently unable to attend the session: *Inquisitiones post mortem for Glos. 1625–42*, iii. pp. 63, 68.

Presentments of the Officers

It is presented that:

1   Richard Proben, late of Mitcheldean, labourer, on 10 December 1636 at *Horwood Eaves*[1] in Mitcheldean bailiwick in the king's demesne of his Forest cut down the stump of an oak (*truncum querci anglice the stubb of an oak*), containing one cord of wood, which he carried out of the Forest on his back, with loss to the king 5*s.*

2   James Scott, late of Mitcheldean, labourer, on 10 December 1636 at Lining wood in Mitcheldean bailiwick in the Forest demesne felled green holly trees (*virides aquifolia anglice greene hollies*) and other trees called hazels, containing four horse-loads (*sarcinas anglice burdens*), which he carried out of the Forest on his back, with loss [to the king] 12*d.*

3   Thomas Wallen, late of Mitcheldean, labourer, on 22 November 1636 in Abenhall bailiwick in the Forest demesne cut down a little beech tree, containing ¾ cord of wood, with loss to the king 7*s.* 6*d.*

4   Benedict Jorden, late of English Bicknor, yeoman, on 3 November 1636 at Coverham in English Bicknor bailiwick in the Forest demesne cut down a beech, containing two cords of wood worth 20*s.*, which he hauled out of the Forest with six oxen, worth £6.

5   Thomas Trigg, late of English Bicknor, timberman, on 5 November 1636 in Bicknor bailiwick in the Forest demesne cut down a beech, containing two cords of wood worth 20*s.*

6   Edward Addams, late of Clearwell in Newland parish, miner, on 21 November 1636 at Winnalls (*le Wynnolls*) in Staunton bailiwick in the Forest demesne cut down an oak tree, containing two cords of wood worth 20*s.*, with loss to the king 40*s.*

[*f. 84v.*]

7   The said Edward Addams and Richard Howells, late of Clearwell, carpenter, on 9 November 1636 at Oakwood in Staunton bailiwick in the Forest demesne cut down a timber oak, containing three tons of timber worth 30*s.*

8   The said Edward Addams and Richard Howells on 9 November 1636 at Oakwood in Staunton bailiwick cut down an oak, containing one cord of wood worth 10*s.*, with loss [to the king] 20*s.*

9   The said Edward Addams on 20 November 1636 at Winnalls in Staunton bailiwick in the Forest demesne cut down a yew tree (*yudre*), containing one cartload of wood worth 5*s.*, after it had been assigned to the king's use.

10   Thomas Treherne, late of Whitecliff in Newland parish, labourer, on 22 November 1636 at Winnalls in Staunton bailiwick cut up an oak, containing two horse-loads of wood worth 12*d.*

11   William Hewitt, late of Coleford in Newland parish, labourer, on 22 November at Winnalls in Staunton bailiwick cut up an oak, containing two horse-loads of wood worth 12*d.*, with loss [to the king] 18*d.*

12   Oliver Howells, late of Newland, labourer, on 8 November 1636 at Barnhill in Staunton bailiwick in the Forest demesne cut up a log, containing one ton of timber worth 51*s.* 6*d.*, after it had been assigned to the king's use.

---

[1] See above, p. 136*n.*

13   Richard Evans, late of Clearwell in Newland parish, labourer, on 8 November 1636 at Oakwood in Staunton bailiwick in the Forest demesne cut down an oak, amounting to two horse-loads of wood worth 6*d.*

14   Thomas Jones, late of [St.] Briavels, labourer, on 7 November 1636 at *Rusieledge*[1] in Staunton bailiwick in the Forest demesne cut down an oak, amounting to four horse-loads of wood worth 2*s.*, and hauled the wood away with a horse worth 16*s.*

[*f. 85*]

15   Hugh Hopkins, late of Coleford in Newland parish, labourer, on 17 November 1636 at Winnalls (*le Wynnolls*) in Staunton bailiwick in the Forest demesne cut down three oaks, amounting to three horse-loads of green wood worth 18*d.*, and hauled the wood away with a horse worth 20*s.*

16   William Nashe, late of Milkwall in the Forest, miner, on 20 November 1636 at Winnalls in Staunton bailiwick cut down an oak, amounting to two horse-loads of green wood worth 12*d.*, and hauled the wood away with a horse worth 20*s.*, with loss to the king 18*d.*

17[2]   Walter Higgins, late of Walford (Herefs.), cooper, on 8 November 1636 at Moorwood in the Forest demesne took three horse-loads (*sarcina anglice horse loades*) of the king's timber, worth 3s., out of the Forest, and hauled it away with three horses, worth 30s.

18[3]   Silvanus Younge, late of Clearwell in Newland parish, stonehewer, on 26 November 1636 at Winnalls in Staunton bailiwick in the Forest demesne cut down an oak and a beech, amounting to three horse-loads of green wood worth 2*s.*, with loss [to the king] 3*s.* 4*d.*

19   James Hawkins, late of Flaxley, gent., on 10 June 1633 on his land at St. White's, near Littledean within the Forest perambulation, had eight tons of oak timber, which formerly he had hauled out of the Forest.

20   Thomas Wade, late of (?)Mitcheldean,[4] gent., during the last month has kept six pigs pasturing in the king's demesne, which were not ringed in accordance with the forest law and assizes.

21   Richard Eddy, late of Hope Mansell (Herefs.), yeoman, during the last month has kept four pigs pasturing in the Forest demesne, not ringed according, etc.

22   Paul Thomas, late of Lea Bailey Side in the Forest, labourer, during the last two months has kept four pigs pasturing in the Forest demesne, not ringed according, etc.

23   John Phillipps, late of Newnham, labourer, during the last month has kept four pigs pasturing on the Forest demesne, not ringed according, etc.

[*f. 85v.*]

24   John Jeffery, late of Parkend in the Forest, labourer, during the last 20 months has kept four pigs pasturing on the Forest demesne, not ringed according, etc.

---

[1] Possibly in the area of the later Russells Inclosure; cf. *Russell Edge* named at the same period: TNA, E 178/6080, f.15 and v.
[2] MS. misnumbers as 18.
[3] MS. misnumbers as 17.
[4] MS. has *Deane.*

25   Robert Robes, late of Flaxley, labourer, during the last month has kept six pigs pasturing on the Forest demesne, not ringed according, etc.

26   William Parlor, late of English Bicknor, yeoman, between 1 March and 10 April 1636 entered the king's demesne with a hunting dog and killed three does, two of which were pregnant with foal (*gravide anglice with fale*); and he took the meat and disposed it at will and sold the skins to a certain Richard Crowes of English Bicknor.

27   Henry Pumfrey, late of Blakeney in Awre parish, timberman, on 4 July 1636 at *le Copes* in the king's demesne of his Forest entered with a gun, contrary to the law, etc.

28   Benedict Jorden and William Parlor, both of English Bicknor, yeomen, with many other unknown persons about three years ago at the Pludds (*le Pludd*) in Ruardean bailiwick in the Forest demesne entered with longbows (*arcibus longis anglice with longe bogyes*), contrary to, etc.

29   George Wirrall, late of Mitcheldean, labourer, and James [*surname indecipherable*] of Abenhall, labourer, on 5 and 6 December in the king's demesne entered with a gun, contrary to, etc.

[*f. 86*]

30   Thomas Sherer, late of Mitcheldean, butcher, and Thomas Dawe, late of Longhope, yeoman, during the last three years at Lea, in the hundred of St. Briavels and within the Forest perambulation, cut down five oak stumps (*truncas querci anglice…stubb oakes*) on the land of William Steventon, esq., containing by estimation 16 cords of wood, and converted them to charcoal to make iron, with loss to the king and contrary to forest law.

31   William Caple of Gloucester city, mercer, and John Constance of Elton in Westbury[-on-Severn] parish, tailor, his tenant, during the last year at Elton within the Forest perambulation diverted a watercourse in the highway leading from Blackmore's Hale towards Gloucester, contrary to the statute passed and contrary to forest law.

32   Anne, the wife of Giles Mathewes, tailor, James Scott, labourer, William White, labourer, Susan, the wife of Richard Wyniatt, labourer, Mary, the wife of Richard Proben, labourer, Margaret, the daughter of the same Richard and Mary, and Katherine Trigge, spinster, all of Mitcheldean, cut down oak saplings and holly trees in the king's demesne and within the Forest perambulation in order to make a sheephouse, and converted and disposed of them to their own uses, with grave loss to the king, to the destruction and harm of the Forest, and contrary to forest law and assizes.

At this court all the presentments and judgements recorded above were affirmed by unanimous agreement of all the foresters, verderers, regarders, and other officers of the Forest.

(*the names of Bridgman and Berrowe, the verderers, end the record of the court*)

GLOSSARY

Note: Some terms, used only once or twice and in some cases of doubtful meaning, are discussed in footnotes where they occur.

Agistor: forest officer with responsibility for supervising the commoning of animals in the forest and collecting payments made for the same.

Assart: land taken out of woodland or waste; originally denoting land taken for use as ploughland but later used more generally for all land newly converted into farmland. *To assart*: to take in such land.

Attachment Court: in Dean also known as the 'speech court'; a forest court held every few weeks for hearing and indicting offenders against the vert and supervising the taking of wood by those with customary rights.

Bailiwick: in the context of Dean referred to a section of the royal demesne administered by a woodward by right of his/her tenure of an adjoining manorial estate.

Cardboard: timber cut into thin board.

Chase: a tract of land reserved for hunting, but without the officers and laws of a royal forest and often held by a private landowner.

Cinders: waste material left by the smelting of iron ore, particularly that from Roman and medieval workings that was re-used later in the blast furnaces.

Coal: in the 17th century generally used for charcoal (mineral coal was usually then distinguished as 'sea-coal'). *To coal*: to turn wood into charcoal.

Collier: in the 17th century usually meaning a charcoal burner.

Cord: a standard-sized stack or bundle of cordwood.

Cordwood: small timber cut to a standard length (in Dean 4ft 3ins) for use in charcoal pits.

Covert: a wooded area providing shelter for deer and other game.

Deer-Leap: a lowered section in the hedge or paling of a private park adjoining a forest, enabling deer to gain access from the forest.

Eaves: the fringes of woodland; in Dean sometimes an element of place-names in the royal demesne combined with the name of the near adjoining settlement on parochial land, e.g. 'Bream's Eaves'.

Estovers: the customary right to take wood in a forest for the use of neighbouring dwellings and farms; the word was sometimes used only for the right to take wood for firewood (otherwise termed 'firebote') but at other times it was used to cover also wood taken for repairs to buildings and fences (otherwise termed respectively 'housebote' and 'heybote').

Expeditate: to mutilate a dog's feet to prevent it pursuing game; sometimes termed 'hambling'.

Eyre: circuit by itinerant royal judges; in the case of a royal forest a visitation originally made every few years to punish offenders indicted by the local forest courts and to supervise and regulate the forest administration. In the 17th century a forest eyre was more usually termed 'justice seat'.

Firebote: see Estovers.

Hambling: see Expeditate.

Heybote: see Estovers.

Housebote: see Estovers.

Justice Seat: see Eyre.

Mean, Meend, Mesne: a parcel of waste land, often open to rights of common.

Messuage: a dwelling house, usually with farm buildings and yards.

Mine: iron ore.

Pannage: the customary right to pasture pigs; also used for an annual payment made for exercising that right

Perambulation: a circuit of a forest undertaken to identify and establish its bounds; also used for a document setting out those bounds.

Purlieu: land once subject to the forest law, since disafforested

Purpresture: an illegal encroachment on forest land, usually involving the erection of buildings.

Regard: a detailed survey of the state of a forest.

Regarder: forest officer having as his principal function the conducting of a regard in preparation for a visit of the forest eyre.

Royal Demesne: in the context of Dean the usual term for the central area of woodland and waste held directly by the Crown, as distinct from manorial and parochial lands within the Forest bounds

Seal: to mark (with a hatchet or other implement) timber trees for felling for royal use or to be reserved for such use.

Speech Court: see Attachment Court.

Swanimote: in Dean the term was sometimes used for the attachment court, but in the early 17th century it usually denoted a forest court that was convened two or three times a year to hear and indict a range of offences under the forest laws and attended by all the forest officers and representatives from the parishes and tithings within the bounds. A special session was convened in preparation for the eyre of 1634 to hear presentments of all matters covered by the articles of the regard.

Treenail: wooden pin used in carpentry, particularly in shipbuilding.

Verderer: a forest officer, appointed by royal writ and having as his principal function presiding over the local forest courts.

Vert: trees, underwood, and other vegetation in a forest.

INDEX OF PERSONS

Notes. References are to page numbers, with (where relevant) item numbers given in brackets and bold type. Different forms of the same surname are grouped together (the inclusion or absence of a final letter 'e' not noted). No attempt has been made (except with titled persons) to distinguish individuals having the same surname and forename.

Olliver, James, 9, 97 (**717**)
Osborne, Edward, 45 (**14**)
  Thomas, 42
  William, 42
Owen, John, 85 (**550**)

Pacie, Richard, 82 (**497**)
Packer, Gabriel, 58 (**149**), 71 (**339**)
  Thomas, 58 (**149**), 71 (**339**)
Palmer (Palmore, Pallmer), Anne, 58 (**137**),
  71 (**337**)
  Christopher, 86 (**566**)
  Edward, 36]
  John, 78 (**415**)
  Richard, 139 (**42–3**)
  Thomas, 86 (**566**)
Parkhurst, Robert, 129 (**4**)
Parlor, Godfrey, 56 (**123**)
  James, 113 (**21**)
  William, 17–18, 36, 57 (**133**), 81 (**480**), 82
    (**495**), 91 (**643**), 145 (**21–3**), 153 (**26**, **28**)
Parry (Parrie), James, 134 (**66**)
  Thomas, 59 (**158**)
Parsons, Richard, 60 (**177**), 94 (**680**)
  Samuel, 81 (**467**)
Partridge, Alice, 106, 118 (**62**)
  Edward, 35, 60 (**174**), 118 (**62**); *and see* Wheeler
  George, 61 (**183**)
  John, 34
  Thomas, 118 (**62**)
Passmore, James, 80 (**459**)
Payne, Arthur, 35
  Thomas, 60 (**170–1**)
Pearce, William, 67 (**284**), 113 (**16**)
Pearton, John, 40
Peckover, John, 54 (**100**), 89 (**603**), 125 (**116**)
Pello, Christiana, 82 (**494**)
Pembroke, earls of, xiii; *and see* Herbert
Penn, Richard, 134 (**56**)
  William, 133 (**53**)
Perkins, William, 51 (**78**), 52 (**87**), 113 (**17**)
Perrgrove, William, 62 (**188**)
Perry, John, 40
Phelps (Phellps), Christopher, 76 (**391**), 134 (**66**)
  Edward, 84 (**529**)
  Joan, 132 (**34**)
  William, 91 (**638**)
Phillipps (Phillippes), David, 68 (**298**)
  John, 42, 63 (**206**), 122 (**98**) 152 (**23**)
  Henry, 35, 120 (**82**)
  Robert, 31, 35, 120 (**84**)

Thomas, xxix, 51 (**74**), 63 (**207–8**), 92
  (**651–2**), 145 (**17**)
  William, 35, 65 (**240**), 105, 120 (**81**)
Philpott, Arthur, 38
  William, 37–8, 104
Phips, John, 72 (**350**)
Pinnock (Pynnocke), John, 90 (**626**)
  Thomas, 90 (**620**)
Pirke, *see* Pyrke
Plowden, Edmund, 14 & n
Pope, Giles, xxviii, 58 (**137**), 136 (**13**)
Potter, James, 113 (**16**)
Poulter, John, 67 (**286**)
Powell, David, 32
  Edward, 73 (**369**)
  James, 123 (**100**)
  John, 73 (**362**)
  Richard, 31, 113 (**16**)
  Simon, 40
Prater, William, 66 (**259**)
Preddye, John, 144 (**7**)
Preist, Walter, 139 (**51**)
Price (Preece), John, 4, 30, 41, 117 (**59**)
  Thomas, 147 (**4**)
  William 147 (**3**)
Pritchard (Pritchett), James, 87 (**581**)
  John, 80 (**460**, **463**), 83 (**502**, **510**), 84
    (**528**), 88 (**588**, **598**), 89 (**604**), 145 (**26**)
Proben, Margaret, 153 (**32**)
  Mary, 153 (**32**)
  Richard, 151 (**1**), 153 (**32**)
Probert, Elizabeth, 132 (**28**)
Prosser, Christopher, 86 (**565**)
  John, 77 (**408**), 92 (**660**)
  Meredith, 77 (**405**)
Pullen (Pullin), Eleanor, 89 (**614**)
  John, 60 (**177**), 94 (**680**)
  Luke, 93 (**665**)
  Richard, 49 (**60**), 92 (**658**)
Pumfrey, Henry, 128 (**9**), 148 (**17**), 153 (**27**)
Purefoy (Purefie), William, 129 (**3**)
Purnell, John, 54 (**101**)
Pury, Thomas, xxix
Pychard, John, 45 (**22**)
Pynnocke, *see* Pinnock
Pyrke (Pirke), Robert, 60 (**173**, **176**), 73 (**365**)
  Thomas, 78 (**427**)

Rashford, James, 55 (**106**)
Ravenhill (Ravenhall), Henry, 33, 39
Rawlings, John, 103 (**786**)

Somerset, Henry, earl (later marquess) of
    Worcester, xxxvi, 37 & *n*, 130 (**12**), 139 (**44**)
 Henry, marquess of Worcester (later duke
    of Beaufort), xxxvi
Somner, John, 91 (**633**)
Soult, Thomas, 73 (**366**)
South, George, 31, 111 (**10**)
Sowdley, Christopher, 77 (**406**)
Sparks, Thomas, *see* Lokyer
Springe, John, 68 (**288**), 85 (**538**), 90 (**619**)
Stafford, Henry, Lord Stafford, 111 (**11**)
 Henry, 73 (**355**)
Stayner (Steyner), John, 4, 30
Sternhold, Thomas, 74 (**377**)
Sterry, Thomas, 70 (**324**)
Stevens (Stephens), Christopher, 35
 John, 33, 38–9, 141 (**12**)
 Julia, 122 (**98**)
 Richard, 33, 39
 William, 38
Stevington (Steventon), William, 60 (**178**),
    118 (**68**), 153 (**30**)
Steyner, *see* Stayner
Still, Stephen, 82 (**483**)
Stirley, William, 103 (**799**)
Stratford, Anthony, 32, 35, 71 (**336**)
Stroude (or Freeman), Richard, 122 (**95**)
Sugar, John, 69 (**302**)
Surrey, earl of, *see* Howard, Thomas
Swanley, Anne, 61 (**181**)
 John, 73 (**356**)
Swayne, Thomas, 91 (**644–5**)
Swift, John, 105
 Sara, 136 (**10**)
Symonds (Symons), Edmund, 121 (**88**)
 John, 36, 70 (**312**), 106, 123 (**103**)
 Thomas, 148 (**21**)
Talbot, Gilbert, earl of Shrewsbury, 129 (**2b**)
Tayloe, Thomas, 42
Taylor (Tayler), George, 62 (**203**)
 James, 85 (**541**), 143 (**4**)
 John, 55 (**104**), 92 (**655**), 146 (**34**)
 Roger, 39, 104
 Thomas, 45 (**21**)
Teage, John, 148 (**15**)
Terret, Richard, 36
Thomas, Charles, 64 (**233**), 69 (**303**)
 Edward, 45 (**19**)
 James, 65 (**241**)
 John, 59 (**161**), 70 (**313**)
 Llewellin, 63 (**213**)

Morgan, 66 (**269**)
 Paul, 79 (**437**), 148 (**16**), 152 (**22**)
 Richard, 7, 64 (**227**), 138 (**39**)
 Thomas, 101 (**767**)
 William ap, 82 (**484**)
Thorne, Alexander, 34, 117 (**57**)
 Christopher, 117 (**57**)
 George, 140 (**4**)
Throckmorton, Sir Baynham, xiv, xvii,
    xxxv, 4–5, 18, 29–30, 36, 53 (**96**), 74
    (**375–6**), 94 (**687**), 101 (**775**), 126 (**120**)
 Sir William, 18, 51 (**78**), 53 (**96**)
 family, xxxvi
Tilman (Tylman), Thomas, 42 (**2**), 87 (**569**)
Tilsley (Tilslow), John, 71*n*
 Philip, 8–9, 46 (**34**), 59 (**154**), 71 (**341**)
Tilton, William, 42
Tims, James, 92 (**653**)
Tipper, —, 10
Tippett, Richard, 38
Tomes, John, 149 (**28–9**)
Tomlins, Richard, 86 (**552, 563**)
Tomlinson, Enoch, 145 (**18**)
Tompkins (Tomkins), John, 67 (**281**), 87 (**583**)
 Richard, 100 (**748**)
Tompson, Leonard, *see* Beare
 Richard, 79 (**440**), 131 (**18**)
Townsend, Hugh, 134 (**55**)
Treganoe, William, 30
Treherne (Trehearne), John, 137 (**19**)
 Thomas, 98 (**730**), 137 (**19**), 151 (**10**)
Tresteed (Tristed), James, 123 (**102**)
 Tristram, 57 (**135**), 131 (**22**)
 William, 80 (**455**)
Treswell, Robert, 18, 44 (**6–7**), 49 (**57 &
    *n***), 61 (**184–5**), 75 (**383**)
Trevor, Sir Thomas, xvi, 3–4, 13, 15, 21
Trewell, Robert, 70 (**325**)
Trigge, John, 41, 83 (**503**), 84 (**520**), 86
    (**560**), 137 (**23**)
 Katherine, 153 (**32**)
 Thomas, 70 (**310**), 76 (**388**), 82 (**491**),
    137 (**24–5, 28**), 144 (**13–14**), 151 (**5**)
 William, 42
Tripp, Charles, 104
Trippett, Charles, 41, 107, 117 (**53**)
 Joan, 107, 14 (**109**)
Tristed, *see* Tresteed
Trotman, —, 6
Tucker, Christopher, 32, 35
 John, 84 (**524**)

INDEX OF PLACES

Notes. Places are in Gloucestershire unless otherwise indicated. Places that were in the royal demesne in 1634 are mostly grouped under 'Dean Forest royal demesne'. References are to pages, with (where relevant) item numbers given in brackets and bold type.

INDEX OF SUBJECTS

Note. References are to pages, with (where relevant) item numbers given in brackets and bold type.

THE ROYAL DEMESNE OF THE FOREST OF DEAN: SKETCH MAP OF *c.* 1680
(TNA, F 17/7)
[*see reproduction inside back cover*]

The purpose of this sketch map, entitled *'A Description of the Forest of Deane as it lyes in sev[era]l parcels w[i]th the Inclosures'*, was to locate new enclosures formed in the demesne woodlands as nurseries for ship timber in the early 1670s. It is undated but can be identified as from *c.* 1675–1680: the six new keeper's lodges in the demesne were completed in 1675 or 1676, and Sir Baynham Throckmorton, named at Clearwell, died in 1680. (Others named include, at Harthill near Hewelsfield, the marquess of Worcester, who became duke of Beaufort in 1682).

Though some 45 years later in date, the map illustrates the boundaries of the demesne and disposition of place-names much as they were at the time of the eyre; the picture was somewhat obscured later by the replanting of the demesne in large, new inclosures in the first decades of the 19th century.

The map, which is aligned with west at the top, shows the central tract of the demesne with its various detached parts called the Hudnalls, the Fence, and Bearse common (all adjoining St Briavels parish), the Glydden (within Newland), and Walmore common and Northwood green (within Westbury-on-Severn). The alienated Mailscot wood, adjoining the Wye on the north-west of the demesne, is left outside the boundary, and Abbots wood, south-west of Littledean, the status of which was in dispute at the period, is also excluded (causing Blaize Bailey to the east of it to appear as if detached from the demesne).

No roads are shown within the demesne, the anonymous mapmaker evidently regarding the main streams in their valleys as more useful points of reference; but some landmarks on the principal routes are marked, including, on the ancient 'Dean road' crossing the demesne between Lydney and Littledean, Deadman's Cross where it forms a junction with the Parkend–Gatcombe road and Soudley ('Coudly') bridge where it crosses Soudley brook, and, on the Littledean–Coleford road, the crossings at Cinderford bridge and Fox's bridge. The 'Jack of the Yat' oak, which stood by the Mitcheldean–Monmouth road near Worral Hill and survived until the early 20th century as one of the largest and most ancient trees of the Forest (see Hart, *Royal Forest*, p. 212), was already a noteworthy landmark.

The map is reproduced with the kind permission of the National Archives. The size of the original is approximately 50.5cm x 39.5cm.